First Language English
for Cambridge IGCSE®
Teacher Resource Pack

Jane Arredondo

OXFORD
UNIVERSITY PRESS

OXFORD
UNIVERSITY PRESS

Great Clarendon Street, Oxford OX2 6DP

Oxford University Press is a department of the University of Oxford.
It furthers the University's objective of excellence in research,
scholarship, and education by publishing worldwide in

Oxford New York

Auckland Cape Town Dar es Salaam Hong Kong Karachi
Kuala Lumpur Madrid Melbourne Mexico City Nairobi
New Delhi Shanghai Taipei Toronto

With offices in

Argentina Austria Brazil Chile Czech Republic France Greece
Guatemala Hungary Italy Japan Poland Portugal Singapore
South Korea Switzerland Thailand Turkey Ukraine Vietnam

Oxford is a registered trade mark of Oxford University Press
in the UK and in certain other countries

British Library Cataloguing in Publication Data

Data available

ISBN: 978-0-19-838907-1
10 9 8 7 6 5 4 3 2

MIX
Paper from
responsible sources
FSC
FSC® C007785
www.fsc.org

Printed in Great Britain by Bell and Bain Ltd, Glasgow

Acknowledgments

® IGCSE is the registered trademark of Cambridge International Examinations.

> ® IGCSE is the registered trademark of Cambridge International Examinations.
>
> Past paper questions are reproduced by permission of Cambridge International
> Examinations. Cambridge International Examinations bears no responsibility for the
> example answers to questions taken from its past question papers which are contained in
> this publication. The questions, example answers, marks awarded and/or comments that
> appear in this book and CD were written by the author. In examination, the way marks
> would be awarded to answers like these may be different.

Cover image courtesy of Kendal (acrylic on card), Powis, Paul (Contemporary
Artist)/Private Collection/The Bridgeman Art Library.

The authors and publisher are grateful for permission reproduce the following
copyright material:

Angela Clarence: extract from 'Travelling in the Desert', *The Observer*, 21.5.2000,
copyright © Guardian News & Media Ltd 2000, reproduced by permission of
GNM Ltd.

Dorothy Dunnett: extract from *Scales of Gold : Travelling in the Desert in the 15th Century* (Michael Joseph, 1991, Penguin, 2000), copyright © Dorothy Dunnett 1991,
reproduced by permission of Penguin Books Ltd.

Joan Fallon: extract from *Between the Sierra and the Sea* (Vanguard Press, 2011),
reproduced by permission of the Perseus Books Group.

Kristin Gleeson: 'Anahareo and Grey Owl', copyright © Kristin Gleeson 2013, first
published in this book by permission of the author. Extract from *Selkie Dreams*
(Knox Robinson, 2012), reproduced by permission of the publishers.

Sarah Harrison: extract from *A Flower That's Free* (Warner, 2000), copyright ©
Sarah Harrison 1984, reproduced by permission of The Orion Publishing Group,
London.

Ted Hughes: 'Full Moon & Little Frieda' from *New Selected Poems 1957- 1994* (Faber,
1995), copyright © Ted Hughes 1995, reproduced by permission of Faber & Faber
Ltd, and from *Collected Poems*, copyright © 2003 by the Estate of Ted Hughes,
reproduced by permission of the publishers, Farrar Straus & Giroux, LLC.

International Ecotourism Society: 'Dos and Don'ts While Travelling' from www.
ecotourism.org, reproduced with permission of the Society.

Clive Jeremy and Roger Chapman et al: extract from 'Tropical Forest Expeditions'
(RGS-IBG, London, 2002), reproduced by permission of the Royal Geographical
Society with IBG.

Martin Luther King Jr: extract from 'I Have a Dream', 28 August 1963, copyright
© Dr Martin Luther King Jr., © renewed 1991 by Coretta King Smith, reprinted
by arrangement with The Heirs of the Estate of Martin Luther King Jr., c/o Writers House as agent for the proprietor, New York, NY.

Nathan Kinser: 'Heart of the Crowd: A Study of the Motives of the Peasant Class
in the French Revolution' (1999) reproduced by permission of the author and of
Eric Wake, University of the Cumberlands, www.ucumberlands.edu.

Laurie Lee: extract from *As I Walked Out One Midsummer Morning* (Penguin, 1971),
copyright © Laurie Lee 1969, reproduced by permission of Curtis Brown Ltd,
London, on behalf of The Partners of the Literary Estate of Laurie Lee.

Mervyn Morris: 'Little Boy Crying' from *The Pond* (New Beacon Books, 1973, 1979),
copyright © Mervyn Morris 1973, reproduced by permission of New Beacon
Books Ltd.

Hattie Naylor: extracts from *Ivan and the Dogs* (Methuen Drama, 2010), copyright
© Hattie Naylor 2010, reproduced as audio by permission of United Agents,
www.unitedagents.co.uk.

Téa Obreht: extract from *The Tiger's Wife* (Weidenfeld & Nicolson, 2011), copyright
© Téa Obreht 2011, reproduced as audio by permission of the publishers, The
Orion Publishing Group, London and of The Gernert Company on behalf of the
author.

Jane Revell and Susan Norman: 'The Drought' from *In Your Hands, NLP for teaching
and learning* (Saffire Press, 1997), reproduced by permission of the authors and
the publisher.

William Saroyan: extract from 'The Summer of the Beautiful White Horse' from
My Name is Aram (Harcourt, 1940, Penguin 1944), copyright © William Saroyan
1940, 1944, reproduced as audio by permission of the Wm Saroyan Foundation
and the Trustees of Leland Stanford Junior University.

G P Taylor: extract from *Shadowmancer* (Faber, 2003), copyright © G P Taylor 2003,
reproduced as audio by permission of the author c/o Caroline Sheldon Literary
Agency Ltd.

Dylan Thomas: 'Memories of Christmas' first published in *The Listener*, 20 December 1945, from *Quite Early One Morning* (J M Dent,1954), copyright © Dylan Thomas 1945, copyright © New Directions Publishing Corp 1954, reproduced as audio
by permission of David Higham Associates and New Directions Publishing Corp.

Although we have made every effort to trace and contact all copyright holders
before publication this has not been possible in all cases. If notified, the publisher will rectify any errors or omissions at the earliest opportunity.

Any third party use of these extracts outside of this publication in any medium is
prohibited, and interested parties should apply directly to the copyright holders
named in each case for permission.

Contents

1 Travellers' tales

This first unit is designed to encourage students to reflect on their thinking skills and participate in class discussion. Use the Talking points and Speaking and listening tasks to help you get to know each other. During the first weeks, also do a lesson on learning styles so students are aware of how they acquire and use information. The prose and poetry texts in this unit relate to a wide range of locations to reflect the passages from the many English-speaking countries used in the exams.

Spend some time at the start of the course explaining exactly which exam components students are preparing for and what they will be expected to do in the exams. Ask them to take notes and keep them as a handy reference so they can see how everything they do in the course relates to the exams.

Point out that neither drama nor poetry appear in Language assessments, but both can be developed for coursework assignments. Other coursework ideas are featured in the Student Book and many of the passages in the Student Book and Workbook can be developed into individual activities for coursework components.

Unit starter

Student Book, page 3

The story **"Asclepius and the two travellers"** on page 3 of the Student Book provides an excellent discussion topic to get students thinking. It's an appropriate introduction to the course because effective reading, writing, listening and speaking skills require good thinking skills. Use the **Talking points** that follow the passage to encourage students to think about how they see life as individuals. Do they tend to have a positive or a negative outlook? Encourage students to explain their reasoning throughout the exercise.

Some students may struggle with this and, if they come from diverse backgrounds, may be reluctant to share their ideas in the first instance. If so, set the questions for homework. At the start of the next lesson give students 2–3 minutes to discuss their findings in pairs before asking them to feed back to the class.

Travel writing

Student Book, pages 4–15

This section presents different types of travel writing and provides resources for introducing students to writing for different purposes and the importance of good writing skills, the relevance and importance of good reading skills, and how to use reading and writing skills in summaries.

Introducing writing skills

Workbook, pages 4–5

Explain the importance of being able to write well, not only for the exams and coursework, but also in future academic studies and professional careers. Relate this idea to the specific requirements of the course. If your class is doing the Coursework Portfolio, explain the nature of the three different assignments.

You could use the **Writing skills questionnaire** on pages 4–5 of the Workbook, which requires students to think about what and how they write on a daily basis, and what writing styles they expect to need in the future. If this is set for homework, follow up with a class discussion. The task does not need to be marked but you will find it useful to see what students have written; not all are forthcoming (or entirely honest) in front of their peers so time spent looking at their preferences and opinions is time well spent.

Noticing details: Moving through time project

At some point in Unit 1, do a Moving through time project. This activity will help students become more aware of their environment and should improve their descriptive writing skills. They need notebooks and pencils: ideally they should not use electronic devices for note-taking. The more practice they have with old-fashioned handwritten note-taking the better, as this forms an important part of their Reading and Directed Writing assessments. Introduce the project by asking: What do we see as we move through time?

Brief students to make a note of anything that grabs their attention during a 24-hour period. Suggest ideas: billboards, advertisements, birds, flowers, litter, odd human behaviour, bristles on a toothbrush. The point is to take note of things that seem random and irrelevant but actually form part of their day. Explain that they need to take note of what they see with their eyes but do not always stop to process or consider, and then think about how much of this is actually worthy of comment.

Arrange a feedback session in small groups on the following day. Give the groups 5–10 minutes to discuss their findings. Prompt them as necessary to keep the activity engaging and lively. If you have a large class, you could ask groups to report on just one item each that grabbed their attention and to explain why it was meaningful. At a later date, perhaps once a week, students can share with the class what else they have noticed and considered in their environments.

Finally ask students what they have learned from this activity and how they can apply it to their writing. Hopefully they will make comments about being more inquisitive and observant of the world around them, paying attention to the minutiae of life, writing about what they see and experience. Of course, there are many more possibilities.

Introducing summary writing

Student Book, page 4

Before students attempt their first written summary they should understand the purpose of the exercise. Write the following questions on the board, giving students 2 minutes to discuss their answers in pairs or small groups before reporting back to the class.

- What do you think is meant by the term *summary*?

- Why do you think writing a summary is such an important skill?

Spend some time eliciting why summary writing is such a useful skill. Make sure students understand it is a skill they will use throughout their academic careers and later in the workplace in the form of memos, minutes and emails.

Explain that students need to answer a Summary question on one text for both Core and Extended Reading Passages. Although Extended students are no longer required to work with information from more than one text, obtaining information from two texts is a very useful skill and can be applied to the Directed Writing task or for coursework. It is also especially useful for students doing English Literature.

Point out the **Summary skills panel** on page 4 of the Student Book; it will help students adopt a systematic approach to writing a summary. There are numerous tasks in English (Language and Literature) where students are asked to use a text in different ways: to find words and phrases to answer questions, then to compare and contrast; or to answer questions, then find information to be used in an empathic writing task. Using different coloured pencils helps students to separate relevant points and retrieve them more quickly under exam conditions. They should avoid highlighters because highlights cannot be deleted and tend to obscure information that may be required later. For example, for Reading Passage questions they can use one colour to underline information for Comprehension and Language questions and another colour to identify information for the Extended response (letter, diary entry, etc.).

Identifying essential information

Resource 1.1

Write the following two statements on the board, or hand out or display the task on **Resource 1.1**.

- For his 16th birthday the boy called Tom, who was very fond of music, was given a new guitar, a flute and a mouth organ. (25 words) Keeping essential information, reduce this sentence to about 10 words.

- Our neighbours' dog, which is black and white, barks all the time and it will bite anyone that goes near it. (21 words) Keeping essential information, reduce this sentence to about 7 words.

Ask students to read each sentence carefully and consider what essential information it conveys. Give them about 5 minutes to work independently on the tasks before sharing examples as a class.

In the first task they need to generalise: e.g. Tom was given musical instruments for his birthday. (7 words); Tom was given three instruments for his birthday because he likes music. (12 words); Music-loving Tom was given (musical) instruments for his birthday. (8 or 9 words)

The second task contains one essential piece of information – the dog is dangerous: e.g. Our neighbours' noisy dog is dangerous. (6 words)

Hand out two strips of paper per student (different colours if possible). Ask them to write a long sentence on one strip and a short summary of it on the other. Each student needs to keep their summary strip for the next lesson. Collect the longer sentences to use in the next lesson. Each student then becomes the "owner" of an answer and can decide on how well their peers perform. One way to organise the activity is to play a game.

1. Fold the strips with long sentences and put them into a hat or box.

2. One student pulls out a strip and reads the long sentence to the class while you write it on the board.

3. Give students a set time to write a summary sentence.

4. Nominate students in turn to read out their sentences. The original owners decide if each summary is close enough to their original summary to award points. Allow 5 points for an answer that exactly matches the owner's summary or has the same number of words, reducing this to 1 point for the nearest correct answer.

5. Continue for 15 minutes, depending on the size of your class or the degree of interest and attention, then award merits/credits to the student with the most points.

"Wanderings in South America"

Student Book, pages 4– 5

Before reading the passage on page 5 of the Student Book, ask students to consider what they think the text will be about from the title alone. Read the text as a class.

Review summary writing and/or use the **Summary skills task** on page 4 of the Student Book. Elicit what students already know about summarising: e.g. concise sentences, formal language, impersonal tone, etc. Prompt and recap as necessary. Alternatively, you could set the Summary skills task for homework to give students more time and then take feedback at the start of the next lesson. The details they should identify are:

a. Ingredients: wourali vine; bitter-tasting root; stalks of two kinds of bulbous plants (with green and glutinous/sticky juice); large, black ants with a venomous sting; small, red ants that nest under leaves and have a nettle-like sting; Indian pepper (grown round huts); pounded fangs of (deadly) Labarri and Counacouchi snakes.

b. Method:

- scrape the vine and root and place the shavings in a leaf colander

- pour water over the shavings (until it has a coffee-like appearance) into a pot

- bruise bulbous stalks and squeeze their juice into the pot

- bruise and add fangs, ants and pepper

- place the pot on a slow fire and bring to the boil

- add more wourali vine juice and remove scum with a leaf

- leave the pot over heat until the liquid reduces to a thick brown syrup.

Introducing reading skills

Student Book, page 6

This is a good opportunity for students to reflect on how they read. They need to be aware of why they need to demonstrate their understanding of a text, what examiners are looking for and how this helps their studies across the curriculum. Draw their attention to the **Reading skills panel** on page 6 of the Student Book to help them adopt a range of strategies for reading to identify information.

Quoting and paraphrasing

As students work through the reading tasks in this unit they should become aware of when it is appropriate and necessary to quote in an answer and when they should paraphrase, as in a summary. The **SQuEE technique** described on Page 6 of the Student Book is a variation of the PEE technique (point/example/explanation). However, the SQuEE technique is more sophisticated and appropriate for Language tasks because it requires students to comment on a writer's choice of words (the effect). Remind students that they must never quote in a summary but instead they should paraphrase the writer's words.

Answering Reading questions

Workbook, pages 6–8

To give students practice in comprehension and retrieval of information, you could ask them to read the article **"Mystery of Alexander Selkirk, the real Robinson Crusoe, solved"** on page 6 of the Workbook and answer the questions that follow. Suggested answers:

1. **a.** The most compelling evidence is a part of a pair of navigational dividers.

    b. The author could have used *convincing, forceful* or *persuasive* instead of *compelling* or *the strongest* instead of *most compelling*.

    c. This evidence is compelling because the dividers could only have belonged to a ship's master or navigator such as Selkirk.

    d. The discovery of the dividers was the deciding factor in suggesting that Selkirk stayed on Aguas Buenas.

    e. Postholes were also found, which suggest that Selkirk built two shelters.

2.

*   Where he came from: Lower Largo, Fife, Scotland.

*   Biographical details: he was born in 1676, the younger son of a shoemaker, and went to sea at an early age.

*   Where he was marooned: a tropical island in the Pacific, thought to be Aguas Buenas.

*   What he had with him on the island: "some practical pieces" and mathematical instruments, including, it is thought, navigational dividers; also a gun.

*   How he passed his time: he chased and shot goats for meat and skins; it is thought he built two shelters; he watched for approaching ships.

*   His rescue: he was rescued by Captain Woodes Rogers in 1709.

*   Other interesting details: student's own ideas.

Answering summary questions

Workbook, pages 9–10

Before students move to the next section in the Student Book, you could ask them to work through this section in the Workbook, which guides them through the process and culminates in asking them to write a summary of the short text provided. Suggested answers:

1. **a.** Keywords might include: summarise, conditions, evidence found, how Selkirk survived alone.

    b. Conditions: totally alone and isolated ("desert island", "marooned"); hot days and warm nights ("tropical island"); evidence found: "evidence of a campsite"; how Selkirk survived alone: lived off land and sea ("surviving on what nature alone can provide"; Aguas Buenas = good water); found hope and support in prayer ("praying for rescue").

    c. Students should think what the writer's words suggest: e.g. "surviving on what nature alone can provide" suggests he survived on sea-food and fish. The eight points:

*   tropical island (mild/warm temperature and vegetation for food and shelter)

*   campsite (Selkirk was a practical/ resourceful man)

*   "some practical pieces" suggests that he had some useful equipment

*   postholes suggest he used tree trunks to make a shelter

*   by a freshwater stream (he had drinking water)

*   shot goats for food (and their skins)

*   had a gun

*   was able to make himself clothing (from skins).

2. Make sure students use the eight points from their notes, organising them into a cohesive, logical structure for the summary. Award 1 mark for each point (up to 8 in total) and up to 7 marks for style and accuracy (total of 15 marks).

Colour-coding parts of speech

Student Book, page 276

This might be a good opportunity to introduce students to the technique of colour-coding the different parts of speech. Explain that colour-coding nouns, verbs, adjectives and adverbs is very useful in preparation for discussing how writers use language to create specific effects. It also helps with learning to understand syntax. The technique can be used in more sophisticated textual analysis, in exam-style Language questions and in Literature tasks.

Explain or model the technique on the board. Depending on your class, you could introduce this technique just for identifying verbs and nouns and then move on to adjectives and adverbs. More able students may be better suited to going straight into identifying all four parts of speech. Emphasise how important it is to always use the same colours: red for nouns, blue for verbs, yellow for adjectives and green for adverbs.

"Children of the Stars"

Student Book, pages 6–7

As a class, read the passage on page 7. Ask students to practise their reading skills by doing the **Reading task** on page 6. They should record three examples of facts and three examples of opinion or personal impression. To get them used to thinking and working quickly, set a time limit of 5 minutes for each task. Encourage them to write in note form, using bullet points. Share responses as a class.

Ask students to do the **Writer's craft task** on page 6 and examine the travel writing techniques used by the writer in the article. Draw their attention to Clarence's techniques:

- balance between historical/geographical details and facts with personal impressions

- use of an arresting first image for a would-be traveller (sense of being the only person there)

- writing in the first person to show her personality and interests through observations

- use of humour (the yellow grubs and "I just wasn't hungry")

- use of anecdote (the tarantula)

- expands out of the ordinary subject matter (history of the Waroa Indians)

- gives the main impression that this is a fascinating/exciting place to visit, where you aren't surrounded by other tourists.

Speaking and listening: Travel and tourism

Student Book, page 8

Discuss why people have always been travellers and then move on to how and why people travel nowadays. The **Speaking and listening task** on page 8 of the Student Book will serve as a good starting point to get discussion flowing. Also ask: How does travelling for business differ from travelling for pleasure?

Daniel Defoe's travel writing

Student Book, pages 9–10

Make sure students understand the difference between a journey or voyage and an expedition (point out the definition of *expedition* on page 8 of the Student Book).

Emphasise the importance of terminology, word choice or defining terms in essays and in conversation. Point out that definition boxes often appear on the pages of the Student Book and that there is a Glossary at the back.

Discuss the idea that many people enjoy reading about travel but never go anywhere; some might spend hours watching television programmes about foreign places they will never visit. Introduce the idea of vicarious experience: e.g. television as a substitute for real life. This can be extended to how and why people read novels or watch films. Lead discussion to the fact that people have wanted to read about other people's travels and adventures since books became available as popular entertainment. Lead into the success of Daniel Defoe's novel *Robinson Crusoe* and his non-fiction travel writing.

As a preliminary activity to work on Defoe's travel writing, students could research and record five facts about him. Alternatively, you could add to the information on page 9 of the Student Book. Daniel Defoe was born in 1660 in London, England. He trained for the Christian ministry but abandoned this career, served as a soldier and then started a hosiery business before becoming a prolific writer. He travelled widely in Europe for his hosiery business and was recruited by the government to act as a spy, a role in which he delighted. Defoe's first publication appeared in 1688. In 1719 he turned to fiction, writing *Robinson Crusoe*, based on the true account of a shipwrecked mariner, Alexander Selkirk (see Workbook, page 6). He followed this success with various novels and then turned to travel books, including the vivid *Tour Thro' the Whole Island of Great Britain* (1724–27). Defoe is regarded as one of the founders of the English novel. Before his time, fiction was primarily written in verse or in the form of a play, but Defoe and, to a lesser extent, Samuel Richardson, developed a new form of storytelling, which remains with us today. He can also be credited with being one of the founding fathers of English journalism.

"Tour Thro' the Whole Island of Great Britain"

Student Book, pages 9–10; Resource 11.1 (a–d)

Review the bullet points that characterise modern travel writing on page 9 of the Student Book. As a class, read the two passages on pages 9 and 10.

Ask students how the bullet points relate to Defoe's writing and to write down one quotation from Defoe to exemplify each technique. Give them a maximum of 10 minutes to get used to finding evidence in timed conditions.

You may find it useful to introduce aspects of the history of English, available on **Resource 11.1 (a–d)**, at this point. Resource **11.1c, New words and new worlds** might be most appropriate here. Ensure students understand that although Norse and Norman French had a significant and lasting effect on Anglo-Saxon English, there are many other adopted words in common use that have come from a wide range of locations. They could do the research task that follows the narrative in this resource. The answers to question 1 are: *shampoo*/India, *cotton*/Arabic, *freckles*/Norse, *yacht*/Dutch.

"On Cornwall"

Student Book, page 10

Referring to the **Question box** on page 10 of the Student Book, write the terms *objective* and *subjective* on the board and ask students to write definitions for both terms as a quick quiz. Discuss the terms in relation to the Defoe passage on Cornwall on page 10. Draw attention to the words "Our manner is plain, and suited to the nature of familiar letters" in Defoe's preface to the second volume of "the Tour" and the subjective way in which he describes the game Hurlers and the Cornish in the next passage: "I confess, I see nothing in it […] It seems, to me […]" (lines 7–11). Ask students: Why might it be difficult for a travel writer to write objectively? Does it matter which viewpoint a writer adopts for travel writing?

"How to Write the Perfect Travel Article" and "Tips for Travel Writing"

Student Book, pages 11–13; Resources 1.2–1.3

There are various websites that would-be writers can access for guidance on how to write a travel article. As a class, read the two examples on pages 11 and 12 of the Student Book.

Ask students to work in pairs on question 1 in the **Tips and techniques box** on page 12 of the Student Book to compare the two sets of guidelines. They could write notes on **Resource 1.2**. Encourage them to work with pace; 10–15 minutes would be long enough. Discuss responses as a class. Li and Bowes disagree on the inclusion of personal mishaps. Li says including personal mishaps can be amusing; Bowes says to avoid them. They agree that travel writing should:

- be factually accurate
- include personal details, perspectives or opinions
- include interesting anecdotes or something out of the ordinary
- have a narrative thread that conveys the big picture
- use language creatively and avoid clichés.

Look back at "Children of the Stars" on page 7 of the Student Book and discuss how Angela Clarence uses her personal impressions to make her writing more readable and entertaining. Look back at Martin Li's advice to "be a quoter" (lines 51–4). How does Clarence's use of quotes (quoting what a local person says) influence the text and/or reader? Ask students to write bullet points on the techniques recommended by Li and Bowes that Clarence uses in her article in response to question 2 in the Tips and techniques box on page 12.

Explain that students are going to do their own piece of travel writing. First, recap on criteria for writing. They could work in groups of three or four to prioritise the criteria on **Resource 1.3**. Give them 2–3 minutes and then take feedback. Lead into discussion on what students consider to be the most important techniques in their writing and why.

As a class, look at the **Writing task** on page 13 of the Student Book and discuss ideas for the three locations. Suggest they use Clarence's article as an example and refer to Li's advice on page 11.

Prompt ideas on how students might write to inform and entertain. Discuss the importance of audience or readers. Encourage them to think about who they are writing for, to have a "reader" in mind and to think about the sort of publication their work could feature in.

If students are writing their articles on a computer, remind them that they must use a spell checker, but that grammar checkers are not always reliable. If they are writing by hand, they must proofread carefully. It is advisable to insist that some creative work is done by hand in preparation for the exams. It is very easy for students to get out of the habit of handwriting; they will need to write quickly and neatly in their exams, so practice is vital.

"The crusade for Crusoe's Island"

Student Book, pages 13–15

Explain that the story of Robinson Crusoe has been made into numerous films and the idea of being marooned on an island has spawned various television series and reality shows. You could also discuss the continuing fascination with the idea of being marooned on a desert island (far from social media and without mobile phone connections) and why the very rich buy islands in the Caribbean, for example. After this, move on to how humans are apt to affect pristine environments or locations such an uninhabited island.

You could point out the link with the article about Alexander Selkirk on page 6 of the Workbook. In addition, if your class has read or will be studying *Lord of the Flies* by William Golding (see Unit 8, pages 212–17 in Student Book), you could develop the theme of living on a desert island more thoroughly. On Golding's island the boys have enough food and shelter available to survive, but they are young children and need to organise themselves before building huts or collecting food. They also have to overcome fear of the unknown without parental care.

As a class, read the article on pages 13–15 of the Student Book. It was taken from the www.geographical.co.uk website, which contains various other useful articles. Ask students to do the **Writing** on page 15, recapping on the techniques they should use. Discuss the article on the Juan Fernandez Islands. Then talk about the writing techniques needed for an article (blog or magazine) and how they can set out the advantages and disadvantages of encouraging tourism in this location and similar environments. Award up to 13 points for the content and up to

12 marks for style and accuracy (total of 25 marks). They should include the following points:

- Advantages: eco-tourism raises public awareness (of value/wealth of biodiversity); it's an important source of income for inhabitants; other sources of income reduce pressure on the land (overgrazing/tree-felling/agriculture).

- Disadvantages: over 130 endemic species are at risk, especially the hummingbird; the island has unique biodiversity; it already suffers from immigrant species such as rodents and goats that destroy vegetation; visitors bring in seeds (and pets) from elsewhere which negatively affect the environment; the island cannot sustain a larger population (food and lodging); creating more/better infrastructure for tourists will damage the environment.

"The Story of Alexander Selkirk"

Resource 1.4

More able students might benefit from looking at the passage on Resource 1.4 from an 18th-century essay about Selkirk by the British essayist Richard Steele. It is also available at www.ourcivilisation.com. Answers:

- Sea-Chest (presumably for the Cloaths and Bedding)

- a Fire-lock (flintlock) – a gun with a flint embedded in the hammer to produce a spark that ignited gunpowder

- a Pound of Gun-powder and a large quantity of Bullets

- a Flint and Steel – when struck against steel a flint edge produces sparks to make a fire

- a few Pounds of Tobacco

- Hatchet and Knife

- Kettle (probably like an open saucepan for boiling water, soup or stew over a fire)

- Bible and other Books of Devotion

- Navigation and Mathematical Instruments

- enough food for two meals.

Holiday brochures

Student Book, pages 16–19

Ask students to do the **Speaking and listening task** on page 16. Encourage them to read the four advertisements on pages 16–18 carefully. Discuss the way each advertisement makes the location particularly appealing. They should order their preferences and then work with a partner to discuss their choice of holiday. Remind them the emphasis is on why; they must explain their preferences, likes and dislikes, and give reasons.

\Ask students to do the **Writing task** on page 19 of the Student Book. Use the advertisements on pages 16–18 as examples. They should work independently or in pairs to create an advertisement, paying close attention to how they describe the location and what it has to offer. Encourage them to use figurative language with a positive slant.

"Banff & Lake Louise"

Student Book, page 19; Resource 1.5

This advertisement on page 19 could be used at various points during the unit. Make sure students can identify the difference between tourism and eco-tourism. Discuss how and why people might choose to go to a remote, unpopulated area as opposed to somewhere with tourist facilities. Discuss the moral and socio-economic aspects of eco-tourism, as well as the negative impact tourists can have on the natural environment to address the **Talking point** on page 19.

The quote from Bill Bryson at the bottom of page 19 of the Student Book is a humorous reminder that going off the beaten track can be dangerous. Bryson's account of his walk along the North American Appalachian Trail in *A Walk in the Woods* is an entertaining non-fiction book that might appeal to students who don't enjoy reading very much. Various websites have passages from the book, along with lesson plans.

Writing a leaflet

Resource 1.5

Ask students to write a leaflet for eco-tourists using the list of do's and don'ts presented on **Resource 1.5** as a source of information. The task requires students to reword the information to suit another format and is similar to Directed Writing questions. Students should only use the information given but the choice of location for the leaflet has been left open. They may choose to write about places you do not consider appropriate; however, when marking focus on the content of the leaflet. Award up to 12 marks for how the information has been used and up to 13 marks for style and accuracy (total of 25 marks).

A writer's choice of words

Student Book, page 20

Make sure students understand the definitions of *paradox* and *oxymoron* on page 20.

"As I Walked Out One Midsummer Morning"

Student Book, page 20

Introduce the passage by telling students that Laurie Lee grew up in a relatively poor family in a very rural English environment after the First World War. His early life is described in *Cider with Rosie. As I Walked Out One Midsummer Morning* describes the journey he made across Spain when he was 19 years old. In this passage he uses a number of paradoxical statements and oxymorons, perhaps to extend the irony of La Granja (the farm) being a very elaborate palace and/or to explain his own conflicting ideas. He is impressed by the location, but ultimately thinks it is rather tasteless or "vulgar".

Ask students to do the **Writer's craft task** on page 20 of the Student Book. Suggest that as statues cannot move students should think about why Lee used the adjective "writhing". Point out that the leaves are on dry ground, but Lee uses the verb "paddling". Prompt students to find other paradoxes and oxymorons. If they need clues:

- fountains rise from dust

- the palace gardens are elaborate and artificial, but it's called "the farm"

- the overall impression is not awe-inspiring, Lee likens it to a suburban garden.

Prepare for the last question by asking: What does Lee's description suggest about the place to you? However, point out that the last question asks for Lee's opinion or point of view.

Dictogloss

Resource 1.6

The passage on **Resource 1.6** appears on the next page in Lee's book and is in direct contrast to his visit to La Granja. He describes a place less than a kilometre from the palace, but it is a very different location and point of view.

This is a good passage for dictogloss, but do not show it to students until they have finished the task and are ready to mark their version against the original. Read the passage to the class once in a normal speaking voice. Ask students to note down basic *wh-* points (who, what, where, when). Read the text again and ask them to make notes on the five senses (what Lee saw, felt, heard, touched, smelled). Organise students into pairs or small groups. Read the text a third time and ask groups to reconstruct the text from memory. Set a suitable time limit.

Ask students to exchange reconstructions. Each pair or group should then peer-mark by reading through the passage on Resource 1.6 and ticking correct phrasing or sentences and remembered points in the reconstructed passage. The pair or group with the closest reconstruction wins or gets credit/merit points.

You could then discuss Lee's attitude to La Granja and how or why he feels differently about being in a more natural environment.

Improving narrative writing skills

Workbook, pages 11–13

As students have done quite a lot on travel and descriptive writing in this unit, they may now enjoy writing a story. If you would prefer them to continue with descriptive writing skills, go to the end of Unit 2 in the Workbook.

Work through the bullet points for narrative writing on page 11 of the Workbook together.

You could stimulate ideas for narrative writing by having a group story-making session. (This is also a good activity for the last lesson of the day, bad weather, days of low concentration or as a light-relief reward after an exam or test.)

1. Organise a large class into groups; if you have a small class do it all together.

2. Explain that they are going to take turns to contribute a sentence to a story, which needs a beginning, middle and end.

3. Each group sits in a circle with one student – the prompt – in the middle. In a whole class activity, the teacher could act as prompt.

4. Going clockwise, each student is allowed to say one sentence only. The prompt must listen for a full sentence and indicate when the next student can add the next sentence.

5. Students can change the direction of the narrative by starting with the words, "New paragraph."

6. It is up to the prompt to decide when the story is ended.

Any activity of this nature can be an invitation to adolescent silliness. If a student cannot make a sensible contribution, point to the next person and the student should then move out of the circle. Sometimes only a warning is necessary; few students like being left out!

When students have written their compositions, award up to 12 marks for content and up to 13 marks for style and accuracy (total of 25 marks). You could take the opportunity for some students to read their work to the class and/or display all the compositions in the classroom.

A poet's choice of words

Student Book, pages 21–2

Remind students that everything they do relating to poetry applies to prose and they can use poetry techniques such as alliteration in their own creative writing.

Core students and those not studying English Literature will also benefit from the literature components in each unit. Encourage them to enjoy the different forms of poetry, prose and drama for their own sake.

"Kubla Khan"

Student Book, pages 21–2

Allow students to read the poem on their own and then read it with them. Discuss the poem's musicality and how the rhythm and rhyme suggest the flow of water. Consider how long vowel sounds are used to slow the pace. This might be a good moment to introduce the terms *alliteration, sibilance, assonance* and *consonance*. The following notes might be useful:

- Kubla Khan was a 13th-century Mongolian ruler.

- Note the magical, romantic associations of folklore.

- It is worth spending time on the phrase "Five miles meandering" (line 25), looking at the long, open vowel sounds and alliteration.

- It is the distant nature of Mount Abora (line 41) not its geographical location (in Abyssinia) that is important. Coleridge is building a picture of a perfect, harmonious world (Utopia), distant in time and space from the hurly-burly of everyday life.

When students are familiar with the poem, explain that it is regarded as an unfinished masterpiece.

Ask them to complete the poem in a maximum of 30 lines. Encourage them to write as the imaginary character in the poem, to think about the persona's mood and time. They need not try to imitate the language of the Romantic era.

Ask students to do the **Writing task** at the bottom of page 22 of the Student Book. You could encourage more able students to practise the SQuEE writing technique: State, Quote, Explain Effect, reminding them of the Reminder box on page 6 of the Student Book. You could model the technique and then ask students to write one or two more examples independently, for example:

S – Initially, Coleridge suggests that Xanadu is a picturesque, appealing place.

Q – "there were gardens bright with sinuous rills, / Where blossomed many an incense-bearing tree."

EE – The adjective "bright" brings a luminous quality to the gardens and, coupled with "blossomed many" suggests that the place is utopia-like, filled with an abundance of trees and lovely smells.

All the poems in this unit could be used for coursework activities. For example, students could finish the poem "Kubla Khan" in prose; write an article about the real Kubla Khan; or write a first-person account from one of Kubla Khan's subjects (e.g. a gardener or architect).

"Travel"

Student Book, pages 23–4; Resources 1.7–1.8

Hand out Resource 1.7. Tell students something about Robert Louis Stevenson. He is most famous for writing the adventure stories which included *Treasure Island* (1883); he also wrote the much darker novel, *The Strange Case of Doctor Jekyll and Mr Hyde* (1886); he wrote many travel books, including *Travels with a Donkey in the Cevennes* and a lot of popular verse. Stevenson's father was a well-respected lighthouse engineer and Stevenson was expected to follow in his footsteps. Robert Louis, however, was of a different temperament and also suffered from ill-health (tuberculosis). He travelled to California in an emigrant ship in 1879 and never returned to live in Scotland. He died in Samoa in 1894.

The poem "Travel" conjures the world Stevenson wanted to see and includes an image of an old man in a "dusty dining room" who only has his pictures to remind him of his travels. Point out that the poem was written at the end of the 19th century; use of the word *negro* was acceptable then, but is not now. Students

could work in pairs to do the **Reading task**, listing the places visited, but they should do the **Writing task** on their own. This task is a narrative, but requires descriptive content. The length of this task makes it suitable for Coursework Portfolio practice. Use the syllabus guidelines for marking such assignments or mark A–F. Students could do a similar activity on a poem of their choice for their Coursework Portfolio.

Ask students to do the **Descriptive writing task** on page 24 of the Student Book, referring to the guidelines on **Resource 1.8**. Award up to 12 marks for content and up to 13 marks for style and accuracy (total of 25 marks).

Self-assessment

Student Book, page 24; Resource 1.9

At the end of the main unit, ask students to recap on what they have learned by answering the questions on the **Self-assessment panel** on page 24 of the Student Book; these are also available on **Resource 1.9**. Give them a minimum of 15 minutes or set this for homework to ensure that students are thinking independently without peer influence. Explain that it is important for them to reflect on what they have achieved but also to identify their weaknesses so that they know what to focus on in future. When you have feedback, you could recap on a particular skill, such as summary writing. Take the time to do that but don't dwell on areas of weakness so early in the course when there is plenty of opportunity to practise these skills in later units.

Literature extension

Student Book, page 25

Introduce Elizabeth Brewster, who was born in Canada in 1922, and this poem, which captures impressions of the rural Canada of her youth.

Read the poem "Where I Come From" as a class. Then look at the way Brewster makes a statement in the first line and then gives examples to elaborate in the rest of the first stanza. Draw out the meaning that something of the places where they live or were born live on in people. The places might be jungles, mountains, seas or cities, but in most of the first stanza Brewster focuses on people in museums, glue factories, offices and subways.

The second stanza shifts to a rural setting and perhaps from the present to the past. It starts by repeating "Where I Come from", followed by various images from the countryside: pine woods, blueberry patches, farmhouses and schoolhouses. The last four lines are central to the poem. They focus on spring and winter and help to explain the main influences on the persona. The metaphor of "the door in the mind" that "blows open" shows how important the sense of place that the persona carries with her is.

At this stage of the course, you may choose to use only the general idea in this poem that each of us carries with us "where we come from". Introduce the idea of cultural baggage – that we literally carry with us ideas, beliefs and perhaps a world view relating to where we come from. If you have a multi-national group of students, this could develop into a fascinating discussion. If you are in a one-nation classroom, encourage students to consider people who live in their community but come from different places, and how their beliefs and ideas may have been shaped in early childhood. You could relate this back to tourism and visiting or living in another country – how we see foreign places and act when abroad.

If you set the **Writing task** on page 25 of the Student Book, remind students that they need to think about the physical aspects of the environment and the way the climate and geography affect the way people think and behave. For example, if they come from a warm country, people may gather outdoors in the evenings to chat or take a stroll, which is only possible during the summer months further north.

2 The world of nature

Many aspects of this unit can be developed into activities for the Coursework Portfolio. Passages and Listening and speaking activities can be used for class discussion, debate and pair work, which can then be developed independently for oral or written assignments.

Unit starter

Student Book, page 27; Resources 2.1–2.2

Start by reading the short myths from **Metamorphoses** and about **Ginnungagap** on page 27 with the class, asking students to relate these to other myths they know that "explain" natural phenomena or how the world came into being. Consider how early man used myths to explain the environment and why. If you want more information about Ovid's *Metamorphoses* or other ancient texts see: http://ancienthistory.about.com.

Move on to the **Talking points** on page 27 of the Student Book. Ask students exactly what they understand by Nature (with a capital N) and look at the definition on page 27. Discuss what Tennyson meant by the expression "red in tooth and claw"; you may choose to explain that he was alluding to the debate over the major scientific and theological concern of Victorian thinkers – Charles Darwin's theories of natural selection, as expressed in *The Origin of Species* (published later in 1859). The expression itself was in common use at the time. Richard Dawkins also uses "red in tooth and claw" in *The Selfish Gene* (published 1976) to summarise the behaviour of all living things in their need to survive and reproduce.

Ask students to work in pairs or small groups to discuss: Is Nature, by nature, cruel? Prompt them to think about the food chain (e.g. lions catching baby deer) and natural disasters. Ask: Is Nature *always* dangerous in some way? Students might give tidal waves, hurricanes or tornadoes as examples. Ways in which people try to tame or change nature might include wind turbines, dams or training animals. The ways Nature constantly proves its power might include tsunami or floods. Discuss fish-farming, battery hen farming, building irrigation and transport canals as ways in which people try to change the natural world for their personal benefit. Assist students to list three other ways, as necessary.

This discussion, as others in the Student Book, could lead to some interesting coursework so encourage students to make notes, including opposing points of view, on **Resource 2.1**. They could fill in the second column in advance, then finish the worksheet in silence afterwards. The questions are also available on **Resource 2.2** for display or they can be cut up so that small groups of two or three students can discuss one question each before feeding back to the class.

Reading skills questionnaire

Workbook, page 14

The Reading skills questionnaire on page 14 of the Workbook reviews and develops the reading skills students were introduced to in Unit 1. Students are asked to think about *how* they read and different ways of reading: active and passive. It is worth reviewing responses so that they can compare and contrast what and how they read. Point out that they already have a wide range of reading skills – glancing at incoming text messages, answering reading comprehension questions, finding information, interpreting and developing it for History, Geography, Business Studies, etc.

Improving your reading skills and Scanning

Workbook, pages 15–16

Having looked at skimming and scanning in class, students could recap, using the notes in **Improving your reading skills** on page 15 of the Workbook. Make sure they understand the difference between, and the importance of, using the techniques outlined here. Ask them to do the **Scanning task** on page 16 of the Workbook independently. Answers:

a. 351;   **b.** 15, 10;   **c.** 53, 59;   **d.** 7;   **e.** 20, 30.

Then discuss how students approached the text and if they were consciously reading in different ways to locate and retrieve information. Outline the importance of learner autonomy and how they are developing skills and strategies for the exams and/ or coursework across the curriculum. You could extend the activity by asking students to identify the adverbial clauses of time. They include "The spring of 2011"; "30 years ago"; "seven weeks before".

Improving summarising skills

Workbook, page 17

Ask students to work independently on this activity. Answers to question 1:

- in 2011 more than a quarter of all butterfly species made earliest recorded appearances
- 15 types of British butterfly to appear weeks before they would have ten years ago
- warmest spring for 351 years – rising temperatures
- climate change
- arriving before nectar is available, there may not be anything for caterpillars to eat, global warming threat to butterflies, they appear before their food source is available (what will caterpillars eat?)

The elements

Student Book, pages 28–39

This section includes poetry, prose and drama relating to the elements: each text relates to how we use the environment for sustenance and energy, or to explain difficult ideas or concepts that affect us socially or personally. All the texts relate in one way or another to the discussions on myths and Nature on page 27 of the Student Book.

Aristotle (384–322 BC) taught that there were four elements: earth, air, fire and water, plus a *quinta essential* or *quintessence* that was supposedly common to all and unified them. See Shakespeare's *Twelfth Night* Act 2 scene 3: "The theory of the five elements was the first chemical theory that had any force in it … "

Earth

Student Book, page 28; Resource 2.3

As a class, read the text and the **Facts about salt box** on page 28 of the Student Book. You could discuss some of the facts before asking students to work in pairs to put them into chronological order. They should cut out and sort the statements available on **Resource 2.3**.

You could extend this task by asking students to write an informative article about salt for a serious Nature magazine or blog. Prompt them to think about the readers/users of magazines such as *National Geographic*. If you have access to a library, devote a lesson to reading serious magazines and journals. A library provides a more academic atmosphere than the classroom. Many students will never have opened or seen *National Geographic* or Humanities and Science journals, but encourage them to read at least one or two articles. It is time well spent because they will see in print (not on a screen) the style of writing they are asked to produce in a range of subjects, including English Language. Encourage them to work on their own in silence.

Guide them in researching more information about the history of salt to add to their existing knowledge. Remind them that they do not need to include all the information, but should leave out anything irrelevant. You could give them the starter: *Since its discovery thousands of years ago, salt has been a valuable item …*

Air

Student Book, page 29

Briefly discuss how we are aware of air, leading around to the words we use for wind and how we measure its speed. You could explain how we refer to wind speeds using the Beaufort Scale. In 1805, Sir Francis Beaufort, an admiral and hydrographer in the British Navy, established a common scale for wind speeds. It is still widely used by mariners and meteorologists all over the world.

As a class, compare and contrast the moods and/or tone of the poems **"Wind Turbines"** and **"Pain"** on page 29 of the Student Book. Then look at form and content. Discuss how the poets perceive and use the wind. Draw attention to Magliaro's use of light, delicate sounds such as "whoosh" and "whirl" and the idea of blades slicing. Consider the pronunciation and meaning of the final word, "Windflower". Explain the literary use of personification.

In "Pain" the wind is a foreboding, ominous presence, with the use of "agony", "despairing" suggesting tyrannical force. Students should think about the idea of a "grim king" and how rage and menace are present in the poem.

Then look at the speech from *King Lear* on page 29. Lear's pace and diction is strong and aggressive. Ask: How does Shakespeare achieve the atmosphere or mood of a violent storm or gale? Remind students that this speech comes from a play and discuss how an audience might react to it spoken on a stage. They might pick up on the mix of harsh exclamatives and onomatopoeic sounds (e.g. "crack", "rage"); the diction associated with torture and pain (e.g. "sulphurous", "thought-executing"). Draw out that the sounds and vehemence of the language would be all the more powerful with an actor's intonation and movement, and therefore sound threatening to an audience. Finally, ask students to think about why an old man wants the wind to destroy "nature's moulds" ("That make ingrateful man").

If you have a class of high flyers and/or your students are also studying English Literature, this may be an opportune moment to introduce the concept of *pathetic fallacy* – how poets and authors use the elements/weather as a metaphor and to create mood.

Fire

Student Book, pages 30–2; Resource 2.4; Recording 1

As a class, read the text above the passage on page 30 and then ask students to read **"How Coyote Gave Fire to the People"** independently. They could also listen to the passage on **Recording 1**. Then ask them to do the **Reading task** at the top of page 32 either in pairs or small groups. Take feedback. Possible responses:

1. Humans need wood in order to survive and keep warm when it's cold. If people do not respect the environment, they cannot learn from it or use its resources wisely. Coyote shows that Nature helps those in need and that those who protect only themselves (the Fire Protectors) have no respect for the natural world and will eventually be defeated.

2. Coyote is patient, biding his time, waiting for the Fire Protectors to sleep; wise in tossing the flame to squirrel; cunning in that he has a plan and asks other animals to help. Squirrel is determined not to let the pain stop her tossing flame to Chipmunk, who is intelligent and forward-thinking enough to pass the flame to wood.

Ask students to choose one of the **Coursework ideas** on page 32 of the Student Book. Point out that they will need to use imagination and think carefully about their use of language for both options. Some students may prefer the first option, but not know a similar myth. Suggest they use the school library and/or www.mythencyclopedia.com, or you could tell them this very short fire myth:

The Admiralty Islanders in the Pacific Ocean have a myth in which a snake asks his human children to cook some fish. The children simply heat the fish in the Sun and eat it raw, so the snake gives them fire and teaches them to use it to cook their food.

Because fire warms and gives off light like the Sun, it often represents the Sun or a Sun god in mythology. In some tales, it is linked with the idea of the hearth, the centre of a household. Fire can also be a symbol of new life, as in the case of the phoenix, the mythical bird that is periodically destroyed by flames to rise, reborn, from its own ashes.

You could take this opportunity to look at stories in the oral tradition in more detail. Read the story "The Drought" on **Resource 2.4** to students and then discuss the importance of storytelling to our ancestors. Give them copies of Resource 2.4 and ask them to answer the questions about how the storyteller makes the tale interesting while using very simple vocabulary. Answers:

1. a. "Suffocating dust."

   b. "And the plants were dying."

   c. "And the people were starving too, for there was nothing to eat."

   d. "Changing from green … they withered and died."

   e. "And do you know what?"

2. Short, simple and minor sentences are used to suggest pauses, hesitation and emphasis as if someone is actually speaking (not considering their grammar before writing words down). Some sentences begin with "And", which gives an oral quality as the story continues.

Water

Student Book, pages 32–9 and 48; Workbook, pages 18–21

Introduce this element by reviewing how humans are utterly dependent on, yet subservient to, water: how people are reliant on rain and rivers, and victims of floods or droughts.

Before or while working on the articles on the Yangtze River, you could set aside at least half a lesson to look at the guidelines for writing to inform in the **Writing skills panel** on page 48 of the Student Book. This style of writing is the basis of many types of text such as feature articles, blogs, etc.; it is also very relevant to speaking and listening skills and how students convey information. Take time to clarify terms such as *impersonal* and *objective*; explain the word *citation* and why citations are important. If necessary, recap on the difference between active and passive verbs, simple and complex sentences. More on verbs and sentences can be found in Unit 11, on pages 281–2 and 291–6 of the Student Book. Be sure to explain that not all informative texts conform to these bullet points: it depends on the purpose of the text and its audience.

"The Yangtze River Three Gorges Project"

Student Book, pages 32–3

As a class, read the article on page 33, paying particular attention to the advantages and disadvantages of building the dam. Discuss how the writer has used data and made it interesting. You could use this opportunity to consider how the article conforms to the guidelines for information texts. You could also ask students to find:

- a phrase written in the present tense: e.g. "the Yangtze River journeys" (line 2) (present tense used for facts)

- two adverbs or adverbial phrases of time: e.g. "For nearly three millennia" (line 16); "Each year" (line 34)

- a sentence that contains two sides of an argument: e.g. "Vessels as large as … years of China's heritage" (lines 65–9)

- reported speech: e.g. "Water, they say, is stronger than stone." (line 82)

Ask students to work independently on the **Reading task** on page 32. Set a time limit. When they have finished, review the article and discuss their answers. Suggested answers:

1. Facts include: the Yangtze's source is in Tibet; it travels over 6,000 miles to the Pacific Ocean; it flows through Shanghai; it flows through gorges, plains, mountains and lakes, over rapids and shallows; about 300 million people live in the Yangtze valley and along its tributaries, etc.

2. Beliefs include: the Yangtze is the main bearer and sustainer of Chinese life and culture; it creates a social and cultural divide; that people should go with the flow; that Nature can be transformed, etc.

3. People say: the Yangtze is the "golden waterway"; that they belong on the south or the north bank; "go with the flow".

4. The writer often includes her opinions by using adjectives such as "tortuous" and "teeming" (line 4); negative words such as "servants" and "slaves" (lines 51–2, in referring to respect for Nature); positive ideas such as halting the river's flow, transforming its appearance, navigating it and driving turbines of industrial growth (lines 52–5, in referring to transforming Nature); the phrase "alter but not ruin" (line 58), etc.

5. The huge vessels indicative of an industrial growth will sail across water that has flooded an area that represents thousands of years of Chinese culture, including an ancient settlement, tombs and palace, which will never be seen again.

6. The people should benefit because the supply of water will be controlled, eliminating floods that destroy crops, homes and livelihoods; from the filtering down of new economic growth; from new job opportunities.

7. a. Less welcome effects on the river: it could ruin the scenery; it will become a busy shipping channel; marine life may be destroyed; silt may be trapped behind the dam; the river may burst its banks or the dam.

   b. Less welcome effects on the people: many will have to move house; they may not get new jobs; they may not be able to use river silt to enrich farmland.

You could extend the work by asking students to summarise the advantages and disadvantages of the Three Gorges Project outlined in Ling's article in less than 100 words. Suggest that they use a green pencil to identify the benefits the dam will bring and red for disadvantages. Emphasise the importance of remembering the stages of summary writing: finding information and making notes before summarising those notes in continuous writing.

"China warns of 'urgent problems' facing Three Gorges Dam"

Student Book, pages 34–5; Workbook, pages 18–19

Ask students to read the article on page 34 in silence and then to prepare a few notes on the problems relating to the new dam. Discuss the questions in the **Speaking and listening task** on page 35. Encourage students to refer back to their notes and the texts, to quote data in support of their views and to paraphrase the writers' opinions.

Similar topics on managing the environment, civil or agricultural engineering, could be developed towards Speaking and Listening Coursework. Students could work in pairs, each partner taking an opposing view on an issue such as the Three Gorges Dam or genetically modified food. These issues could also be explored independently and developed into an informative or discursive/argumentative assignment for Coursework Portfolios.

Move on to the **Writer's craft task** on page 35 of the Student Book to look at how Watts has used data and statistics in his article. Prompt students to explain their answers, supported with examples from the texts. Suggested answers:

1. "in 1992 about 16m tonnes of concrete"; "26 giant turbines"; "capacity of 18,200MW"; "1.4 million people"; "more than 1,000 towns and villages"; "1.5 mile barrier was completed in 2006s"; "Four years ago"; "hundreds of thousands of nearby residents", "1,392 reservoirs"; "300,000 people"; "went into operation in 2003".

2. The author uses numerals with dates, money and time, and spells out numbers as words at the start of sentences and if a number is not exact.

3. Shocking or particularly large numbers are written as numbers for maximum impact; they are easily spotted if skimming the text quickly. Remind students that quantity and number are

adjectives. If students struggle with this task, refer them to page 286 on adjectives of number and quantity in Unit 11.

You could also set the **Descriptive Writing task** on pages 18–19 of the Workbook, perhaps for homework. In preparation, refer back to mood and Nature in the poems on page 29 of the Student Book. Then point out that the mood in each passage in the Workbook is tranquil, with a sense of the past: each river having a timeless or eternal quality. The rivers here contrast well with the texts on the Yangtze River in the Student Book. Suggested answers:

Passage A

Setting: a still, silent river with clear and brown water, mangroves growing along the banks, flat land alongside and steep, stony mountains beyond.

Time: at sun rise.

People: Thornhill is the only person present.

Imagery: includes description of the place, "ferocious" mosquitoes, bird and fish.

Figurative language: "as brown as strong tea" (simile); "needle-like biting part", "silvery sound", "a little bell being struck" (metaphors); "The place held its breath, watching." (personification).

Effect(s) on reader: the overriding impression is of a beautiful, peaceful scene, despite the "ferocious" mosquitoes. Thornhill is the only human present and has time to appreciate the scenery and watch the mosquitoes, bird and fish. The final idea is of the place holding its breath and watching, which could be in tranquil wonder or could hint at forthcoming change.

Passage B

Setting: a slow, old river that flows through willow herb and rushes and past a "many cornered" house with chimneys in a thick white mist in a Tamar valley.

Time: before sun rise.

People: no humans are there.

Imagery: include description of the house, river, animals and birds.

Figurative language: "curled", "sidled", "settled", "chattered", "Morning had come to a slow turn" (personification);

Effect(s) on reader: a scene of peace and tranquillity as Nature goes about its business undisturbed by human beings.

Move on to the **Reading task** on page 35 of the Student Book, which asks students to locate information and make notes that include line references. If they struggle to begin with, refer them to some of the following points and ask them to decide which are hard facts that can be proven and which are beliefs or attitudes to life. Points to be included are:

Need for the dam (advantages):

- to prevent catastrophic flooding
- to take away constant fear that the river will break its banks and destroy homes, livelihoods, harvests and livestock
- to remedy unreliable/unpredictable water supply
- so that people are no longer at the mercy of the vagaries of nature
- to navigate the upper reaches of the river
- to produce energy to help industrial progress and drive turbines for modern industry
- so that large vessels can sail upriver to major inland cities
- to provide new job opportunities
- to make the river more manageable and productive.

Social and environmental problems (disadvantages):

- dam will stop beneficial silt in the river reaching farmland
- water will drown thousands of years of heritage, including an ancient settlement, tombs and palace
- dam will change the landscape
- polluted water will affect fish supplies and water species
- old social divides created by the river will disappear
- over a million people will need to be rehoused
- potential for landslides and soil erosion on slopes
- weight of extra water may lead to tremors and seismic threats or disasters
- huge amount of money required to restore the ecosystem
- middle stretches of river are left with stagnant reservoirs
- drinking water supplies of over 300,000 people negatively affected
- some areas will no longer be able to use water as a means of (free) transport

- those relying on water for an income will lose their livelihoods
- Chinese philosophy of "go with the flow".

Improving descriptive writing skills
Workbook, pages 20–1

Before moving on to the next river article in the Student Book, students may enjoy doing the Descriptive Writing task on pages 20–1 of the Workbook. Ask them to read the information on descriptive compositions carefully and remind them that the travel article on Venezuela on page 7 of the Student Book uses descriptive writing techniques. Ask them to read the passage from *The Impressionist* and do the writing task in the Workbook for homework. Students should remember the guidelines from work in Unit 1 and they will provide useful revision. There is no markscheme for this task but look for a wide, original use of language. Remind students not to write less than 350 or more than 450 words. Gradually they should be becoming accustomed to writing within word limits for different purposes. Similar descriptive passages could be created and developed by individual students for their Coursework Portfolios.

"Ice cold in Alaska"
Student Book, pages 36–9; Resource 11.1

As a class, read the article on pages 36–9 about a raft trip down the Copper River in Alaska. Point out that it is written in the first person and ask students if they think it is a typical piece of travel journalism or feature article for a newspaper. If not, what makes it different? Lead them to look more closely at how the couple see and feel what is around them, and how they interact. Finally, set the **Speaking and listening task** on page 38, ask students to work in pairs and give them a time limit. Regarding the Iveys' "children's school", allow students to decide on the specific age-group of their audience; it should be evident when they give their talk. Finally, ask students how Ivey's article differs from the articles on the Three Gorges Dam.

Introduce the skill of writing to argue and persuade. Set students a time limit of 5 minutes to work in pairs to list as many features of writing to argue and persuade as they can. They will realise that they already know a lot. Share responses as a class. Review the guidelines in the **Writing skills panel** on page 39 of the Student Book and ensure students understand that writing to argue and persuade presents a case and promotes the writer's point of view. This style of writing needs to be logical and convincing.

Ask students to suggest any other useful words and phrases used in writing to argue and persuade, and write them on the board. Discuss how they might use words like *notwithstanding* and *albeit*, and the dangers of using words like *ordinary* and *normal* (especially in an exam).

Point out that students should be aware of bias and how one's environment might shape one's world view (Unit 3 focuses on points of view). You may want to relate this back to the poem "Where I Come From" (page 25 of the Student Book), reviewing how our world view is shaped by home country and/or upbringing (socialisation).

Ask students to do the **Writing task** on page 39 of the Student Book. With the suggested word count, this writing activity can be used as practice for coursework. If your students are not doing Coursework Portfolios, you may want to reduce the word limit. Before they begin, discuss the term "devil's advocate", how it can be employed in debates and its significance in this type of writing. Remind them that whether or not they use this technique, they should always include an opposing point of view in a discursive/argumentative essay.

Emphasise the need to choose one topic and develop it; to be specific and not wander into generalities. Remind students to plan carefully before they begin writing, to write neatly, to conform to the word count and to proofread and edit once they think they have finished. Remind them to define terms: e.g. What is a captive animal – a pet rabbit, factory farm chickens or zoo animals? Are safari parks just big zoos? Remind them to use rhetorical questions very sparingly (although they can be effective in rousing speeches) and never end a formal essay with a question ("What do *you* think?" begs the answer "Rubbish!" or "You're wrong!")

Importance of register

This may be a good time to re-iterate the importance of using an appropriate register. Students who have spent hours preparing for oral assessments can ruin their chances of good marks by constantly saying, *ya' know, kinda, gonna, wanna* or using expressions like *half a brain, know what I mean?, What kinda guy does something stupid like that?* The same applies in written exams: students who have interesting points to make let themselves down by inappropriate use of register, such as " … well he really pushed the envelope that time … " in an essay about Iago taunting Othello about Desdemona.

The history of English on **Resource 11.1** should help students become more aware of how and when they use idiomatic English. At this point, focus on the **New words for the New World (11.1c)** section, which traces the development and expansion of English in North America. You can spend some time in class discussing American slang and register – how *gonna*, *wanna* and idiomatic expressions are used in colloquial speech but not in essays. (Some students may have little contact with formal English outside the classroom and think the dialogue they hear in American movies is Standard English. It is important that they understand how to use different registers, especially if they plan to go on to further education when they will have to write a dissertation.) Introduce students to the **Transatlantic English task** by discussing the word *hoodlum* as used in American gangster movies. How did this word come into being? (Robin *Hood* was an outlaw, although *Webster's Dictionary* says "origin unknown".)

Bestiaries

Student Book, pages 40–1; Resource 11.1

Explain that many expressions still in use date back to medieval bestiaries. The phrase *crocodile tears*, for example, relates to the belief that crocodiles cried real tears while devouring their victims.

As a class, read the text on bestiaries on pages 40–1 of the Student Book. There is also a wealth of information and wonderful examples from the medieval Aberdeen Bestiary at www.bestiary.ca. If your class is also studying English Literature, discuss the prevalence and purpose of animal imagery in the works of Chaucer, Shakespeare and other pre-20th century authors. Relate the extract from the Arundel manuscript on page 40 to the history of English on **Resource 11.1**.

Explain that animal imagery is not confined to poetry or classical literature; we use it all the time. Ask students to work in pairs to answer questions in the **Animal imagery box** on page 41. Then take feedback. Answers:

1. The odd one out is the adjective *mousy*; the others are verbs.

2. *to fox* (trick/confuse); *to hound* (follow/pursue); *to wolf (down food)* (eat greedily)

3. *a snake in the grass* (someone who cannot be trusted): *a wolf in sheep's clothing* (someone who is acting the innocent with evil intent).

You could ask students to compile their own list of animal-related expressions. Suggestions include: *to let the cat out of the bag* (to tell something that should be kept secret); *raining cats and dogs* (in medieval times, cats and dogs would often sleep in the warm loft area of a house; during bad weather heavy rain would bring down the thatched roof, causing cats and dogs to fall as if from the sky). Take feedback and discuss how these sayings may have come into being.

A short history of English

Resource 11.1

At some stage in this unit and before you look at Shakespeare's diction in detail, spend some time on the early history of English, using **Resource 11.1**. The purpose of this text is to demonstrate the breadth of English vocabulary, how words have come into use from a wide range of origins and to demonstrate how we make word choices according to circumstances. Display a map of Britain and read the text as a class.

Focus on the **Word invaders** section. Nominate students to draw arrows on the map showing the "word invasions". Discuss how language is the result of a two-way process with words coming into English from other places, while other English words have become used all over the world.

You could give examples of Norse words that came into English: e.g. *woman/women, husband, brat, skull, rotten, freckles, sky, they/their/them*. You could point out that although the languages of the Vikings from whom the Normans were descended influenced Norman French, it was also influenced by Latin. Expand on the use of different words by lords and peasants in England. The Norman invaders/colonisers held higher social positions than the local population; they were seen to be more educated and wealthier than native Saxons and Celts. Anyone with ambition needed to copy their "betters", which may explain why they used certain words such as *cows* for animals in the fields but used different words, such as *beef*, for the meat on their plates. Explore the differences between *cook/chef, fashion/couture*, etc.

You could ask students to complete the task in this section of the resource, in which they are asked to identify the source of words that mean more or less the same but are employed in different ways. The task is designed to show how everyday or common speech differs from "officialese" or legal and scientific terminology. Answers to question 1 are:

- Old Norse, Old English: smell, ask, job, kingly, folk, forebear, spread, kill, speak, teacher, holy

- Latin, Norman French: odour, interrogate, profession, regal, persons, ancestor, extend, exterminate, enunciate, professor, consecrated.

Discuss how the two columns list words in everyday conversational use and words that are employed in a more formal, official and/or scientific context. Ask students to respond to question 2. (Ask students to keep this worksheet safe for future work in Units 3 and 4.)

Shakespeare's animal imagery

Student Book, pages 42–3; Resource 11.1

As a class, read the information on page 42 of the Student Book on Shakespeare's use of animal imagery, including the listed examples from *King Lear*. Students could work in pairs to do the **Animal adjectives task** on the same page. The answers are: equine (horse); feline (cat); vulpine (wolf); canine (dog); asinine (donkey); aquiline (eagle); leonine (lion).

The **Writer's craft task** on page 43 of the Student Book looks at animal and bird imagery in Macbeth. If your class is studying English Literature, it is worth spending time on this. The animal comparisons and metaphors, and their modern explanations, are:

- "As sparrows eagles, or the hare the lion." (in the same way as eagles/lions are frightened by sparrows/hares – so not frightened at all)

- "The temple-haunting martlet" (the house martin that nests against church walls – meaning that Macbeth's castle is a "good" place (irony))

- "this bird / Hath made his pendent bed and procreant cradle" (This little bird has made a nest for its chicks; perhaps an allusion to Lady Macbeth's childlessness or that this is a pleasant, ideal place to raise young a pleasant place (irony).)

- "Where they most breed and haunt […] The air is delicate." (These birds only nest in places where the air is clean or gentle (irony).)

- "The most diminutive of birds, will fight, will fight, / Her young ones in her nest, against the owl." (Even a tiny little wren will face up to an owl (bird of prey) to protect her young. Macbeth is the "owl", a bird associated with sin and death.)

You could also use this as an opportunity to return to the history of English on **Resource 11.1** and specifically the section on **Shakespeare's English**. Discuss the two main influences on Shakespeare's English, language used to entertain different levels of society in a theatre. It was influenced by Norse, Old French and Middle English, but he had a classical education so he was also familiar with Latin and Greek. You could lead this into the nature of pre-20th century education with its focus on Latin, Greek and the Classics. This will help students when they come to do the tasks in this section of the resource. Suggested answers:

1. Anon, anon! (In a minute or just a minute!); Betimes (At once); To cozen (Cheat); Grizzled (Grey).

2. **a.** sick in the mind, foolish, unwise;

   b. to be thrifty / farming or caring for livestock;

   c. here or come here, depending on context;

   d. the noise and confusion of battle;

   e. fancy that, goodness, what's more, etc.;

   f. a charlatan, trickster, someone not to be trusted;

   g. "I pray thee", meaning please as an entreaty, I beg you;

   h. lovers whose stars were in opposition (people believed the stars and planets controlled their lives);

   i. fed up, cross, ill-humoured;

   j. scoundrel, knave.

Animals and people

Student Book, pages 44–9

Ask students to make a list of animals that people use for work purposes and another list of animals kept as pets. Give them a few minutes to compare lists in pairs and then take brief feedback. Ask them if they feel differently about working animals and domestic animals. Why do we accept that some animals have to work, but others can be literally kept in the lap of luxury?

"Taming the wolf"

Student Book, page 44–45

This article is about how the wolf developed into the domestic dog and also touches on our somewhat complex relationship with these animals. As the vocabulary is quite sophisticated, do a pre-reading session focusing on:

- what wolves and dogs have in common

- how people use dogs (e.g. "seeing-eye dogs", companions, hunting, guard dogs).

Ask students to do the **Reading task** on page 45 of the Student Book.

Students need to rephrase or paraphrase information in the article, an essential skill for Reading Passage questions. Remind them not to quote in a summary unless required to do so in the question. Remind them to use different coloured pencils for different tasks. Award up to a total of 15 marks, as indicated below. Suggested answers:

1. Wolves/dogs may have "adopted" humans and chosen to live in or near human habitation for food, as in modern hunter-gatherer societies. (3)

2. Men (hunters) herded animals into a narrow space, where they speared their prey. Dogs were probably not used for this. (3)

3. The end of the Ice Age caused big game to die out, move north or change habitat. Dogs were probably used to stalk prey, enabling men to catch their food and avoid starvation. (2)

4. Dogs helped to keep campsites clean by eating rubbish; they acted as guard dogs, keeping predators away; they helped people to obtain food. (3)

5. Semi-wild dogs form groups of no more than three and move into people's dwelling space. (2)

6. Recent dating of a tooth has changed previously held belief. (1)

7. The transition occurred over 14,000 years ago or between 14,000 and 14,600 years before the present. (1)

Get students started on the **Scanning and note-making task** on page 45 of the Student Book by giving them a subheading for the first paragraph: Archaeological evidence. There are no clear-cut answers for this part of the task, but students may find it interesting and useful to exchange their lists of subheading with a partner before writing out their summaries. Remind them to write concisely and effectively. You may choose to mark out of 10 for style and technical accuracy or award A–E grades.

"Working Elephants in Thailand"

Student Book, page 46–8; Resource 2.5

This article explains how mahouts are trained. In the **Writing task** on page 47, students are asked to write an informative passage to explain how working elephants are trained. Recap on the **Writing skills panel** on page 48 of the Student Book as necessary. Remind them that the information they need may not be in a linear or chronological form. They will have to sift each paragraph and put the information into chronological order themselves. Numbering points in the order they will use them is essential, especially in exams when there isn't enough time to write a rough draft. If you have a weaker group, you could get them to work independently on planning the summary so that you can support them in numbering and checking points for inclusion before they start to write.

As this section focuses on summary-writing skills, hand out **Resource 2.5** and ask students to exchange their summaries. Encourage them to check the inclusion of relevant points and evaluate their partner's writing style. Make sure they understand that they can award 1 mark for each point up to a maximum of 10 and up to 5 marks for style and accuracy (total of 15 marks).

Narrative writing task

Student Book, page 49

When you set this task, tell students to keyword their chosen question carefully. After a few minutes, ask them which is the most significant key word in each bullet point. They should respond with *episode* and *end*. Ask them to decide where their episode is going to occur in the plot of their (longer) story or how they are going to end (cliff-hanger or closure). The word limit here is similar to written coursework. Mark essays for content, style and accuracy, using an A–F grading. (There is more on writing narrative and ending stories in Unit 9.)

Self-assessment

Student Book, page 49: Resource 2.6

A version of the Self-assessment panel is available for students on **Resource 2.6**. Give them a minimum of 15 minutes or set this for homework to ensure that they are thinking independently without peer influence. Remind them that it is important to reflect on what they have achieved but also to identify their weaknesses so they know what to focus on in future. When you have feedback, you could recap on a particular skill, such as writing to inform, but don't dwell on areas of weakness so early in the course.

Literature extension

Student Book, page 50–3

This optional section focuses on poetry. Explain how and why reading and annotating poems (especially longer ones) can improve language awareness and usage (vocabulary and figurative language).

Poetry anthology

Compiling a poetry anthology and copying out stanzas or short poems helps weaker students or more kinaesthetic (tactile) students to develop their language skills in a less pressured manner, and they often find it an enjoyable activity. Creating poetry anthologies during free activity lessons may start slowly but it becomes more popular. Students can work in the school library or in the classroom if you have a wide selection of poetry books available. Many poems are also available to listen to at www.poetryarchive.org.

An important aspect of this activity is that it is student-led; the teacher may advise and suggest, and help with difficult vocabulary, but otherwise the selection of poems should be the students' own choice. Leave them to work without teacher support during the early sessions so they get used to doing things on their own and develop a sense of ownership. Try to permit a degree of talking; they may be discussing a poet's words or reading aloud something they particularly enjoy – a joy to watch.

The main objective of compiling an anthology is for students to copy the poet's words exactly in longhand. Encourage them to copy out stanzas or short poems, which they can illustrate if they wish. This forces them to focus on the form of the poem: stanzas and enjambment; rhyme schemes; sibilance, alliteration; punctuation, the effect of caesura, etc. Copying by hand also eliminates any temptation to download a poem onto a computer without a second thought.

Students who have previously found no pleasure in poetry often discover they like writing out their own choice of poems and sometimes exhibit a sensibility kept carefully under wraps during lessons. Compiling an anthology is also very good preparation for students going on to do further studies.

"Snake"

Student Book, pages 50–1

Read the poem to the class. It is essentially about the poet – an Englishman abroad – so you should explain something of D.H. Lawrence's background. He grew up in a mining district in the British Midlands and is famous for novels set in this area, notably *Sons and Lovers*. He also travelled widely (Italy, Australia, the USA). The *Oxford Companion to English Literature* says Lawrence "believed modern man was in danger of losing his ability to experience the quality of life. Passionately involved with his characters and the physical world of nature, he wrote of them with a fresh immediacy and vividness."

Discuss the poem as a class. Draw students' attention to how the speaker stood and watched the snake. How many of us would do this? Why do most people (who have grown up in urban settings) shudder at the mere thought of a snake? There is an ambivalence – the "delicacy and horror" of the creature (which is echoed in Hughes' poem on the pike). Recap on the terms *paradox* and *oxymoron* as necessary.

Set a 3–5 minute time limit and ask students to work in pairs or independently to list other animals about which we have conflicting feelings: e.g. the beauty and danger of wild cats; the cuddly appearance and man-eating cruelty of bears.

Support students as they work on the **Writer's craft task** on page 51 of the Student Book. Suggested answers:

1. For the most part, the tone is serious, dignified and contemplative. The mood is created by sibilance ("softly … slack … silently", lines 13–14) and elongated vowel sounds ("two-forked tongue", line 18) suggesting lethargy and the heat of a Sicilian summer; repetition of "and" gives an almost childlike innocence.

2. He likens the slow movement of the snake drinking to ordinary cows at a trough (lines 16–17); later its movement is rapid and it "writhed like lightning" (line 60). Is this because having grown up in an area where there were no snakes, he lacks the vocabulary or because this is really how he sees the Sicilian snake?

3. He speaks of "honour" and "humility" and has an almost reverential tone when saying "But even so, honoured still more/That he should seek my hospitality" (lines 38–9). This tone continues up to and including the reference to the god (line 45). It ends when he contemplates "that dreadful hole" (line 58). Students may have other interpretations, which they should be encouraged to discuss.

4. Lawrence describes the snake as a mythical lord of the underworld, using words and phrases to suggest its god-like qualities: "and depart peaceful, pacified, and thankless" (line 36); "honoured still more / That he should seek my hospitality" (lines 45–6); "looked around like a god" (line 52).

5. Lawrence juxtaposes the voice of reason and cultural expectation ("voice of my education", line 27) with independent thought/opinion ("I confess how I liked him", line 32; "Felt so honoured", line 41); he despises himself for his cowardly action ("A pettiness", line 87).

"Pike"

Student Book, page 52–3

This poem by Ted Hughes is also available at www.poetryarchive.org. Many of Hughes' bird and animal poems focus on the struggle for survival in the animal world. Pikes are predatory and notoriously aggressive. You might like to start by asking students to discuss the violence and violent diction in the poem. The poem divides into three parts, which you can discuss as follows:

*   Stanzas 1–4 describe the fish and include heavily alliterative and almost mono-syllabic opening lines (plosive [p] and harsh consonant [k] sounds in "pike", "killers", lines 2 and 3) emphasise the malevolence and aggressive nature of the pike.

*   Stanzas 5–7 recount what happened to three pikes the poet kept as a child. This shows the fish to be vicious ("red fry to them", line 19); unforgiving ("they spare nobody", line 22); turn on their own ("One jammed past its gills down the other's gullet", line 25). This activity benefits weaker students greatly and they often find it enjoyable.

*   Stanzas 8–11 move from another childhood anecdote to a terrifying image of something rising from "Stilled legendary depth" (line 33). Examine the "voice" and point of view here: Is Hughes dramatising a childhood nightmare or does the sombre, hypnotic language and use of repetition suggest something that has more meaning to an adult mind? It reminds readers of the darkness and evil lurking beneath the often beautiful surface of nature; echoes Darwin's theory of survival of the fittest, just as the pikes kill each other in order to survive; this is as deep and as

complex as the human condition ("as deep as England", line 34). In contrast to the Romantics who revel in the joys of nature, Hughes vividly recognises the horror and cruelty of nature. He remains fascinated by his days spent pike fishing as a child; the pikes represent the dark imaginings of a child ("For what eye might move", line 39); they represent the sinister to be found in nature ("Darkness beneath night's darkness", line 43).

Students often enjoy the gruesome description of how pike eat their own kind. Draw attention to "Killers from eggs" (line 3) and "delicacy and horror" (line 7), and ask students to work in pairs on the **Understanding poetry task** on page 53 of the Student Book. Suggested answers:

1. See examples in the list above.

2. "malevolent … grin" (line 3); "move, stunned" (line 5); "still splashes" (line 40).

If students are also studying English Literature, ask them to work in pairs to analyse the poem. Then have a plenary session to draw together their ideas before setting a typical exam-style question: Explore the ways Hughes describes the fish in "Pike". Remind them to use the SQuEE technique, recapping as necessary (refer to the panel on page 6 of the Student Book). Point out that they need to consider: diction; the poets' point of view as child and adult and how this affects his perception; the unsympathetic tone and language in relation to the aggressive nature of the pike.

Ask students to do the **Speaking and listening task** on page 53 of the Student Book in small groups.

3 Points of view

The focus in this unit is voice; identifying a narrator's point of view (fiction and autobiography), and how poets and authors create mood and tone. This is a good point to show students how narrative voice can be unreliable and how writers and poets adopt or use a persona. Separating the writer from the narrative voice can be something of a revelation for many students. Ask them to think about how descriptions of films often involve using the actors' names and not the names of the characters they are playing, e.g. Johnny Depp is not Jack Sparrow – he plays Jack Sparrow.

An interesting activity to introduce point of view is to set up an unexpected incident in the classroom, then ask students to give witness statements. Arrange for a colleague or student to come into the room to deliver a message and blatantly steal something from a desk or provoke a scene in some way. Once the visitor has left the room, ask students what happened and count the different versions. Don't tell them it was arranged until the very last moment.

Unit starter

Student Book, page 55

Give students 3–4 minutes to consider the **Talking point** on page 55 and discuss their memories in pairs. Take feedback. The emphasis is on finding why certain memories are so strong and how and why we remember quite random details such as the colour of a coat or someone's hair. Ask if students can see/hear/feel/smell something from the past. Ask if certain smells provoke memories (the smell of baking/mown grass/hospital antiseptic). Identify the difference between what is a happy memory and what may have been a traumatic incident. You may need to tread carefully here, so do not push the issue if you or your students feel uncomfortable.

Memories

Student Book, pages 55–56; Recording 3

Read the passage from **"The Tiger's Wife"** to the class or play **Recording 3** without opening the Student Book. Then ask students to read the passage by themselves in silence. Do not let them discuss the passage. Ask them to answer the questions in the **Reading task** on page 56, also on their own in silence. Remind them to quote from the passage to support their views, using the SQuEE technique. Suggested answers:

1. She tells the reader directly ("I am four years old") and indirectly ("I am little"; "my grandfather is bald as a stone").

2. Descriptions of other people suggest child-like simplicity and memory: "a boy with a parrot-shaped balloon"; "a woman in a purple coat".

3. There may be alternative readings and there is no one correct answer, but students must justify their views by quoting or referring to the passage:

   - perhaps the grandfather wants her to recognise danger at a young age

   - wants her to grow up more quickly

   - to see what can happen if you disturb powerful creatures

- his action may relate to where the story is set, implying the child may witness much worse in her life and this is a preparation for reality.

Looking for evidence; register and formal English

Workbook, pages 22–5 and 26

Introduce the passage **"13 April 1809"**, which is taken from a novel based on a real unsolved crime. It would be better not to explain too much about the scene before students have answered questions 1–3. Let them come to their own conclusions first. If this is set for homework, consider how much time students have available; it may be better to set questions 1–3 one day and question 4 later. Before they do question 4, you may want to set the tasks on register and in/formal English on page 26 of the Workbook (and remind students of the work they did in Unit 2 for the Word invaders section of Resource 11.1). Explain that the report for question 4 should be written in very formal English for two reasons: Lavender is writing something that could be used for a trial so it must be succinct and specific; it is 1809 and a detective is writing a report for a superior officer. Students are given a passive verb construction to begin with, so credit further use of this formal report-style use of English.

"Memories of Christmas"

Student Book, pages 57–8; Recording 2

Read the first passage on page 57 to the class and then go through it together. Ask students to look at what Thomas remembers; they could count the number of things he recalls. Ask them to work in pairs to do the **Writer's craft task** on page 57. Suggested answers:

1. There is only one full stop at the end of the paragraph. The effect is lyrical; it accentuates the rhythm of Thomas' voice and the sense of a child's excitement as they wait for Christmas.

2. He remembers holly, robins, pudding (sight); squabbles, carols, tin whistles, Auntie Bessie playing the piano (sound); front room fire (touch); banging crackers, ringing bells, shaking glass bells, mouth-organs (sound); blancmange, oranges (taste).

3. See above.

4. Students may pick up the lyrical quality of the wording. If they have been taught to take a breath at a full stop, they may find the text difficult to read out loud.

Listen to **Recording 2** of the passage on page 58 of the Student Book. Make sure students understand the reference to Hudson's Bay (fur-trading and trappers) and the *Boys' Own* (weekly adventure comic) and the nature of the incident with the cats. Draw out examples of Thomas' use of hyperbole and bathos: reindeers/cats; jaguars, lynx-eyed hunters, moccasined trappers; igloo/house; town-crier in Pompeii / Mrs Prothero. Draw attention to the differences between Mr and Mrs Prothero's reaction to the fire. Ask more able students to identify use of metaphor and simile.

Go back to the first paragraph and discuss how Thomas used, or didn't use, punctuation. Draw students' attention to the effect of the run-on clauses and ask them to say why he might have done this. Ask if, when they were remembering an incident from their childhood, there was a similar sense of everything running together and time standing still.

Ask students to answer the questions in the **Reading task** on page 58 of the Student Book. You could do this as a class activity with students marking their own work (which you will check later). Award a maximum of 15 marks, as shown in brackets below.

1. They heard Mrs Prothero banging the dinner gong and (eventually) shouting fire. It's odd that they ran into a house that was on fire. (2)

2. Jim, Mrs Prothero's son (1)

3. They were waiting for cats / had made snowballs to throw at cats / were pretending to be Hudson Bay trappers / pretending the local cats could be trapped for their fur. (3)

4. December (in Wales) is "white as Lapland"; cats were "sleek and long as jaguars"; "Mrs Prothero was announcing ruin like a town-crier in Pompeii". The similes make a winter afternoon in a Welsh garden sound very exciting; they remind us that the author was a child; they evoke exciting childhood memories; they give a sense of adventure and excitement. (2)

5. Thomas had a tremendous imagination even as a child; he invented exciting games and must have read a lot to get ideas about Hudson's Bay and dangerous animals such as jaguars. He makes humble domestic cats seem very dangerous, so the boys are brave to face them. (2)

6. Mrs Prothero was banging the gong and shouting about doom and destruction. (1)

7. Mrs Prothero cries "Fire", announces "ruin" and bangs the gong as a warning or cry for help. Mr Prothero says "A fine Christmas!" (irony) and waves/smacks the smoke with a slipper. (4)

8. This requires a summary of the passage. Remind students to keyword the question, to number the relevant points in the passage in the order required to answer the question, etc. You could hand out or display **Resource 3.1** to remind them how to approach writing the summary.

Extended student activity

Student Book, pages 55–6 and 58

Ask students to look at, compare and contrast the narrative voice in the passage from *The Tiger's Wife* and "Memories of Christmas (2)". The first passage is fictional, the second autobiographical. Ask: How, where and why do they differ?

An unforgettable character

Student Book, pages 59–61; Resource 3.2

Ask students to read the passage **"Lalla"** on page 59 independently, so that they can form their own opinions. Avoid giving too much help if possible. Once they have read the text, point out that Ondaatje also varies his sentence structure for effect.

Ask students to answer the questions in the **Reading task** on page 60 of the Student Book. Suggested answers:

1. She is "casual and irresponsible"; extremely busy; an eccentric "mad aunt"; a practical joker; poor.

2. He remembers Lalla searching for children, yelling their names, always saying "yes"; their embarrassment at the "mad aunt"; her dramatic practical joke of the goat on the table at the expense of having food to eat.

3. Descriptions should include (a) Lalla's long black clothes; (b) her generosity and love of practical jokes; (c) she bought them stilts, included all the children, rescued them from extra tuition, played practical jokes, made people laugh.

Ask students to re-read the passage and then do the **Writing task** on page 60 of the Students Book to produce the transcript for a radio interview with

Ondaatje. Hand out the framework on **Resource 3.2**, for guidance. Point out the **Reminder box** on page 61. Explain that this task is typical of Directed Writing questions, which provide text to read and annotate according to the question and then used in a designated writing style. Award up to 10 marks for content and up to 15 marks for style and accuracy (total of 25 marks).

Improving Directed Writing skills: points of view

Workbook, pages 27–9

Ask students to read the guidelines on how discursive and argumentative writing differs on page 27 of the Workbook. Explain that the task on page 28 asks them to construct a logical argument/discussion using the planning sheet on page 29 and that they will be credited for evidence of planning and also editing. As always, individual flair improves the final mark. If students need extra practice at constructing a logical argument, ask them to underline the topic sentences in their work, write them out as a list and check that they lead through the argument to a specific conclusion. Award up to 12 marks for content and up to 13 marks for style and technical accuracy (total of 25 marks).

This task could also be set at the end of this unit after students have read the short story "Flight" on pages 76–9 of the Student Book.

Mood and tone in fiction

Student Book, pages 62–3; Resource 3.3

Make sure students understand the terms *mood* and *tone*, reminding them of the Glossary at the back of the Student Book. Discuss how mood and tone are created using the text on page 62.

Ask students to read **Passage A** independently and then work in pairs to answer the **Writer's craft** questions below. Take feedback. Suggested answers:

1. The corn tries to fight the wind but is eventually defeated ("weakened leaves", "wearily sideways" like a dying animal); the sun "shone redly" like an angry enemy, frustrated; the "prying" wind "dug cunningly" like a coyote or wild dog, a manipulative and strong force.

2. It indicates foreboding, the onset of tragedy, the loneliness of the wind, that the land is now empty.

Move on to **Passage B** from *Bleak House* on page 63 of the Student Book. Dickens' style may be a challenge for some students, so explore diction with the class. You can ask them to use a dictionary for words such as *mire* (line 5), *tenaciously* (line 14), *defiled* (line 17), *nether* (line 28); however, this is a good opportunity to discuss how to infer or guess meaning from context and how to deal with difficult vocabulary under exam conditions.

Hand out or display **Resource 3.3**. Ask students to work in pairs or small groups to consider what the phrases suggest to the reader and how they create mood and feeling. You could give each group a different phrase or ask them to consider all of the phrases. Encourage them to use the colour-coding system for analysing the writer's choice of words (red/nouns; blue/verbs; yellow/adjectives; green/adverbs) so they see that not only adjectives create atmosphere. Give them about 5–10 minutes and then discuss as a class. Suggestions might be:

- "black drizzle": very light rain; dark, miserable weather

- "mourning": to grieve; express deep regret for; perhaps someone's died

- "death of the sun": metaphorical; must be a dark day if even the sun has died; suggests late afternoon, dusk; extreme darkness

- "general infection of ill-temper": contamination or corruption morally; everyone around is ill-mannered

- "crust upon crust of mud sticking": disgusting, horrible conditions; battling through mud

- "Fog everywhere": oppressive; dark; sinister; metaphorical or physical blindness.

Spend a few minutes looking at all the references to fog and how Dickens has given it an almost tangible presence. Once you are happy with students' contribution and understanding, read the whole passage again and ask students to write a SQuEE answer to the question: What atmosphere or mood is Dickens trying to create with his words in this passage? Review answers as a class.

Mood and tone in poetry

Student Book, pages 63–4; Resource 3.4

Ask students to read the poem on page 63 of the Student Book and then do the **Writer's craft task** on page 64. Hand out **Resource 3.4** and

encourage students to find three to five examples per category, differentiated according to their ability if necessary. Support them as they decide on their own words to summarise each writer's tone or mood. Suggested answers:

1. **Dickens:**
   Nouns: smoke, chimney-pots, drizzle, soot, snow-flakes, death, sun, dogs, mire, horses, blinkers, passengers, umbrellas, ill-temper, foot-hold, street-corners, day, deposits, crust, mud, points, etc. **Adjectives**: soft, black, full-grown, general, new, green, defiled, waterside, great, small, ancient, wrathful, close, shivering, little, nether, misty. **Images**: flakes of soot as big as snowflakes; death of the sun; splashed to their very blinkers; jostling one another's umbrellas; crust upon crust of mud, waterside pollutions of great (and dirty) city, etc.
   Wordworth:
   Nouns: earth, soul, majesty, city, garment, beauty, morning, ships, towers, domes, theatres, temples, fields, sky, air, sun, splendour, valley, rock, hill, calm, river, will, God, houses, heart.
   Adjectives: fair, dull, touching, silent, bare, open, bright, glittering, smokeless, first, deep, sweet, mighty.
   Images: morning worn like a garment; bright, glittering ships and buildings; creeping of the sun's first rays; the river gliding; houses sleeping; the city as a mighty heart lying still.

2. Dickens' city is down-beat, as he shows how smoke, soot, mud and especially fog pervade the city and affect people's lives; the tone or mood might be described as dismal, chillingly foggy. In contrast Wordsworth's city is gloriously peaceful and beautiful, as he describes the early rays of the sun lighting up the city in a tone that reflects morning splendour.

3. "Death of the sun" in *Bleak House* suggests late afternoon/evening and the dying of the day lends itself to pessimistic feelings; "beauty of the morning" in *Westminster Bridge* infers a time of optimism and new beginnings.

4. In 1853, London's population was rising fast and the Industrial Revolution was at its height; factories were growing, industry booming, railways and shipyards expanding, all of which brought pollution and poor living conditions. *Bleak House*: "tiers of shipping and the waterside pollutions of a great (and dirty) city […] Fog lying out on the yards, and hovering

in the rigging of great ships". On the other hand, in 1802, London's population was about 1 million and although the city was expanding, the railway hadn't yet been built and the effects of the Industrial Revolution had yet to be felt: the city was still in touch with its natural environment. "Westminster Bridge": "Ships, towers, domes, theatres, and temples lie / Open unto the fields, and to the sky". The manner in which these two texts were written is also very relevant here; Wordsworth was a young man full of hope for the future; Dickens was older, more worldly wise perhaps, and saw the hurly burly and pollution of London differently because he himself was under pressure.

"Death of a Naturalist"

Student Book, page 64

Allow students to listen to Heaney's recording of the poem on http://video.pbs.org or www.youtube.com.

Ask students to do the **Writer's craft task** on page 64, exploring the ways Heaney uses words and images to convey a changing point of view. Remind them to quote from the poem to justify their interpretations and ideas. They might track the changing point of view as follows:

Lines 1–4: the opening is oppressive and somewhat grotesque: "festered", "rotted", "sweltering", "punishing" – the sort of things a young boy may revel in or not notice at all.

Lines 5–10: the beauty of frogspawn in its natural environment: "delicately", "dragon-flies, spotted butterflies", "best of all" – this diction suggests the boy is still young.

Lines 10–21: the excitement and intrigue that nature arouses in a young mind: "every spring I would fill jampotfuls of the jellied specks", "Miss Walls would tell us how", "You could tell the weather by frogs too" – reference to the teacher and her voice show he is still at Primary or Elementary school.

Lines 22–34: he returns to the tone set at the start of the poem (cyclical) – frogs are now disgusting and obscene, grotesque, threatening: "angry frogs", "gross-bellied frogs", "obscene threats", "blunt heads farting" – reference to the bass chorus may be because his own voice has deepened or is changing, meaning he is now an adolescent and has a different outlook on life.

If your students enjoy this poem or have difficulty identifying the different perspectives, look at "Blackberry Picking", another poem from Seamus Heaney's collection *Death of a Naturalist*, which describes a boy's joy at the mess of picking blackberries set against a teenager's realisation (and disillusionment) that fruit rots and nothing lasts.

Points of view in a short story

Student Book, pages 65–7

Ask students to read the short story **"Her First Ball"** independently. Do a *wh-* analysis as a class to establish who goes to the ball, who is at the ball, what Leila sees and feels. Suggested responses:

- Where the story is set: the cab journey; "Ladies"; drill hall.

- When the scene or event takes place: unclear, almost swept along in the moment, like a waltz ("Exactly when the ball began Leila would have found hard to say").

- Whose "voice": third-person narrator; free indirect thought ("Oh dear, how hard it was to be indifferent like the others.") We hear Leila's point of view.

- Who the narrator is speaking to: private thoughts ("Oh, how marvellous to have a brother!")

- What the speaker is talking about and his/her point of view: experience of the ball, Leila's nervousness and longing for someone to look after her ("Oh, how marvellous to have a brother!"); through to ball etiquette, disappointment of the "fat man"; through to the joy of the mysterious man at the end.

- How we hear what the narrator is thinking or feeling: dynamic verbs ("breaking", "scattering", "spinning", "tossed"); hyperbole ("most beautifully slippery"); long vowel sounds and imagery ("He was tossed away on a great wave of music", "she floated away like a flower that is tossed into a pool").

- What you feel about the story: personal response.

Read the story aloud to the class so students can hear the lilting diction used for the waltz music and Leila's excitement in the free indirect thought. Draw out how the author presents Leila's point of view. If appropriate, ask them how they felt about going to their first party.

Ask students to answer the **Reading questions** on page 67 of the Student Book. Suggested answers:

1. Leila is in a reverie of anticipation and imagining ("the bolster on which her hand rested felt like the sleeve of an unknown young man's dress suit"); she is overcome with excitement and curiosity which she tries to mask ("Oh dear, how hard it was to be indifferent like the others! She tried not to smile too much; she tried not to care.")

2. The Sheridans have been to balls before and seem more indifferent ("as usual", "I've never known your hair go up more successfully than it has to-night!"); the women in the Ladies are excitable ("cried", "wailed"); exclamation marks ("pass them along!") convey excitement; "the crush" suggests that guests are eager to progress to the drill hall.

Ask students to do the **Writer's craft task** on page 71 of the Student Book, reminding them to use the SQuEE technique. Suggested responses:

1. Students should look at the use of diction: dynamic verbs, hyperbole ("marvellous"; she would "die at least"); consonance and long vowel sounds ("gazing", "gleaming", "golden"). Even the ladies powder room is seen as an exotic, exciting place with a "great quivering jet of gas".

2. Movement (and excitement) is created through repetition of verbs: lifted, carried, tossed/tossing, patting, smoothing, tucking, pressing, quivering, gliding; and "waltzing-lamp-posts … " (line 8).

Related texts

For point of view, narrative voice and use of free indirect thought, look at *The Lumber Room* by Saki. If considering narrators, look at Lockwood in *Wuthering Heights* and/or the opening of *To Kill a Mocking Bird* by Harper Lee.

School in the past and present

Student Book, pages 68–72

Many students may not know anything about one-room schoolhouses or that they still exist in many rural environments around the world. Take a few moments to elicit what they think happens in a school like this, who attends, how children are taught, etc. Read about one-room schools and "dame schools" in the text on page 68 of the Student Book.

Ask how students would feel about teachers moving into their homes for a few months each year!

Read through **"The Nine Parts of Speech"** on page 68 and explain the old method of learning by rote. Then move on to the **Speaking and listening task** on the same page. Organise students into pairs and set a time limit. You could take feedback on question 1 before moving on to question 2. Depending on time available you could organise the pairs into fours for question 2. This will take longer but elicit more discussion about what is pedagogically important nowadays.

The material on pages 69–72 of the Student Book could be developed independently for Coursework Portfolios and/or be used as a group discussion topic for Speaking and Listening Coursework. (There is also an interview with Rafael Selas, a young Spaniard who gave up a high power job in Miami to run an NGO for children in Kenya on pages 56–7 of the Workbook.)

As a class, closely examine the photograph of the ragged school on page 69 of the Student Book. Ask: What is familiar and what is unfamiliar? You could use this as a way into the **Writing task** on page 69, along with time spent doing some research (in the library or for homework) into the Ragged and Industrial Schools in London in the 19th century. The following website would give students a useful starting point and also help them with the **Talking point** on page 72: www.hiddenlives.org.uk. The website www.maybole.org has a fairly graphic description of the students teachers had to deal with in 19th-century city schools and would also help students with the Writing task:

"A volunteer teacher tells you how boisterous the children are 'all of them ragged and dirty and some of them revoltingly so, and who were spending the Sabbath in lounging about the streets and yards or playing games (not of the most innocent kind). When ushered into the first classroom, they whistled, sang, shouted and yelled until better sport presented itself […] The girls' appearance was unrefined in the extreme; their answers to the teachers' questions revealed a state of ignorance truly deplorable.' "
(From *A Child's World*, by James Walvin)

Once students have a more detailed understanding of the history of ragged schools, they can start planning their account. Encourage them to plan thoroughly, e.g. using a mind map with a strand for each of the bullet points in the Writing panel. Refer them to the guidelines set out in the **Writing skills panel** on page 69 of the Student Book. Allow them to discuss their ideas in pairs, but emphasise that they need to practise writing the account independently.

"First Day at School"

Student Book, pages 70–1

Ask students to read the passage on page 70 and then do the activities on page 71. Suggested answers to the **Reading task**, for a maximum of 10 marks, as shown below:

1. When the herd boys threw stones at Mwihaki and she was left crying, Njoroge came over and comforted her: it "felt like soothing the weeping child". (2)

2. He is a "Njuka", a newcomer. (2)

3. He wants them to call him by his name: "I am Njoroge." (2)

4. Mwihaki's sister is a teacher and she could report them. (2)

5. He feared her because she beat a boy and "the stick broke into bits". However, he knows the boy was wrong to bully a Njuka and so, in that sense, he deserved the punishment. (2)

Suggested answers to the **Writer's craft task**:

1. There are lots of simple sentence structures, perhaps reflecting the child's voice ("The school looked a strange place. […] It looked haunted"); simple use of punctuation with full stops and exclamation marks to show tension ("whack! whack!"); many sentences beginning with personal pronouns (e.g. *they, he*).

2. "She burst out."; "He did not know what to do."

3. They increase the tension and drama of the extract and reflect the simplicity of the child's viewpoint.

4. Ngugi Wa Thiongo used it to portray the simplicity of a child's point of view; it allows the reader to experience the events from Njoroge's point of view, that of innocence and naivety.

Take feedback from students' work on the writer's craft, particularly discussing the effectiveness of Thiongo's use of short simple sentences. Explain that students are going to rewrite the scene from Mwihaki's point of view, as outlined in the **Writing task** on page 71 of the Student Book. Discuss how Mwihaki might have felt taking Njoroge to school and defending him from the other boys. Encourage students to re-read the passage and identify details

they want to use. Explain why they need to plan their writing and, if there is time, suggest they discuss their plans in pairs or small groups before starting to write.

Rwebigaga School

Student Book, pages 72

Ask students to read the text and look at the photograph on page 72, before discussing the **Talking point** below. If you have the time and resources, spend a lesson in the library or an IT room where students can research current policies and laws for children of poorer families. A useful starting point could be www.unicef.org. You could ask students to present their ideas and policy plan as a speech to the class. They could then vote on the speech with the most convincing ideas and arguments.

Points of view in poetry

Student Book, pages 73–5; Resources 3.5–3.6

Although there are no poems in the exams, the **Speaking and listening task** on page 73 of the Student Book gives students valuable practice in expressing their thoughts and justifying their ideas or interpretations. The poems on pages 73 and 74 will also give students further opportunity to develop their analytical skills.

"Little Boy Crying"

Student Book, page 73; Resource 3.5

Ask students to work in pairs to discuss the **Speaking and listening task** on page 73. The poem is available on **Resource 3.5** for students to annotate. Take feedback. Suggested answers:

*   You can hear the little boy as a child and the boy grown up.

*   Where: is unclear, irrelevant.

*   When: after a shower or rain storm.

*   Whose: "voice": the adult voice of reason and the viewpoint of a three-year-old boy

*   Who: the narrator is speaking to a child, possibly his son, and relating his feelings to a wider audience.

*   What: the speaker is talking about a childish tantrum; chastisement by a parent; the child's sense of resentment; the father's sense of guilt, desire to hug the child, knowledge that the child must learn how to behave so he has a parental duty to be severe at times.

- How: diction choices ("contorting", "frustration", "howls", "spite"); quick plosive sounds ("slap"); metaphorical imagery ("ogre towers"); reflective voice ("not yet").

- What you feel about the poem – personal response.

"Before the Sun"

Student Book, page 74; Resource 3.6

Students can practise their skills further by working with a partner to analyse this poem, which is also available on **Resource 3.6** for annotation. Remind them that they need to support their views by quoting from the poem and encourage them to use the SQuEE method. The voice in the poem tells us that the boy chopping logs is 14 years old (line 13). The final stanza includes the first-person *I* and *me*. Prompt students to decide whether the boy is the narrator or whether the older man is looking back on his youth.

Descriptive and Narrative Writing task

Student Book, page 75

When setting this writing task, remind students they have advice on Narrative and Descriptive Writing on Workbook page 11 and 20. Suggest that they time themselves to do the task. Award up to 13 marks for content and structure of the story or description and up to 12 marks for style and accuracy (total of 25 marks).

Self-assessment

Student Book, page 75; Resource 3.7

A version of the Self-assessment panel on page 75 is available for students to fill out on **Resource 3.7**. Give them a minimum of 15 minutes or set this for homework to ensure that they are thinking independently without peer influence. Remind them it is important to reflect on what they have achieved, but also to identify their weaknesses so that they know where they need to improve. Review skills such as writing to argue or an interview as necessary.

Literature extension

Student Book, pages 76–9

This section is designed to help students also studying English Literature, but it could also be used as a springboard for Coursework Portfolios. As a class, read the passage **"Flight"**. Guide students through the **Question box** on page 79. Suggested answers:

- It doesn't matter that we don't know the grandfather's name. The focus is on the theme and notion of "flight": the youngest granddaughter growing up and leaving the nest, while the grandfather feels betrayed and alone ("Can't we keep her a bit longer?", "they had forgotten him again") until he learns to accept her flight ("Now you can go").

- The author does let us see other characters' points of view: the daughter's viewpoint through her dialogue with her father ("Leave Alice alone. She's happy"); Alice's view ("Go and tell!", "he saw the tears run shivering off her face"). Seeing how Alice feels at the end of the story adds poignancy and shows how much she cares for and respects her grandfather.

- The grandfather's age may affect his point of view. His grandchild is now a woman – a sense of his time running out. There is also a sense that he doesn't want Alice to end up like his other granddaughters ("serious young matrons"). He mutters that Alice will "come to something quite different". He wants to save her from this fate; his experience and age inform his judgement and feelings.

Move on to the **Writing task** on page 79 of the Student Book. The question leaves students room to think about the story and examine their ideas in writing. Remind them to quote from the text to justify their opinions. Also remind them of the importance of legibility; they may write quickly but they must take care with spelling, punctuation and keeping their handwriting neat so people can read what they have to say. There are no "correct" answers, so credit well-reasoned, well-supported analysis and interesting ideas.

4 "All the world's a stage"

The focus in this unit is theatre and drama as performance. Although there is no drama in the Speaking and Listening Test or Coursework, acting out scenes will help students to improve their speaking skills. Extracts from plays can also be developed into prose responses for Coursework Portfolios. It isn't necessary to work through the unit as a whole; you may prefer to dip in for play extracts or passages throughout the course.

Encourage students to take roles and act out scenes; this will improve speaking skills and help diminish adolescent self-consciousness. The information on the history of theatre can be used to improve students' analytical skills. They should come to see that even modern soap opera involves universal characters and eternal concerns about the human condition. The comparison of Kathakali, Noh and Kabuki dance-dramas is designed to improve processing information and cultural knowledge; the optional Shakespearian insults activity is a fun way to broaden language awareness and help to develop speaking skills of pace, pitch and projection.

Unit starter

Student Book, page 81; Resources 4.1–4.3

Before discussing the Talking points on page 81, you could have a more general discussion about what drama is. Ask who has been to the theatre: explore students' experiences and share your own with them. If possible, ask them to compare live performance with television and film. Remind them that television and film are relatively recent inventions, but people were watching drama in Ancient Greece and street theatre was a significant form of entertainment in medieval times. Theatre has always been a means of exploring human relationships and commenting on social concerns, such as the abuse of power.

Many students assume that "doing Shakespeare" is boring and/or difficult, so you may like to open this unit with Shakespearian insults on **Resource 4.1**. This activity requires open space, so book the drama studio or hall if possible. If not, consider safety and move desks and chairs to the edges of the room. Cut up the insults on Resource 4.1 and give one to each student. Ask them to practise their insult on their own (quietly) in different ways, e.g. softly, quickly, sternly, angrily etc.

Select two or four of the more voluble members of your class and ask them to address each other in pairs using their insults; the rest should watch. Ask all students to find a partner and create a very short scene, using their insults. After about 5 minutes, select pairs to act out their scenes, then ask the rest to comment on whether they find the language truly insulting or surprising in any way.

Finish with a serious question: Why do people take pleasure in watching other people fight verbally or physically in films and television? Ask how and why so much television and film includes very real verbal abuse and physical violence. Lead into the idea of vicarious experience.

Give students 5 minutes in pairs to consider the **Talking points** on page 81 of the Student Book. Suggested responses:

- This introduces the idea that we are rarely ourselves, all of us "play" parts and act in ways we consider acceptable/expected, etc.

- This will depend on students' backgrounds and experiences.

- Seven stages would be infancy, childhood, adolescence, young adult, middle age, late middle age, old age.

Students are often very enthusiastic to reflect on how their own lives might be played out. Ask them to do the **Writing task** on page 81 of the Student Book. Give them sufficient time to think about the task but avoid letting them discuss it; it should be done independently to avoid bragging, intimidation or embarrassment. Ask them to finish for homework.

In the next lesson, hand out Jaques' monologue on **Resource 4.2**. Read it through with the class and ask them to compare Jaques' view of life in the 16th century to modern life. If you have Extended students or they are studying English Literature, take longer over Jaques' language and ask for modern equivalents. Ask how many of the ideas remain unchanged ("creeping like snail / Unwillingly to school"; the young executive and "the bubble reputation"; the elderly being "Full of wise saws").

Ask students to work independently on the **Theatre Language task** on page 81 of the Student Book. They can peer-mark the answers given on **Resource 4.3**.

Kathakali, Noh and Kabuki

Student Book, pages 82–5: Resources 4.4–4.5

As a lead into the topic of dance-drama, you could ask students to research Kathakali, Noh and Kabuki before the lesson, directing them to the following websites: www.indianfolkdances.com, www.britishmuseum.org, www.britannica.com.

As a class, read the article on **"Kathakali dance-drama"** and then set the **Reading task** on page 82 of the Student Book. Suggested answers:

1. 1. Classical story plays from Hindu epics; 2. What is important in life; 3. Larger-than-life costumes denote character; 4. Hand signals and facial expressions convey emotions and attitudes; 5. Applying the make-up is an art in itself; 6. Preparing for a performance takes many hours; 7. Kathakali is still popular and attracts international interest.

2. Ancient Greek drama provokes thought about human nature, which is similar to thinking about what is important in life.

3. Students' own opinions.

As a class, read the articles on **"Noh theatre"** and **"Kabuki"** on pages 83–4 of the Student Book. Invite students to comment or add any information from their research. Ask them to work independently to complete the **Reading task** on page 85, filling in the grid on **Resource 4.4**. You could allow them to peer-mark, using the answers that are available on **Resource 4.5**.

Ask students to re-read the information on traditional Japanese theatre, then do the **Directed writing task** on page 85. They need to plan an informative article for an entertainment blog on traditional Japanese Noh and Kabuki theatre.

They should include the following points:

- how each type of theatre began

- what an audience can expect to see in performances

- why they think Noh and Kabuki are still popular.

They should write between 350 and 450 words. Award up to 10 marks for content and up to 15 marks for style and accuracy (total of 25 marks).

Move on to the next **Writing task** on page 99 of the Student Book. Ask students to think about how and why special effects are used in films: What do these special effects add to the experience or pleasure of the film? Go through the bullet points in the Writing task. Explain the idea of spectacle in drama and film (e.g. the larger-than-life / impossible events in *Mission Impossible* movies) and refer back to dance-drama they researched. At this stage they need only be aware of what constitutes spectacle; the concept is discussed in greater detail later in the unit. Also pay attention to the relevance of considering the audience, referring them to Reminder box on this page.

Exploring the writer's craft

Workbook, pages 30–3

Ask students to read the passage **"A wildlife spectacle"** on pages 30–1 of the Workbook and answer the questions that follow. Some Core students may find this challenging and need help, but more able, Extended students should try to do it independently. Allow about an hour for the questions that follow and remind students that they must quote to support their answers. The questions provide good practice for compulsory Extended Reading Passage questions. Suggested answers:

1. **a.** Warfare – 3; **b.** Background history – 4; **c.** Anecdote 1 – 5; **d.** Paradox – 6; **e.** Anecdote 2 – 7; **f.** Spectacle – 1; **g.** Film stars – 2.

2. Award 2 marks for each question.

   a. Clarke is using cinema or theatrical diction, so uses the word *flashback* to refer to kites or some unspecified thing/event seen before.

   b. "homing down" suggests kites are missiles or weapons programmed to land on this farm. The verb "firing" (like rockets or jets) is used in the previous sentence.

   c. This is more than a natural event; it is dramatic, colourful, exciting, frightening.

   d. Kites study the area like soldiers or lookouts watching in hostile territory.

   e. It is worrying the buzzards, which normally take their prey and feed before kites do; the natural order is threatened by the kites hovering above.

   f. This alliteration suggests the greedy or unruly behaviour of crows.

   g. Accept answers including the words *oxymoron* or *paradox* but not *opposites*; beauty and violence are not opposites.

   h. Clarke is extending the metaphor of warfare: gorse like barbed wire (a First World War image) enhances the idea of kites as a dangerous enemy.

   i. Accept answers that refer to colour, fire, spectacle, showing off (the word comes from Old French *flamboyer* = to blaze).

   j. This refers back to the beauty above and the repetition of consonance in "gorging" heightens the author's ambivalent feelings and the paradox of beauty and danger.

3. Award 2 marks for each question.

   a. For example: "minesweepers clearing the ground" (line 16); "outriders taking the risk" (line 17); "the angelic host blazes down" (line 26).

   b. For example: "Such lazy grace, such beauty, such savagery!" (lines 45–6); "elegant circles, fell on the body and gorged" (line 52).

   c. For example: "falling on flesh" (line 1); "monstrous machine" (line 36); "causing consternation" (lines 37–8); "aisled and alley-wayed" (line 49); "an old sheep seeking" (lines 49–50).

   d. There are many examples, but students must explain the author's diction and image.

   e. The combine harvester "growled up and down the field" (line 37) extends the imagery of danger and/or threat (to small rodents).

Theatre in Ancient Greece

Student Book, pages 86–9

Briefly introduce Ancient Greece, its location and epoch. Explain why it is important to know something about this period of history. (There is a section on the Olympic Games in Unit 8 and various other references throughout the Student Book.)

"Aristotle's analysis of theatre and tragedy"

Student Book, pages 86–7

When you read through the bullet points for Aristotle's definition of theatre, point out that students have already examined some of these aspects: character and spectacle in Indian and Japanese dance-drama; diction in the Shakespearian insults and Jaques' monologue.

As a class, discuss the **Talking point** on page 87 of the Student Book. Draw out that plot is still the most important factor, always dramatic and often controversial; reversals of fortune are common and suffering is commonplace, resulting in audience pity; complications are resolved and there is usually a happy ending; modern plays are not often centred around one character like ancient drama; dialogue and the delivery of lines is important; nowadays minor characters often fulfil the role of the chorus when they talk about the protagonists' situation in separate scenes; spectacle is still an important element in modern entertainment.

Lead into television series and soap operas: how viewers relate or empathise with certain characters; plots include ancient stories of love, hate, jealousy; characters are universal, e.g. the betrayed wife, the mistreated or misunderstood son, the corrupt leader or magnate.

Introduce the **Reading task** on page 87 of the Student Book by explaining that films and television programmes create different types of fear in an audience. Ensure students can distinguish between being afraid of something, fearing for someone and fearing that something will happen to someone. Move on to discuss how and why we are usually on the hero's side in a drama and how script-writers use this to create fear and pity when the hero makes a tragic mistake or becomes the victim of circumstance. Leave students to examine question 2a independently, then take feedback before they tackle question 2b.

Greek tragedy and modern soap operas

Student Book, pages 88–89

Start by clarifying the difference between a television or radio serial and a series. Ask students if they watch and enjoy soap operas and what it is about these programmes that make them so popular. Even if they do not watch popular soaps, encourage them to discuss their popularity objectively.

As a class, read both articles comparing Greek tragedy with modern soaps. Do students agree that a link can be made? Depending on your class (Core or Extended candidates) and whether or not they are studying English Literature, you may want to develop the following points from the two passages on soap operas: dramatic irony, the recognition scene, fatal flaw, archetypes, the unities of time and place.

The **Speaking and listening task** on page 89 of the Student Book is designed for oral practice for the Speaking and Listening assessments. A topic such as this, where students discuss their thoughts and feelings about a play, film or programme, can also be used as an individual presentation or a pair-based activity for Speaking and Listening Coursework.

Scripts and register

Student Book, page 90–3

Ask students to read the passage on page 90 of the Student Book independently. Check they don't need clarification before you discuss the main points:

- dialogue for different characters and register (gender, age, role and setting)
- how different members of an audience relate to or empathise with different characters and why

- how and why Shakespeare incorporated different types of people in his plays.

Tell students that they are going to write a script and recap on what they already know about scriptwriting conventions. Supplement their knowledge, drawing from the guidelines in the **Writing skills panel** on page 91 of the Student Book. Spend some time talking about the purpose of stage directions and how they appear in scripts. Tell students they may include camera directions if they choose, but they are not essential. If you have a play to hand, look at the script or ask students to turn to page 94 of the Student Book so they can see the conventions in use. Some students may refer to screenplays, but camera angles and tv/film jargon are not necessary.

Ask students to work independently on the **Stage directions task** on page 91 of the Student Book. Then review their answers as a class. Suggested answers:

1. The witches speak in verse form; in rhyme; in doggerel ("A drum, a drum! / Macbeth doth come"); in riddles ("Lesser than Macbeth, and greater"); with exclamation ("Hail!"). Macbeth and Banquo speak some blank verse; paradox/oxymorons ("So foul and fair a day"); interrogatory ("Live you?"); commanding ("Speak", "Stay", "Tell").

2. Students may have a variety of ideas to create scenery and the sound of wind.

3. A metal sheet or a rolling cannonball was used to create the sound of thunder.

Organise students into groups of five for the **Speaking task** on page 92 of the Student Book. Prompt them to consider how Macbeth and Banquo react to the witches and how their words suggest their different reactions. Draw out that Macbeth is much more authoritarian and commanding, yet he is more believing and regrets that the witches disappear. Banquo concludes that the witches are of no substance and dismisses both them and their prophecies.

Spend some time after each performance, encouraging each group to say what they felt were the key components of their performance and what they really wanted to emphasise to the audience. Ask for feedback from the class on how well these aims were achieved.

Using English: proverbs and clichés

Workbook, pages 34–5

Before students go on to explore classic British drama in the Student Book, set this language awareness task on proverbs and clichés. Remind them of the importance of using interesting and original language in their writing and avoiding clichés when speaking. Award 2 marks for each part of question 1; give 1 mark for each interesting or sensible answer in questions 2 and 3. All the expressions in question 4 are over-used, although not all students may be familiar with them. Award 2 marks for each interesting or sensible answer in question 5.

Classic British drama

Student Book, pages 94–9

Introduce Priestley's play **"An Inspector Calls"** with details from the top of page 94 and ask students to read the passage quietly to themselves. Discuss the passage and draw out what happened in the scene and what students think about each character. Then choose a confident student to read each part or ask for volunteers, and read the script again. Encourage students to use as much appropriate expression as they can. You could stop the reading at certain points to invite comment from the class on how effective specific sections are or where there could be improvement.

Organise students into groups of four and ask them to do the **Discussion task** on page 99 of the Student Book. Take feedback. Then ask students to find the adverbs Priestley uses in his stage directions, as outlined in the **Adverbs task** on page 99. Answers: massively, uneasily, suddenly, dryly, miserably, harshly, stormily, sternly, steadily, hysterically, slowly, searchingly, bitterly, eagerly, calmly.

Depending on the size of your class, ask students to get into groups or begin the **Writing task** on page 99 of the Student Book as a whole class activity. Encourage them to consider how the language would change if, for example, they were setting the play in 21st-century Australia, 19th-century Paris or pre-Civil War Spain. Ask how they will convey cultural and/or class differences in their scenes. Close the discussion and ask students to plan their letters independently.

Modern drama: "Ivan and the Dogs"

Student Book, pages 100–3: Recording 4

This play was a BBC Radio 4 production in October 2010; it was extremely moving so it is worth checking whether it is available to download from www.bbc.co.uk. The play is based on the true story

of a boy in Moscow; it begins when 11-year-old Ivan is promised a dog by his foster mother if he will tell the story of his earlier childhood. His story tells how at the age of four he walks out of his parents' flat, away from their arguments, to live on the streets of Moscow where he is adopted by a pack of wild dogs. He spent two winters with them in a city where life was cheap, children fought for territory and the homeless froze to death. The boy and dogs develop an extraordinary relationship; Ivan learns that only the dogs can really be trusted.

As a class, read the script on pages 100–1 of the Student Book or listen to **Recording 4**. When reading the script, ask students to consider how and why Ivan speaks as he does. Draw out that it could be because of his age, of his lack of education, he spent two years at a formative age speaking only to dogs. Ask them how they think adults failed the boy and, apart from what we read here, how they think he really survived.

Ask students to read the article on page 102 of the Student Book, then answer the questions in the **Reading task** on page 103. Remind them to write in full sentences and support their opinions with evidence. Award marks as shown below up to a total of 20 marks. Suggested answers:

1. It has been staged at the Drum twice. (1)

2. It is very physical theatre with members of the company playing the dogs. (2)

3. Physical theatre is restrictive and can't show what things mean for Ivan and how they affect him. (2)

4. She solved this by using monologue. (1)

5. A monologue allows us to hear and understand a character's experiences. (1)

6. The play is spoken by Ivan to the audience; an actor takes the part of Ivan later in his lifetime, looking back and relating how it shaped him. (3)

7. Her diverse background in mime and radio writing provided a range of approaches from physical to textual. (3)

8. The music and set design reinforce the words and projections make the experience very real for the audience. (3)

9. Audiences are moved because Ivan's story is relevant to their own lives. (2)

10. Ivan's childhood gives them a different way of looking at their own childhoods and connects the audience to their own experiences. (2)

Comedy

Student Book, pages 103–5

Taking care not to let this turn into a joke-telling session, ask students to think about something they thought was very funny when they were small but now seems just silly. If students have younger brothers or sisters, elicit how small children find trivial things amusing and how this can be annoying for older siblings. If you have a multinational class, move on to how different cultures have different types of humour. If you have a one-nation class, ask students to compare British television comedy with American humour, for example. End the discussion noting that our perception of what is funny changes and largely depends on where we have been brought up. Try to bring into the discussion slapstick and visual gags in silent movies, puns and more sophisticated wordplay in modern comedy.

As a class, read the passage on **"Commedia dell'Arte"** on pages 103–4 of the Student Book and briefly discuss the idea of improvised comedy, slapstick and knockabout humour. Ask: Is this type of humour common to most cultures? Why do people laugh at someone else's misfortunes or physical discomfort? Go on to review a recent popular comedy and what it has in common with *Commedia dell'Arte*. British students should see the link with pantomime; other nationalities may see a link with circus clowns.

If your students are doing a Shakespeare play, encourage them to analyse the nature of the comic relief, e.g. how and why it is there, or not.

Ask students to do the information retrieval **Reading task** on page 105 of the Student Book, writing their answers in full sentences. You could

mark out of 10, giving 2 marks per question. Suggested answers:

1. It began during the 14th century in Italy as improvised street theatre.

2. A quick discussion took place between the performers, who chose their subjects and characters. Then a "situation" was set up and acted out.

3. The original slapstick humour was developed more intricately for maximum entertainment.

4. Stock character types, incidents and visual humour are still popular.

5. Students' own responses.

As an optional Reading task, ask students to develop their answers to the Reading questions into a short article for a school magazine on the content and history of *Commedia dell'Arte*. They should write between 200 and 300 words, using their own words as far as possible. Award up to 10 marks for content and up to 5 marks for style and accuracy (total of 15 marks).

Self-assessment

Student Book, page 105; Resources 4.6 – 4.8

A version of the Self-assessment panel on page 105 is available for students to fill out on **Resource 4.6**. Allow a minimum of 15 minutes or set this for homework to ensure that they are thinking independently without peer influence. Remind them that it is important to reflect on what they have achieved but also to identify their weaknesses so that they know what to focus on in future.

To end this unit you could give students the wordsearch on **Resource 4.7**, which tests their knowledge of some of the key terms associated with theatre. The answers are available on **Resource 4.8**.

5 Family and friends

This unit focuses on close relationships, and different forms of love and friendship, using fiction, drama, poetry and news reports. There are scenes from two famous plays, poetry from different epochs, grammar and vocabulary tasks. Students will be asked to write to inform and discuss for different purposes. You may be doing this unit at the end of the first year of the course or at the beginning of the second, so students should now be sufficiently comfortable with each other to talk about personal views and feelings. However, as elements in this unit touch on family issues, be sensitive to their feelings and don't push them to participate in discussions if they seem uncomfortable. At this point in the course give them more time to work on their own unaided. They need to become more aware of their study and exam skills, and less reliant on you for help, especially with new vocabulary.

Unit starter

Student Book, page 107

Ask students to consider, in pairs, the implications of the quotation in the **Talking point** on page 107. Allow 1–2 minutes and then share different views and open it up for class discussion. Work in a similar way on the quotations in the **Speaking and listening task**. Allow a few minutes for students to review their own responses before opening up the discussion.

Happiness in Bhutan

Student Book, pages 108–9

Ask: Why does mass media dedicate so much space to royal weddings? Are people genuinely excited by these events or are they "media events"? Spend a few minutes discussing how royal marriages were arranged historically (to expand and consolidate territory) and why future monarchs and members of a royal family were obliged to marry "wisely". You could then ask students if they think royals should continue to marry royals and why many princes/princesses nowadays choose commoners as partners. Bring discussion back to the role of the popular press in royal weddings and then read about **"Royal Wedding in Bhutan"** on page 108 of the Student Book. Set the **Writer's craft task** on page 107. Suggested answers:

1. The writer uses the present tense when commenting on the present situation ("Wangchuck […] is a keen basketball player") and for direct speech ("It's great!").

2. The writer uses the past tense when recounting events ("He then placed an embroidered silk crown … ") and when giving information about past events ("Bhutan's Dragon King, who studied in … ").

"Bhutan's 'Gross National Happiness' index"

Student Book page 109

Before reading the next article on Bhutan on page 109, ask students what they think a "gross national happiness index" is. How can happiness be measured? Introduce ideas such as truancy statistics (happy at school), low divorce rates, longevity. Ask students to read the article and then do the **Writer's craft task** on the same page. Check that their paragraphs include the following points:

- Register: D'Arlon's article is more informal ("She and the king started dating"); Nelson's article is formal ("This was to be measured").

- Word choice: D'Arlon is sensationalist ("longtime girlfriend", "massive statue"); Nelson is detached and business-like ("proposed", "measured […] economic development").

- Style: D'Arlon is tabloid style ("king marries commoner"); Nelson is factual and informative ("There are many aspects of social life … ").

- Tone: D'Arlon is casual and light-hearted ("Jigme likes to keep it more free and easy."); Nelson is impersonal and detached ("Pavan K. Burma […] said the spread of the idea […] reflects …)".

Move on to the **Speaking and Listening task** on page 109 of the Student Book. Its purpose is to enable students, who at this age can be very inward-looking, to see how things that affect one personally can be developed to exemplify or reflect a social trend. Ask them to work in pairs and make notes in response to the three bullet points. After about 5 minutes, organise the class into groups of four to six. Choose one person in each group to be spokesperson, asking them to collate ideas and opinions and act as arbiter. Allow another 10–15 minutes for discussion within the groups.

Take feedback. Draw attention to the following: they started the activity on a micro-scale by looking at issues that affect them personally; they then looked at wider issues from a personal perspective of cause and effect; finally, they considered the same issues from a more objective standpoint on a macro-scale. Write the words *microcosm* and *macrocosm* on the board. Tell them this is a useful way of approaching a topic when asked to write to inform, discuss, argue or even give a persuasive speech: go from a personal viewpoint and expand it to examine it from an objective point of view. Point out that mind maps are a good planning strategy for this.

End the lesson by telling students that they are going to read (see below) about how social changes in the distant past affected a girl growing up in Japan in the 1960s and how changes in social status over a long period of time directly affected personal relationships within her family.

Interpreting the meaning of new words

Workbook, pages 36–40

Explain that the two passages come from the autobiography *Geisha of Gion*, which is a form of writing to inform and entertain. Set the tasks for homework in two stages. Question 1 is a challenging (Extended) Language question; students may need up to an hour. Allow the use of dictionaries, but remind them that answers must be in the context of the passage. Award 2 marks for each part of question 1 except (c), which is worth 3 marks (total of 15 marks). Suggested answers, although accept alternatives in context:

1. a. The military rulers who had governed the country for 650 years were ousted.

    b. The old feudal system was destroyed.

    c. the perpetual squabbling between aristocrats/lords

    d. the burdensome obligations/tasks expected of him in his position/role

    e. extremely important/life-changing decision

    f. giving up the land

    g. being poor but keeping up appearances.

Question 2 on Workbook page 39 is similar to the Extended response required in Reading Passages questions. To complete the diary extract, students need to read and annotate the text on Workbook page 38 according to the bullet points. They must demonstrate understanding of the passage; discuss what is thought, felt and imagined (empathic task); develop ideas and opinions where relevant. They must write in the designated style and register: the diary entry may use a limited informal register because both parents are well-educated from upper-class families; slang is not really acceptable. Award up to 15 marks for content and up to 5 for style and accuracy (total of 20 marks).

Topic sentences

Resources 5.1–5.2

Most students will have covered topic sentences already, but they are so fundamental to planning for all writing styles it is worth recapping either here or later in the unit. As a class, read the introductory text on **Resource 5.1**. Then ask students to read the passage and do question 1 on **Resource 5.2**. Suggested answers:

1. "Gertrude Bernard … town in Canada."

2. "During her stay … Robin Hood."

3. "With trapping … public's attention."

4. "As a celebrity … stylishly bobbed hair."

5. "Later in life … 1983."

Draw attention to how the content of the passage can be reconstructed from these topic sentences then ask them to write a suitable subheading for each paragraph in the text in response to question 2.

Families in Ancient Egypt

Student Book, pages 110–15; Resources 5.3–5.4

Point out that the passage on page 110 of the Student Book is a blog article – an account of someone's life, using writing to inform and entertain. As a class, read this passage and the short passage on page 111. The first passage provides a good opportunity to look at the use of *would* with the infinitive. Look at the first example quoted in the **Writer's craft task** on page 111 in situ in line 4. Then ask students to find another example ("would be young" (line 9) / "she would adorn herself" (line 34)). Explain that *would* is a modal verb and recap modals using the Reminder box on page 111. Examples in the passage are *could* (lines 10, 47, 55); *might* (line 31). Students should then do the rest of the Writer's craft task on their own. Suggested answers:

2. A man would be able to marry when he was considered to be old enough and able to support his spouse and any future children.

3. Sibling – brother or sister; spouse – husband or wife.

Move on to the **Summary writing tasks** on page 111 of the Student Book. If you are uncertain which students will be doing the Core assessments, set the Extended task here for all of them, unless they still struggle with summary writing. Note that the Core passage is longer than students will encounter in the exam.

For the Core task, after students have made their notes, hand out **Resource 5.3** and ask them to check their own notes. Once they are sure they have included relevant points, ask them to write out their notes in continuous writing as succinctly as possible. Collect the summaries for marking. Award up to 10 marks for relevant points (having checked their notes, all 10 points should be there!) and up to 5 marks for style and accuracy (total of 15 marks). This approach will boost confidence and emphasises the importance of locating relevant information in a text. You could use a similar

approach with Extended students using **Resource 5.4**, which includes points they need to include for up to 15 marks for content.

"Who was Cleopatra?"

Student Book, pages 112–15; Workbook, page 41

Ask students what they know about Cleopatra and why she is famous. Lead discussion round to the belief that she was a forceful, perhaps charismatic leader at a time when it is often assumed that men were in charge of all forms of government. This may be why she is still a popular figure in historical fiction and films. Read the passage on pages 112–13 of the Student Book as a class.

The next section involves work on past perfect verbs. If students have difficulty with tenses, you could ask them to work in pairs on the task on **Using English: irregular verbs** on page 41 of the Workbook or refer them to page 281 of the Student Book. Answers:

a. run/sank;

b. woven/grown;

c. driven/slain;

d. fallen/broken;

e. drawn/written.

Review responses and discuss confusions and incorrect answers in detail. Remind students how what they hear people say isn't always correct: use *you should of* and *he did good* as classic mistakes.

Move on to the work on past perfect verbs in the **Writer's craft task** on pages 114–15 of the Student Book. Suggested answers:

1. The verb "had hoped" suggests that Cleopatra's rule was not going as well as she would have wished.

2. The author used the present tense to suggest Cleopatra's iconic status; the image of her tumbling out of an unfurled carpet is world famous and emphasises her impact on the world stage.

3. Other examples include: "to sneak herself", "jam-packed", "set about the business".

4. Modern use of English: "To solidify her grip on the throne" (lines 79–80); Familiar, newsworthy events: "Cleopatra's foreign policy goal" (line 112).

5. • Film versions are full of chronological (time) / historical mistakes; are fictionalised; give an unrealistic picture; use incorrect details or costumes.

- Cleopatra changed herself / her personality according to who she was with or what was happening.

6. Students should know from the passage that "Philopatris" means "she who loves her country" and cite evidence of this: she learned the Egyptian language, was determined to uphold Egypt's autonomy against the Roman Empire and established trade with the East in order to expand Egypt's investments and capital.

Before they start the **Writing task** on page 115 of the Student Book, ask students how a biography for a web page might differ from a biography in an encyclopaedia or full-length biographies in a library. Explain that because it is shorter the language has to be succinct and also more entertaining. They may have done this kind of writing before, so ask how their approach will be different now. They should identify some of the points in the **Writing skills panel** on page 115 or make reference to the article about Cleopatra, especially on audience, use of interesting data and entertaining but factual style.

This task provides a good opportunity for students to research a famous person or event that can be developed independently for Coursework Portfolios or used as the basis of a talk for Speaking and Listening practice or oral coursework. There is more on biography and a sample of a student's written coursework on page 199 of the Student Book.

Using a dictionary or thesaurus

Workbook, pages 42–4

Set this language activity for homework. Explain to students why they need to know how to use a dictionary or thesaurus well: to become more conscious of how they use words in relation to audience and register; to be constantly expanding their vocabulary; to learn ways of identifying the meaning of new words from syntax and context; to employ new language in their writing. Ask students to read everything carefully before they do the tasks. Suggested answers:

1. **a.** tell
   b. Accept sentences with changed syntax that include: inform her of; apprise her of; acquaint her of; state that; reveal that.

2. Accept answers in full sentences only.

3. **a.** spoken;
   b. speak;
   c. speak;
   d. ask;
   e. replied/responded;
   f. spoke;
   g. said;
   h. saying;
   i. ask;
   j. spoke;
   k. talk/chat;
   l. talked/chatted;
   m. told;
   n. tell

Family and loyalty

Student Book, pages 116–7; Resource 5.5

Ask students to read the extract from *Macbeth* on their own. Then read it aloud to the class and ask students to identify the reasons Macbeth gives for not killing King Duncan. This could be an oral class activity or set as a written assignment. In either case, students should give line references and support their interpretations. The reasons are:

- the king is Macbeth's kinsman (line 14)
- he is a subject of the king, so murder will be high treason and regicide (line 14)
- Macbeth is the king's host, so he should be taking care of his welfare (line 15)
- the king is a good / "meek" person and a good and virtuous ruler, so Macbeth has no reason to even dislike him (lines 17–20)
- Duncan's death will cause sorrow and great pity; "tears shall drown the wind"; no one will accept or understand such a terrible deed (lines 22–6)
- the only reason Macbeth can see is his own ambition (which he predicts will bring misfortune) (lines 26–9).

Read Seamus Heaney's poem **"Follower"** with the class. You may need to explain the words relating to ploughing with a team of horses.

Students should write their answers in full sentences and give line references where relevant. The answers are as follows, but accept alternatives supported by evidence from the poem:

1. Father is a big man, broad-shouldered (line 2), he wore hob-nailed boots. He was a highly skilled ploughman (stanzas 2 and 3). He must

have been a patient and caring father because he tolerated his son following him about, chattering ("yapping") all the time; he picks the boy up and carries him on his broad shoulders when the child falls over in the soil while he is ploughing (lines 14–15).

2. The boy wanted to be like his father. He says his father was "An expert" and stanzas 2–3 explain his skill.

3. The speaker says he was a nuisance because he was always "tripping, falling, / Yapping" and literally under the father's feet (line 13).

4. The father is now elderly and no longer as sure on his feet as he was. Now he is the one who is "stumbling". The last two lines may have a more metaphorical element in that the boy, now a grown man, feels guilty about not taking better care of his father.

Hand out **Resource 5.6**, which presents the diagram in the task on **Different forms of love** on page 117 of the Student Book. Make sure that students understand the different forms already given and ask them to add to the diagram. You could prompt them with ideas as necessary, e.g. pets or animals; the environment; a particular cause such as saving whales; love of a particular poem or song; hero-worship of a sports or film star; loving one's job, etc.

Human emotions

Student Book, pages 118–9; Resources 5.6–5.9

Ask students to read the three poems on page 118–9 and then work in pairs to annotate them to identify the human emotions involved in each poem. The poems are available on **Resources 5.6–5.8**. Herrick's poem is a sincere declaration of love by Herrick to Anthea, whom he loves wholeheartedly, offering to obey her every wish because she commands every part of him; like Romeo he will "dare / E'en death" to be with his loved one. Little Frieda is loved by Ted Hughes, her father; Hughes' love of nature is also present; love is revealed through the imagery, e.g. "warm wreaths of breath". Draw out that "Full Moon and Little Frieda", which is a metaphysical poem, is not full of (what are now) clichés or passionate exclamations of love; it is more subtle and includes far more than love for just one person. The odd one out is Blake's famous poem "A Poison Tree", which is about emnity, hate and anger, and the need for people to discuss their differences.

Move on to the **Synonyms for love and hate task** on page 119 of the Student Book. Ask students to suggest synonyms for the words *love* and *hate* and write them on the board. When they run out of ideas, encourage them to see if a thesaurus prompts other options. Suggestions for *love* include: worship, devotion, caring, keenness, fondness, tenderness, passion; for *hate*: detestation, revulsion, disgust, loathing, repulsion, dislike, despise. Look at the diagram on page 119 and establish how the grading works: from indifference through to strong emotions. Hand out **Resource 5.9** and ask students to add the synonyms on the board at the appropriate level of their diagram. Insist they work independently to arrive at their own decisions without influence. After they have finished, they may compare diagrams with partners, discuss diagrams in small groups or consolidate the activity as a class.

The proposal

Student Book, page 120

If your class is doing *The Importance of Being Earnest* or will be reading it in the future, take a few minutes to explain how Oscar Wilde used this drawing-room comedy to poke fun at his audience; that superficially it appears very silly, but that is because he believed the way the aristocracy of his time behaved was frivolous, meaningless and hypocritical. Nominate two confident readers to read the short scene to the class and then ask students to do the **Speaking and listening task** on page 120.

If you have time, organise a short debate with one group for and the other against romance being about uncertainty. Give them 5–10 minutes to share ideas in their groups and then hear both points of view. If your class is large, have smaller groups of six to ten. Take feedback and ask students to vote on the motion: "The essence of romance is uncertainty."

Happy ever after

Student Book, pages 121–2

The poem "Marrysong" examines a relationship after years of marriage. Before reading the poem, you may want to ask students to make a few notes on how they think a romance turns into enduring love and how the notion of love might be different after 10 or 20 years of living together. Depending on class dynamics, take feedback or leave the issue until after you have read the poem and discussed content and imagery.

After reading "Marrysong", discuss the poet's use of imagery. Is geography a surprising choice of analogy? Remind students of the following expressions: "You don't know where you are with him/her" and "You have to tread carefully with him/her". Ask them to do the **Reading task** on page 121 of the Student Book. Suggested answers:

1. The verb "to learn" is open to interpretation; students should consider the fact that we don't or can't learn relationships as we do Maths or Chemistry.

2. The wife has metaphorically barricaded anger within her, buried it deep ("walled anger of her quarried hurt"); natural imagery conveys extreme change of emotion and elongated vowel sounds contrasting with clipped sounds emphasise a positive change ("cool water laughing where the day before there were stones in her voice").

3. It's a geographical metaphor, suggesting his wife encompasses an expanse of different feelings and that her emotions change without indication.

4. He chose this imagery to convey that his wife is like a different country with another landscape day by day. It emphasises the notion of dramatic shifts in temperament or mood; that marriage is a journey with an unreliable map, unforeseen challenges and obstacles to be overcome.

5. Short statements suggest rapid changes; no sooner has he "charted" than the terrain shifts and that which was mapped is once again wilderness (look at the idea of "*wild*erness"). There is no clear path ("Roads disappear"); his "map (is) never true". Short statements act like relating simple facts of life.

6. As the speaker tries to know what direction his wife is moving in, what she's thinking, she shifts and moves even further away. The short sentences reinforce the distance between the couple and the sense of futility in trying to "read" your spouse.

Using English: splitting infinitives

Workbook, page 45

The purpose of the activity is to remind students how we often speak and write differently. Suggested answers:

a. to explain briefly

b. to follow to your leader obediently and loyally

c. to express his true emotions eloquently

d. to apologise humbly

e. to describe clearly and accurately

Family values

Student Book, pages 122–4; Recording 5

Listen to **Recording 5** of the first part of William Saroyan's famous short story **"The Summer of the Beautiful White Horse"** on pages 122–3. Point out that the writer hasn't used speech marks for dialogue, perhaps to reflect a dreamlike stream of consciousness or memory effect. Do a brief *wh-* analysis to make sure students understand the content of the story without going into it too deeply; students will have to resolve the end of the story later for themselves. Briefly discuss the boys' personalities. Draw out that Mourad seems to be tempted by greed and passion, while Aram seems honest and anxious to uphold the beliefs and values of his Armenian tribe, to be proud, truthful and never steal.

Set the **Writing task** on page 123 of the Student Book, making sure students understand the Reminders on the same page and that they need to be careful how they use the narrative voice. Ask them to read through the **Writing skills** guidance for short stories on page 124 before they start planning. Insist they use correct speech marks in their stories, unless you have a class of high-flyers, who could experiment. However, point out that in exams they must use correct punctuation at all times to prove that they know how to use speech marks, etc.

Once students have written a first draft, ask them to go back to the Writing skills panel on page 124 to see what they have used it effectively and to identify anything that has been overlooked. Leave them to go on independently as they should be developing a degree of self-discipline by now and it will help them to consolidate the information for retrieval and revision.

Award up to 13 marks for content and up to 12 marks for style and accuracy (total of 25 marks). Look for a first-person narrator (Aram, not Mourad) and a clear ending or resolution; interesting use of language; correct references to setting; how the narrator solves his feelings about the stolen horse; references to family loyalty and fraternal love (for the crazy cousin); the joy of riding the wonderful horse early on a beautiful morning. The best essays will incorporate something of Saroyan's style (with speech marks).

Matchmaking

Student Book, pages 125–7; Resource 5.10

There will be an opportunity to discuss arranged marriage later, so ask students to read **"The Matchmaker"** on page 125 without preamble. Let them work out what is happening for themselves: this is good exam practice. Once they have finished reading, discuss the content of the passage to clarify any confusion but avoid doing too much on the use of language. Set the **Reading task** – either Core and/or Extended – on page 126.

Answers and marks for the Core Reading tasks:

1. Award up to 15 marks as indicated below:

   a. The voice is the nostalgic adult voice of a Chinese woman ("When I was older, I came to recognise this as a Peking accent."). (1)

   b. She is two years old. (1)

   c. Huang Taitai is her mother-in-law to be. (1)

   d. The matchmaker says she is a "strong horse" who will grow up to serve her Huang Taitai well in old age. (2)

   e. They never hear stories from the cities of men successfully choosing their own wives, only told stories where bad wives "throw their old, crying parents out into the street". The mothers are afraid so they choose wives for their sons who will look after the elderly and treat them respectfully. (3)

   f. It is possibly a butterfly. (1)

   g. The marriage doesn't work out well for the girl ("even if I had known I was getting such a bad husband"). (2)

   h. The narrator is dutiful and resigned / accepting about what happened ("I had no choice now or later"). There is a sense of regret (but "That was how backward families in the country were"). The culture meant people believed popular myths or gossip; living in the country meant they had little or no opportunity for progress and liberal thinking was forbidden. Nevertheless, there is also a sense of anger or bitterness that girls were sent to look after their parents-in-law and husbands, and she clearly disliked everything about the boy she was chosen for. (4)

2. Students must use the passage for information and respond clearly as the girl's mother or father. Reference to the child's future home, future in-laws, especially the mother-in-law

should be made. The content of the final paragraph should be incorporated in some way. Award up to 10 marks for content and up to 5 marks for style and accuracy (total of 15 marks).

Marking the Extending Reading tasks:

1. Students should use a journalistic style and incorporate details from the passage relating to points (a), (b) and (c). There is no word limit, but students should not write more than 350 words. Award up to 10 marks for content and up to 5 marks for style and accuracy (total of 15 marks).

2. Students can choose two of the following senses: sight, sound, touch, smell. They must address points (a), (b) and (c), quote and explain fully how the author has used imagery relating to the two senses. Award up to 15 marks.

Before students start the Writing task on page 126 of the Student Book remind them that coursework should never be used as a soap box to air personal opinions; they must always try to present both sides of an argument, which is why practising the discursive writing technique is important.

Ask students to copy and keyword the question for the **Writing task** on page 126 of the Student Book. Before they start planning their writing, they could spend a few minutes discussing the issue in small groups or as a class. Hand out the planning framework (**Writing skills panel** on page 127) on **Resource 5.10** and encourage students to plan their writing on the sheet. Award up to 12 marks for content and up to 13 marks for style and accuracy (total of 25 marks).

"Saving Richard Parker"

Student Book, pages 128–9

Ask students to read the passage from *Life of Pi* on page 128 in silence. Try to avoid any discussion of the book or film before they do the **Reading comprehension task** on page 129. Ask students to answer the questions independently, if possible, but if they are struggling with the content of the passage, help them to interpret what is happening and why the boy tries to save the tiger. Insist they provide evidence for their ideas at all times. The reasons Pi tries to save the tiger are below, but accept any alternatives supported by evidence:

- Pi is a child on his own in a traumatic and very dangerous situation

- being alone, it is natural that he would respond to a familiar face

- Richard Parker was part of Pi's "extended family" (line 39) in the zoo; Pi grew with the tiger, although it was in a cage

- the tiger looks "panic-stricken" (line 15) and it is natural for us to want to save a drowning creature

- Pi may feel a sense of responsibility (the tiger belongs to his family), he encourages the tiger as an adult might encourage a child, saying "Don't give up" (line 11).

Using English: sinister words

Workbook, pages 46–7; Resource 5.11

This vocabulary work extends the focus on students' use of language. Do the wordsearch activity to end this unit as a fun way of recapping on previous work on synonyms. The answers are supplied on Resource 5.11. As an extension activity, give them a blank 16×16 grid and ask them to compile a similar wordsearch with numbered clues using synonyms. This can be completed as homework and handed out in the next lesson for another student to do.

Self-assessment

Student Book, page 129; Resource 5.12

A version of the Self-assessment panel on page 129 is available for students to fill out on **Resource 5.12**. Give them a minimum of 15 minutes or set this for homework to ensure that students are thinking independently without peer influence. Remind them that it is important to reflect on what they have achieved but also to identify their weaknesses so that they know what to focus on in future. When you have feedback, you could recap on a particular skill such as writing to analyse.

Literature extension

Student Book, pages 130–3

The story **"Circus Cat, Alley Cat"** can be handled in different ways. On the surface it is an amusing anecdote, which Core students can read and then discuss the animal imagery and references to cages. Extended students should read the story by themselves and then be asked "What is this story about?" They should be able to identify some or all of the following:

- a child's perspective

- family ties

- missionaries trying to do good

- charity

- how one can never tame a wild creature

- theme of colonialism.

Start by asking students to read the story and then discuss their impressions. Depending on your class's academic level, point out that the story is full of animal and circus imagery, and it is also an extended metaphor for colonialism in India (British Raj) and how the British sought to "tame" wild "Mother India". Then ask them to do the **Exploring the passage task** on page 133. The questions require students to find information or make inferences from the evidence they are given. Remind them to support their views by quoting from the text for questions 2, 3 and 4; to examine their ideas before they write; to explain their interpretations or ideas fully in writing.

6 Living in a material world

This unit focuses on Directed Writing related to aspects of the material world such as gold mining, grading diamonds and the history of money; it also includes more literary texts using figurative language. There is a short story in the Workbook, which functions as an extended metaphor for human greed. As you work through the material, encourage students to use their analytical or thinking skills in relation to modern lifestyles in wealthy countries and as a means of identifying a writer's intentions or the theme and secondary meaning of literary texts.

Unit starter

Student Book, page 135

Discuss the **Talking points** on page 135 as a class. The verse comes from "The Money Song" in *Cabaret*, a musical set in Germany during the 1930s depression. Ask students if they think there is any truth behind it. Mention how morning news broadcasts include data from stock exchanges around the world each day. Address the bullet points as a class or organise students into groups. Round up the topic by asking if students are in agreement on one of the bullet points and, if so, which and why.

Hard cash and flexible finance

Student Book, pages 136–7

Introduce the activity on **Categorising information** on pages 136–7 by looking at the photographs; make sure students understand the difference between cash and credit (cards). Point out the definition for *wampum* on page 137. Set the pairwork, making sure students know what they need to do and modelling the categorising of one or two examples if necessary. Explain that the clue is in the wording *hard* cash (as in shells, coins or bartered goods – something of immediate value) and *flexible* finance (notes that represent gold or money held in a bank that can be used as a form of obtaining credit or an overdraft).

Consolidate understanding by asking students to write down this definition:

Credit (n.): a system of doing business by trusting that a person will pay at a later date for goods or services supplied; the power to buy in this way; the amount of money in a person's bank account or entered in an account book as paid to the holder.
Oxford Study Dictionary

Answers:

*   History of money: a, d, g, i, k, m, n, p, r, t.

*   History of credit (flexible finance): b, c, e, f, h, j, l, o, q, s.

Ask students to do the **Speaking and listening task** on page 137 of the Student Book. Point out that they should each talk about ten different points and encourage them to use their own words as far as possible. There is much more on the history of money on: www.historyworld.net and http://library.thinkquest.org. The sorting, retrieval and rewording are transferable to Directed Writing questions or Coursework Portfolios.

Wealth

Student Book, pages 138–41

As a class, read the passage from **"The Great Gatsby"** on pages 138–9. Then ask students to do the **Reading tasks** on page 139. Whether students are doing the Core or Extended question, advise them to make notes before doing the writing tasks so that they include all relevant points. Remind them not to quote from the text in their letters. Point out the guidelines on how to write a letter of complaint in the **Writing skills** panel on page 141, working through the advice with them as necessary.

Suggested answers for Core Reading task:

1. **a.** The Gatsby's Rolls Royce brings people from the city (New York); his station wagon picks them up from the train station; people arrive in their own cars "parked five deep in the drive".

   b. In the afternoon his guests dive from the "tower of his raft", sunbathe on the beach or aquaplane behind one of his motorboats.

   c. On Mondays a team of eight servants clean up and repair damage to the house and gardens after the weekend's party.

   d. Gatsby's garden looked like a Christmas tree because it had lights strung around it.

2. Letters will vary, including in tone: some will reflect the excitement and lavishness; others will moan and itemise how much work is involved in clearing up, repairing damage and running around after the guests. If students moralise on behaviour they must include specific complaints or reasons.

Suggested answers for Extended Reading task:

1. Letters should reflect the content of the passage and the atmosphere it creates while putting forward a series of the student's own arguments. The two elements should be intertwined. They might include the following points:

   • noise, with reference to the big band and voices like an opera

   • lights, with reference to the garden decoration

   • the mess, possible mention of rats and left-over food left at back door

   • cars, with reference to constant entrance and exit of Rolls and station wagon; private cars entering property cars; the nuisance and danger

   • morality, with reference to people being out of control; wild behaviour

   • the lavishness, including any details such as the extravagance of food, the huge numbers, all those oranges, modern gadgets, number of servants

   • the letter could develop into an argument on social responsibility.

2. Students should comment on the following:

   • Lights and colours of the party: extravagance ("enough coloured lights to make a Christmas tree"); symbols of luxury and wealth (motor boats, aquaplanes and the Rolls Royce); bold colours, that could be garish and tasteless ("halls and salons and verandas are gaudy with primary colors"); it seems the light could be seen from space ("the lights grow brighter as the earth lurches away from the sun"); people are constantly moving around ("sea-change of faces and voices and color under the constantly changing light")

   • Sounds of the party: the orchestra described as a "whole pitful" shows Gatsby's wealth; personification of the air suggests that the party is full and busy ("air is alive with chatter and laughter"); there's a metaphorical sense that voices are becoming increasingly more excitable and enthusiastic ("opera of voices pitches a key higher").

Move on to the **Summary writing tasks** on page 140 of the Student Book. For the Core task, award up to 10 marks for content and up to 5 marks for summary style and accuracy (total of 15 marks). Core summary notes: cars (expensive Rolls Royce); luxury food; property (large house with private beach); motor boat and water-skis; parties; servants; hiring caterers and garden marquees; lighting and electricity; new electric kitchen gadgets; entertainment (orchestra); socialising (theatre).

For the Extended task, award up to 15 marks for content and up to 5 marks for summary style and accuracy (total of 20 marks). Extended summary notes: as for Core summary, plus how Gatsby spends his time: expensive leisure pursuits such as water-skiing; sunbathing; buying motor boats and fancy cars; giving extravagant parties; going to theatre/cabaret/musicals; socialising; expensive clothing (implicit).

Now students are thoroughly familiar with the content of the Great Gatsby passage, ask them to start the **Letter of complaint task** on page 140 of the Student Book by reading the student's letter. They should be able to identify mistakes in the content and how the style or organisation of the letter can be improved. Answers should mention:

- Mistakes: Gatsby does provide transport for his guests and they park in his drive, not "blocking (the neighbour's) drive" or on the street. There is no reference in the text to taxis, but this could be inferred from the fact that cars park "five deep".

- Style and organisation: The style is polite and addresses the issue, but the letter is badly organised, suggesting lack of planning. "Last but not least" reiterates the mention of noise and lights and is by no means the final comment.

Practising Reading Comprehension

Workbook, pages 48–51

Students could read **"The Phoenix"** on pages 48–51 of the Workbook. Make sure they understand the story. Encourage them to discuss the motives of all the people involved: Lord Strawberry, Mr Poldero, Mr Ramkin, visitors to the zoo and the press. Ask: Why was the bird caught, kept in captivity and encouraged to die? Who would have benefited? Remind them to answer the questions in full sentences. Suggested answers:

1. **a.** As a hobby or rare, precious acquisition

   b. It was "the finest aviary in Europe", large with good conditions.

   c. As an unusual attraction for his zoo and to get more visitors

   d. In a cage, reasonably well fed and well treated to start with

   e. "Udge" could mean character or personality.

   f. Reference to the woman eaten by a crocodile suggests visitors want something more sensational than a boring bird; the phoenix is "too quiet, too classical".

   g. To get more people to visit his Wizard Wonderland

   h. He provides scented wood for its nest; halves its food rations once and then again; turns off the heating; gives it unpleasant companions; puts cats in the cage; turns on a water sprinkler; jeers at it himself; the bird becomes ill and demoralised, and is kept in appalling conditions.

   i. He starts a publicity campaign when the bird is losing feathers and looks about to die.

   j. They die in the fire.

   k. Students must justify their opinions.

2. **a.** The bird is "civil and obliging" and polite; it adapts to its conditions and tolerates children; it is quiet and not a show-off.

   b. It is now "as capricious as Cleopatra" – described in hyperbolic, show-business language.

Students should select words and phrases and explain their effect on the reader.

Gold and the Midas touch

Student Book, pages 142–7; Resources 6.1–6.3

As a class, read the article **"The Devastating Costs of the Amazon Gold Rush"** on pages 142–3. Then ask students to answer the questions in the **Reading task** on page 144. For question 1, award marks as shown below, up to a maximum of 25 marks. Suggested answers:

1. **a.** The phrase "gold rush" means urgency to get gold. (1)

   b. This gold rush is taking place in the Peruvian rainforest. (1)

   c. It is one of the most biodiverse regions in the world, is unspoilt and includes countless varieties of species and trees. (3)

   d. Unlike ranching or logging, the rainforest destruction goes much deeper, miners are destroying the forest 50ft down and rivers are contaminated. (3)

   e. Mercury is leaked into the rivers which is "taken up by fish" and "enters the food chain"; deforestation has increased six-fold, which means that the area accounting for 15% of photosynthesis is being destroyed; there is a large barren area where rainforest is only visible in the distance, an eye sore that could affect ecotourism in the area. (6)

   f. "surge" is the sudden increase in the demand and urgency for gold; "a hedge against losses" is a means of reducing risk in investments as gold holds its value; "the insatiable appetite for luxury goods made from the precious metal" is the greedy/unappeasable need for inessential and expensive products made of gold (6)

   g. There are a lot of legal documents needed to obtain a permit, including engineering specifications, statements on how the environment will be protected, how native peoples will be protected and how the land will be returned to a natural state. (2)

h. Tourists might want to visit for the tranquillity and peace in a natural environment, to explore and to discover insects and animals unique to the area. (3)

For question 2, award up to 15 marks for content and up to 5 for style and accuracy (total of 20 marks). If students peer-mark, they could refer to the list of points on **Resource 6.1** when awarding marks for content.

Practising reading comprehension

Resource 6.2

If students would benefit from reading comprehension practice or they are doing an oral activity related to the gold mine text, you may want to use **Resource 6.2**, which offers a passage on rain forests and a set of comprehension questions. Award marks as shown on Resource 6.2. Suggested answers:

1. The "crowns" of branches act as canopies and filters, breaking the force of the rain.

2. The leaves are thick, tough and glossy.

3. Epiphytes are climbing plants such as orchids.

4. Birds have adapted to certain areas of the forest and stay in their own "zone".

5. The soil is barren and lacking in nutrients.

6. Volcanic regions and river floodplains have more fertile soils and can support human life.

7. They mean that despite poor soils, lack of sunlight, etc. wildlife and insects flourish.

8. He means the food chain.

9. Count up to nine of the following and accept alternatives within the text: branch canopy, birds, insects, mammals, fat leaves, climbing orchid/flowers, lianas, mat of connecting roots, trunks with flared "buttresses", dark areas, light rain, clearings.

Speeches

Student Book, pages 144–5; Resource 6.3

Explain that now students are going to write a persuasive speech about gold mining in Peru. First, you could read to them Martin Luther King's famous "I have a dream" speech on equality for its tone and style. It is available on **Resource 6.3** or you could find an audio version on www.youtube. com. Let them listen without the words in front of them. Ask them to describe the tone and how King achieved this. Then hand out copies of Resources 6.3. Ask them to underline or highlight

features of persuasive writing. They should identify: alliteration, tripling, imperatives, repetition, emotive language, hyperbole. Then discuss how and why these techniques are used as a class. Be prepared for comments on King's use of the word *negro*, which was more acceptable in 1963 than it is now. There are two more famous speeches and guidance on speech-writing techniques on Workbook, pages 73–6.

Return to the **Writing task** on page 144 of the Student Book. Ask students to make brief notes on both topics and then choose the one they feel more strongly about. Explain that points noted for the other topic can be incorporated into their speech as a form of argument. Direct attention to the **Writing skills panel** on page 157 of the Student Book and briefly talk them through the main points, especially the logical, personal, emotional and social strands mentioned in Aristotle's analysis. Insist that they re-read independently to consolidate understanding. Encourage them to refer back to their answers to the Reading task on page 144, as well as adding their own ideas. If they have looked at Martin Luther King's speech, clarify that they don't have to write a rousing speech, but it must be convincing, have meaningful arguments and persuade listeners to their way of thinking. Set aside one lesson for the writing process, to be finished as homework, and a second lesson for students to give their speeches to the class. Award up to 13 marks for content and up to 12 marks for style and accuracy (total of 25 marks).

"Midas and the River Pactolus" and "Metamorphoses"

Student Book, pages 146–7

Introduce the two passages: the first, on page 146, is a 21st-century blog article on precious metals; the second, on page 147, is about an ancient text by Ovid. Explain that both texts were written to inform, albeit using different techniques. The second passage recounts Ovid's fable (an etiological myth explaining a real phenomena); the blog examines the fable in the light of scientific knowledge.

After reading the passages, ask students to do the **Writing task** on page 147 of the Student Book. Award up to 10 marks content and up to 15 marks for style and accuracy (total of 25 marks). Possible content:

- Midas was king in ancient times.

- His story may have been told to explain rich alluvial deposits in the River Pactolus.

- The god Bacchus/Dionysus wanted to reward Midas by granting him a wish.

- Midas wished that everything he touched could be turned to gold.

- The wish was granted but absolutely everything he touched, including food and his daughter, was turned to gold.

- Midas begged Dionysus to release him from the wish and was told to bathe in the River Pactolus.

- When Midas bathed, he washed away his curse (and gold) into the river.

- The myth may have started to explain the real King Midas' great wealth.

- The River Pactolus is known for its gold-coloured specks of electrum.

- This area of ancient Lydia was rich in electrum.

- Lydians are said to have invented and used gold coins in the 7th century BC.

Using English: new words for new inventions

Workbook, pages 52–3

Before you set this activity, point out that language is constantly changing to incorporate new ideas and inventions. The word *blog*, for example, is a new construction; 20 years ago a *mobile* was an ornament hanging from a ceiling. Ask students to name a few other new words that have come into being in the past half-century (e.g. *hi-fi, i-pod, to text* as a verb). For question 1 accept logical responses and award extra points to students who have taken the time to investigate the words. Draw attention to the fact that all these are compound nouns (you could direct students to page 277 in the Student Book if necessary). For question 2 accept logical or interesting answers that are adequately explained.

"Diamonds are forever"

Student Book, pages 148–52

Start this section by referring students back to the photograph on page 134 of the Student Book. Ask: Why are cars like this considered to be "luxury items". Introduce the term *conspicuous consumption* and ask students to make a short list of goods they consider to be luxuries. If the discussion develops into an argument over name brands, explain that they are right to see name brands as an intrinsic part of luxury items. Finally,

ask them to write a wish list of three expensive items they hope to buy for themselves or someone else during their lives and to write one sentence to explain (honestly) why they want these things.

Ask students to read **"Selecting a diamond"** on page 148 of the Student Book in silence. Then ask them, if they have got diamonds on their wish lists, to add which type or shape of diamond they would prefer. For those without diamonds on their lists, you can have a fun but useful 5 minutes asking them if, in the future, they might buy one for someone else, and, if not, why not. Explain that this information has been written to explain the grading of diamonds by the Rio Tinto mining corporation, which also sent out the press releases on pages on 150 and 151. They can read more about press releases in general in the **Reading skills panel** on page 149.

Do a short-term recall quiz. Ask students write down what the following words mean in relation to diamonds: cut, clarity, colour, carat (don't spell it out). Give them 5 minutes and then ask them to swap papers and peer-mark against the information on page 148.

Ask students to do the **Writer's craft task** on page 149 of the Student Book. Suggested answers:

1. **a.** An opportunity to bid on exceptional diamonds not publically available

   b. Different groups of diamonds available

   c. People who buy diamonds for future gain/value

   d. People who want to buy and the price they offer

   e. Enthralled, fascinated, interested

2. **a.** The most unique sale of diamonds in the world that very few people are invited to take part in

   b. Worth noting because of its totally unique intensity of colour

   c. Long established and new markets for diamonds

   d. From a confirmed, verifiable mine

   e. Eagerly looked for/searched out

"Press releases 1 and 2"

Student Book, pages 150–2

Ask students to read the two press releases on pages 150–1 (the passages are longer than students will encounter in their final assessments). Remind them that they wrote an official report (by a detective) in Unit 5. Explain that they are going to write another report, in response to the **Writing task** on page 152, and they need to use a similar, formal and objective style with a degree of persuasion here as well. Point out the **Writing skills panel** on page 152 and suggest they could also use the information on page 148. Reiterate that before writing their report, they should make notes on the two press releases, organise their notes carefully and choose subheadings for each section of the report. Remind them that a carefully worded conclusion is essential to complete the task. Award up to 10 marks for content and up to 15 marks for style and accuracy (total of 25 marks). Possible content:

- This is a large collection of 55 of the world's most exclusive pink diamonds.
- The diamonds are distinguished for their incomparable intensity of colour.
- There is competitive and persistent demand for Rio Tinto diamonds.
- They are from a provable and well-respected company.
- Diamonds are revered for their richness of colour.
- Lot number one, Argyle Mystra is particularly precious.
- There is a high level of interest from both established and new markets.
- Jewels are rare.
- Rio Tinto is world renowned for being the number one reliable and constant supplier of pink diamonds.
- A 12.76 carat diamond, the Argyle Pink Jubilee, has recently been mined.
- The diamond will be assessed and then bids will be made at the Argyle Pink Diamonds Tender later in the year.
- It has taken 26 years of mining for pink diamonds to uncover a gem like the Argyle Pink Jubilee.

Using English: relative clauses

Workbook, pages 54–5

Explain that students are going to look at the difference between defining and non-defining relative clauses, and related punctuation. This will help them to become more actively aware of how they construct sentences and how they can shorten long sentences to make their writing more succinct and effective when there is a word limit. Set the activity, which guides students step by step. Answers:

1. **a.** that we stayed in on our school trip to London; **b.** who showed us round the Tower of London

2. **a.** which I've read before; **b.** while being evacuated during a war; **c.** who lived in what used to be called Burma when he was young; **d.** whose real hero is a carthorse called Boxer; **e.** who is very hardworking.

3. Defining: c, e; non-defining: a, b, d.

4. Students should pay close attention to how they punctuate their sentences.

Fair Trade goods

Student Book, pages 152–3

Before starting this topic, ask students to find out one or two pieces of information about Fair Trade goods in their country. If they have never heard of Fair Trade, ask them what they think it involves. Ask them to read the web pages on page 153. They should try to find out: which shops sell Fair Trade goods; which goods are most popular; which Fair Trade goods, if any, their country produces and exports. They could start their research with the websites on page 153 of the Student Book. Ask them to bring their notes into the next lesson.

Ask students to work independently on the **Writing task** on page 152. As a reminder, write on the board: *purpose, audience, register*. If students are going to do the Directed Writing assessment, set a word limit of 350–450, but otherwise leave it open with a maximum of 800 words. Award up to 10 marks for content and up to 15 marks for style and accuracy (total of 25 marks). Content should demonstrate investigation and reasoning; style should demonstrate purpose, audience and register. This activity could be developed independently for oral or written coursework so leave students to work on their own as much as possible.

Money and matrimony

Student Book, pages 154–7

As a class, read the passage from *The Importance of Being Earnest* on pages 154–7. Then ask students to address the question at the top of page 154: What is actually happening in this scene? Direct discussion round to arranged marriages and ask them to explain what Lady Bracknell is trying to ascertain (that Jack can more than provide for Gwendolen; that his social status is acceptable; that she herself will benefit from the alliance in terms of social class and property). If possible, watch the same scene from the 2002 film to give students a sense of the director's interpretation and characterisation. There are clips on www.youtube. com. Ask students to answer the **Reading task** on page 157. Suggested answers:

1. Lady Bracknell is interviewing Jack to see if he is eligible enough to marry her daughter Gwendolen ("I am quite ready to enter your name, should your answers be what a really affectionate mother requires.")

2. He can offer "between 7 and 8 thousand a year", mainly in investments, a country house with 1500 acres and a house on the "unfashionable side" of Belgrave Square.

3. Hear students' views based on literature and history. Wilde uses irony and caricatures to create humour in a comedy of manners, yet there is an underlying critique of the real world of the upper classes and their snobbery.

4. Students may have quite personal views and you could have a stimulating debate on this issue.

Ask students to do the **Writing task** on page 158 of the Student Book. They need to select a title and match it to a specific writing style for a blog or magazine article. They should write about the luxury goods, precious metals and gems mentioned in this unit. They may also use information obtained from a daily newspaper or research, which should be cited appropriately. Award up to 10 marks for content and up to 15 marks for style and accuracy (total of 25 marks).

Self-assessment

Student Book, page 158; Resource 6.4

A version of the Self-assessment panel on page 158 is available for students to fill out on **Resource 6.4**. Give them a minimum of 15 minutes or set this for homework to ensure that they are thinking independently without peer influence. Remind them

that it is important to reflect on what they have achieved but also to identify their weaknesses so that they know what to focus on in future. When you have feedback, you could recap on a particular skill such as writing a report.

Literature extension

Student Book, page 159

Each of these poems uses precious stones or gold as symbols and metaphors. Ask students to read Rossetti's poem on page 159 and identify what, for her, was of greatest value. If they have trouble understanding why flint is valuable here, explain how it was used to make a fire. Hood was writing in the first part of the 19th century, but his poem mentions Tudor queens (not in chronological order). You could ask students why he mentions these queens at all. Answers should relate to Bloody Mary and/or Good Queen Bess (Elizabeth 1) and pirates; religion and blood. Take feedback.

Ask students to read the poems again and make brief notes, in pairs, on how the poets use rhyme, couplets, symbol and metaphor. Take feedback. Ask: What do these poems have in common? Answers should relate to people's values; how gold and precious stones are only objects whose value is established by what people are prepared to pay or do to acquire them.

Practising Directed Writing

Workbook, pages 56–8

Set this task for homework or do it during a lesson as exam practice; it also gives good practice for summary skills. Advise students to keyword the question and do a *wh-* analysis of the interview with the question in clearly in mind. The focus of the question is on the founder of Anidan, so answers should include the following points: Selas' background; how and why he went to Lamu Island; how he set up the charity; who he helps and why; what Anidan provides and has a achieved. Award up to 13 marks for content and up to 12 marks for style and accuracy (total of 25 marks). After writing task, students could find out more about Anidan on www. anidan.org.

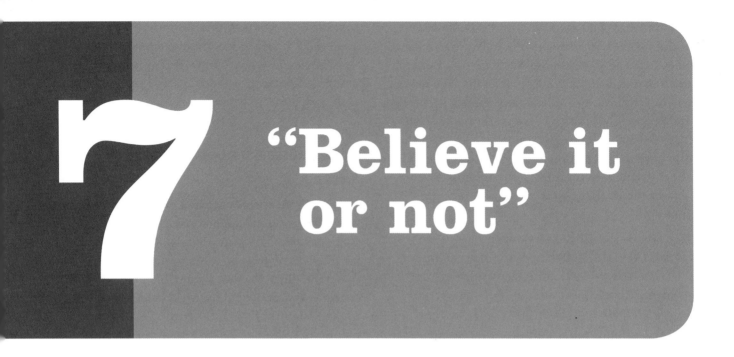

7 "Believe it or not"

This unit reviews and extends awareness of the writer's perspective in media texts, fiction and non-fiction. This includes a close look at print journalism: students will examine media texts of a serious and sensationalist nature and read literary travel writing, as well as online blog reports. Some texts are very accessible, but there are more challenging tasks for more able pupils. It would be useful to have a range of English language newspapers available in the classroom so that students can see how different reporters and papers approach the same topic or event. They could also watch how different television channels present the same event on one particular day, discuss how some media presents a more global point of view and how this affects viewers.

they consciously suspend disbelief when reading fiction. Later in this unit they will examine how fantasy writers create believable worlds, but for now draw out that fiction isn't entirely untrue because it (generally) involves real human experiences and emotions. Encourage students who say they never read fiction outside school to explain why. Before leaving Byron's stanza, draw students' attention to how he suggests that we use fiction, or in his case narrative verse, to learn "truths" about our world.

Move on to the **Speaking and listening task** on page 161. You could stimulate thought for question 1 by suggesting students think about ghosts or extra-terrestrial beings. Mix students up for question 2, asking them to move around the room; when you call "stop", they must work with whoever they are next to.

Unit starter

Student Book, page 161

Discuss the **Talking point** on page 161 as a class. Students might refer to examples of ways truth can be stranger than fiction from news reports, their own experiences and stories from their own and other countries. Recent history might include tsunami, earthquakes, hurricanes and other natural disasters; human acts of kindness and atrocity; bizarre eye-witness accounts of paranormal activity.

The stanza from Byron's "Don Juan" on page 161 presents fact and fiction as opposites. Ask students if this is really the case or whether fiction needs to contain sufficient fact to make it believable. Ask if

News reports and articles

Student Book, pages 162–9; Resources 7.1–7.2

As an introduction to this section, display **Resource 7.1**. Discuss the questions and responses as a class. Suggested answers:

- People want to know the daily news for interest, to be informed, because it's relevant to their job, etc.

- They can find out from printed and online news, the Internet, TV, radio, etc.

- Ask for a show of hands.

- The layout is different and the content may be edited differently.

- Show students the difference in headlines for the same news report from a daily paper and the online equivalent. In online reports there is no banner headline to attract the attention of passers-by; readers have already chosen what they want to read so less space is given to headings and subheadings.

As a class, read the rubric on page 162 of the Student Book and clarify any new points. Students may be familiar with the idea of sensational journalism but may be less familiar with the more serious press. Write *investigative journalism* on the board and ask them what they think it means. Then write *human interest stories* and ask how these differ from investigative reports or articles. Explain that both types of journalism are used in print and broadcast media, but some newspapers and broadcast programmes favour one type or the other. Also introduce the idea of "journalese" and how puns or wordplay are used in headlines.

Read the passage "Mexico takes stock after major quake" on page 162 with the class and ask students to do the **Writer's craft task** on page 163. Award up to a total of 15 marks, as indicated below. Suggested answers:

1. Mexico assesses and analyses the current situation after the earthquake. (2)

2. Short paragraphs are easier to read quickly and look more appealing. (1)

3. Mexico will stay cautious, observing other signs of danger in case of an after tremor. (2)

4. Mexico is assessing the exact nature of the damage, both economically and personally, caused by the earthquake. (2)

5. Mexico earthquake – 7.4 (Richter scale); damaged buildings, no fatalities; 11 people injured; more than 1 minute; 800 houses damaged in southwestern state of Guerrero; strongest since 8.1 earthquake of 1985; 18 aftershocks. (8 marks)

Improving Directed Writing: news reports and articles

Workbook, pages 59–60

Ask students to read about newspaper reports and articles, and then do the **Directed Writing task** on page 60 of the Workbook. Remind them that they need to use their summary skills in tasks like this: they should annotate the text for relevant details, make notes and then write out their notes in the

designated style. Award up to 10 marks for content and up to 15 marks for style and accuracy (total of 25 marks). Points for inclusion:

- Major earthquake south-western Mexico
- No fatalities
- 7.6 on the Richter Scale
- Epicentre in Guerrero state
- Also near Pacific Coast holiday resort of Acapulco
- Not as bad as previous earthquakes in Acapulco
- No tsunami, but possible after-shocks
- Building shook in Mexico City
- Office workers ran from the buildings
- Residents fled from built-up areas
- Traffic came to a standstill
- Quote by Esteban Garcia can be adapted

Students doing Coursework Portfolios could take a news report such as this and develop it into a longer article. A similar incident or event could be used by two students for oral coursework, either as an interview or conversation.

Human interest in news reports

Student Book, pages 163–9; Resource 7.2

The second Mexico report on pages 163–4 is another example of online news. It combines informative reporting style with direct quotes and human-interest stories in very short paragraphs for immediacy. Ask students to do the **Writer's craft task** on page 165. Suggested answers:

1. There is more detail in the Bangkok Post report, which uses direct and indirect speech, and personal accounts of the natural disaster to make it more emotive. *Euronews* states the facts with brevity.

2. The reporter includes information about President Obama's daughter because she is someone many people know about so they will relate to the event in a more personal way: even famous people cannot escape natural disasters.

3. There is direct speech from various people, eye-witness reports and human interest in Malia Obama. The breadth of direct speech and human interest evokes readers' sympathy and interest, disbelief and amazement.

Explain that students are going to write their own newspaper report in response to the **Writing task** on page 165 of the Student Book. Make sure they understand the differences between news reports and news articles, referring to the **Reading skills panel** on page 166. Clarify they are going to write a news report, not an article that explores, informs and discusses. Ask them to read through the guidelines in the **Writing skills panel** on page 165 on their own. You could also let them glance through the daily newspapers.

Hand out **Resource 7.2**, which contains relevant notes on the Mexico earthquake that they could include in their reports. (If you have a class of high-flyers use the resource for marking and leave students to find the information themselves.) Support them in planning and writing their reports independently, but leave them to finish the task in silence. Award up to 10 marks for content and up to 15 marks for style and accuracy (total of 25 marks).

Using English: adjectives and adjectival phrases

Workbook, pages 61–2

This activity would be useful before students read the next section of the Student Book.

Encourage them to use colour-coding, which will help them to analyse more literary texts and the writers' use of language. Answers:

1. **a.** wonderfully relaxing; **b.** blissfully warm;
    c. it was heated and decorated with shells;
    d. it was quite small but had a huge mouth and needle sharp teeth.

2. Students should use the words in brackets as adjectival phrases.

3. Check students have written only one sentence for each topic and punctuated it correctly.

Reports on Kiki

Student Book, pages 167–9

It may be useful to point out Humphrys' reputation as a radio broadcaster and investigative journalist and give a short biography so students can better appreciate the content of his article about Haiti on pages 167–8 of the Student Book. You can find out more about him at http://www.bbc.co.uk/programmes/b006qj9z/presenters/john-humphrys. Before they read the article, clarify the meaning of "icon" in the context of the article heading. Ask students to read in silence and then recount what they found interesting, shocking or surprising. Ask if they agree with Humphrys' analysis of a human-

interest story – that emotive photographs are often remembered, but not the circumstances of the tragedy that surrounds them.

Ask students to do the **Reading task** on page 169 of the Student Book. Suggested answers:

1. The reference reinforces the fact that sometimes real news can be more astonishing and shocking than a Hollywood movie.

2. Memory is short and fickle; we retain positive ideals, images that give us hope, but sometimes forget the hardships and dangers selfless people confront to help those in need.

Ask students to do the **Writer's craft task** on page 169 of the Student Book. Suggested answers:

1. Students might choose: "His huge brown eyes sunk into his face tell of the suffering"; "bodies in the streets; the buildings crushed". Emotive images and words help the reader to conjure a picture of suffering; "bodies" is an unquantifiable collective noun, suggesting the volume of those killed; "crushed" is a highly emotive verb which evokes pity.

2. Humphrys has discussed how Kiki is used to evoke pity and now mentions the girl Wideline with rhetorical questions that draw the reader into the text, making us examine our own responses to media coverage of this or any other disaster.

Move on to read the introduction to an article from *The Sun* on the same subject on page 169 of the Student Book. Then ask students to answer the questions in the **Question box** on the same page. Encourage them to use the SQuEE method to explain and support their choices. Words such as "rubble", "tomb", "joy", "beams" in *The Sun* article uphold Kiki's status as a "miracle" child or an "icon of hope"; the effect is uplifting; there is "joy" and his "smile lit up the darkness". Other aspects of the rescue presented by Humphrys are not included.

Legendary monsters

Student Book, page 170–9; Resources 7.3–7.5

Write *cryptid* on the board and ask students to explain what they think it means (a definition is on page 170 of the Student Book). Then direct them to the **Talking points** on page 170. If there is a local "monster" in your area, ask students what they know about it. Display pictures of the Loch Ness Monster (available on Google images) and ask students to describe what the creature looks like in their own words without using the word "monster".

Read the reports of sightings of different monsters on pages 170–1 of the Student Book and then hand out **Resource 7.3**. Briefly recap on the use of the word *diction*, if necessary. Ask students to fill in the grid, in pairs, as outlined in the **Writer's craft panel** on page 171. Emphasise that they are looking for similarities and differences in style and diction, as well as content. Point out how the headlines use sensational wording, modal verbs (*could*), question forms ("Is this … ?") and phrases such as "reputed to be". The content includes brief descriptions. Suggested answers are available on **Resource 7.4** in case you want students to check their own or a partner's work.

Iceland's Loch Ness Monster

Student Book, page 172

Move on to the *Daily Mail* article about Iceland's Loch Ness Monster on page 172 of the Student Book. Ask students to locate all the phrases that the reporter uses so that he doesn't make an actual claim or factual statement ("Belief in"; "which is said to reside"; "Legends say"; "believed to be"). Set the **Reading task** on page 172. There is no word limit, but point out that they are not asked to do the whole project. Award up to 10 marks for content and up to 5 marks for style and accuracy (total of 15 marks).

Mokele-Mbembe

Student Book, pages 173–5

As a class, read the first blog article on Mokele-Mbembe on page 173 of the Student Book and discuss content. Ask students to read the second passage on pages 174–5 on their own. Ask them what, if anything, in the second text proves the cryptid does or does not exist. Draw attention to the source of these passages: the first is about a television programme, the second is by an anthropologist. Does the source of the articles lend them credence?

Direct students to the **Writing task** on page 175 of the Student Book and ask them if there is enough in the two passages for them to imagine what it would be like to be on an expedition in this part of the Congo. They can use their imaginations but also need to take relevant information from the two Mokele-mbembe texts. Before they plan and write, recap on techniques: e.g. fact, opinion, rhetorical questions, emotive vocabulary, assertive statements. Award up to 10 for content

and up to 15 for style and accuracy (total of 25 marks). However, be flexible because students are imagining a fictitious expedition. You could award points for the use or adaption of content details such as:

- Mokele-Mbembe means "one who stops the flow of rivers".
- It has a grey-brown body with a long neck and small head.
- The earliest account of the creature dates back to 1776.
- Just before the Second World War, a German explorer, Lasnitz, reportedly saw an animal with a long neck and alligator tail.
- People in canoes that come anywhere near it are, according to legend, destined to die.
- Fascination stems from an alleged link of the creature to the dinosaurs.
- In appearance, it resembles a sauropod with its long neck, teeth and huge size.
- Gibbons refutes evidence from a number of explorer accounts, saying that there is no evidence that Mokele-mbembes exist.
- Marcellin Agagna changed his story a number of times.
- Herman Regusters and his wife Kia are the only people to have observed the long neck, yet there were 28 other explorers with them.
- Rory Nugent's photos are 'alleged'.
- Jose Bourges observed a large hump-back animal searching for food along the bottom of the lake.

"On Yeti Tracks"

Student Book, pages 176–9

Introduce Bruce Chatwin, British writer of the passages on pages 176–8 of the Student Book. He travelled the world and wrote various books and novels, the best known being *In Patagonia* and *On the Black Hill*. More able students should be able to identify the more literary quality of Chatwin's prose compared to other travel texts in the Student Book. As you read through the passages with the class, draw attention to how Chatwin describes a very distant, unknown location so his British readers can get an idea of what the views, vegetation, etc. are like. Show how he juxtaposes the exotic with the mundane or well-known for effect.

You could ask all students to do the **Core Reading task** on page 179 of the Student Book as it is quite challenging; even more able students sometimes miss details. The questions, including those for the Extended Reading task on page 179, are similar to those in Reading assessments. For Core Reading question 1, award marks as shown below (total of 20 marks). Suggested answers:

1. **a.** The two types of Yeti: the *mih-teh* which kills people and the *dzu-teh* which kills only animals. (2)

    b. Yak are too big for a man to kill with bare hands. (2)

    c. The first rhetorical question (line 65) shows a genuine sense of puzzlement where western reason and rational scientific explanation is lost. This is immediately followed by a second rhetorical question to reinforce Chatwin's bewilderment and that of all westerners. (3)

    d. Yeti footprints are like huge feet turned back to front (lines 72–3) and have a giant big toe (line 116). (2)

    e. Chatwin's explanation is that the Yeti is a "creature of the Collective Unconscious", imagined by man, perhaps invented by those who live in fear or have extreme beliefs or personality types. Chatwin also suggests it could be due to a lack of oxygen at high altitude. (3)

    f. He is shocked and excited, " 'Look!' (he) blurted out." The exclamatory sentence emphasises his surprise; the verb "blurted" alludes to Chatwin's excitement to relate what he's seen. " 'Look at them!' " shows how eagerly he wants Elizabeth to acknowledge his discovery. (2)

    g. The juxtaposition of her indifference, "'Oh yeah?' drawled Elizabeth, and went on watching the shelldrake" makes Chatwin's discovery all the more surprising. Elizabeth is watching a bird familiar to British readers; it also portrays Elizabeth as the rational, sceptical westerner: she clearly doesn't believe Chatwin's discovery. (3)

    h. Chatwin's travels take him far and wide, to visit the unknown, see the miraculous, but he interprets what he sees according to his western upbringing when trying to explain the inexplicable: if something can be explained rationally then fear of the unknown is eradicated. (3)

2. Students should use the text and their answers above to write the letter. It should include what is thought, felt and imagined from a fist person perspective. Award 10 marks for the content of the letter and 5 marks for style and accuracy (total of 15 marks).

The **Extended Reading task** on page 179 of the Student Book asks students to take a scientific approach and write a journal entry. Point out that does not rule out comments on the beauty of the location. The word limit is 250–350 words, so they need to be brief. They should include what was thought, felt and imagined in the set location. For question 1, award up to 15 marks for content and up to 5 marks for style and accuracy (total of 20 marks).

Possible points for inclusion:

*   Khumbu Ylha, the Sacred Mountain of the Sherpas, had an awesome beauty above the clouds.

*   We climbed alongside the Ngozumpa Glacier into a bright landscape of snow, rock and frozen green lakes.

*   We saw shelldrake ducks, pale pink rhododendrons and birch trees.

*   One monk described the yeti as being taller than a man with yellow eyes, lots of hair and long arms.

*   Lakpa Doma, a Sherpa woman, described the yeti as having yellow eyes with enormous brow-ridges and concave temples.

*   It could have been dangerous at high altitude, with a lack of oxygen, snow and glaciers.

*   We were battling with the elements: snow, ice and wind makes eyes water (vision unclear).

*   Yeti could be an invention of the imagination and folklore.

*   But we saw footprints 15 inches long, showing jumps of at least 8ft in the air, impossible for other native species to have jumped that high.

*   Chatwin was keen to find some logical explanation for the footprints but the Sherpa said they were like yeti footprints.

2. Award marks as shown below (total of 15 marks).

    a. Words that conjure distance and grandeur could be: "torrent"; "track zigzags up a cliff" (height); "Streams of snow were blowing off the summit"; "rearing its triangular peak"; "throne". Students must explain diction and usage adequately. (5)

b. Vegetation is described for its colour, familiarity to British readers; to create setting. As above, diction must be explained for its effect. (5)

c. We are told about the beautiful location. Chatwin then introduces strange and colourful monks to create a sense of unreality, then tells the story of how two ordinary women (the aunts) saw a yeti. Details of size and ferocity are included to consolidate idea that yeti are not a children's fairy tale; they are dangerous. (5)

Exploring where poems come from

Workbook, pages 63–4

This activity is designed for more able students. So far, this unit has only looked at different forms of prose, all of which have a specific purpose. Explain that students are going to consider how and why poets write poems – where poems come from. The questions ask them to explain the poets' use of words (in prose). There are no specific answers, but they must justify their comments and refer to the context of each quotation.

Narrative prose

Student Book, pages 180–3

When you introduce this section remind students of the work they did on point of view in Unit 3. If they are studying English Literature or reading set texts in class, briefly discuss the narrative voice in at least one text, drawing attention to how readers relate to events in the plot and characters according to what the narrator tells them. As a class, read the text on page 180 of the Student Book and then check understanding before moving on to the Showing and telling section on page 181. At some point in this section draw attention to the genre of fantasy and how fantasy authors create a believable world in fiction.

Ask students to read the first passage from *Lord of the Rings* on page 181 of the Student Book. Then ask them to do the **Writer's craft task** on the same page independently and justify their opinions with examples from the text. Tolkein's narrative shows what happens but does not tell the readers what to think, leaving them to draw their own conclusions as to who or what the rider is and the degree of danger in the situation. The language he uses is suggestive, showing possibility rather than assertion so he is guiding/showing the reader, e.g.

"on it sat a large man, who <u>seemed</u> to crouch in the saddle" and "The riding figure sat quite still with its head bowed, <u>as if</u> listening. From inside the hood came a noise <u>as of</u> someone sniffing to catch an elusive scent". The use of "seemed" and "as if" are suggestive, encouraging the reader to explore their own possibilities.

Move on to the second passage from *Lord of the Rings*, on page 182 of the Student Book. Remind students that they have to use the information from the text, so they cannot embark on their own story. They need to think about their character's point of view and personality and how that character feels or experiences the sense of danger or menace (bravely but frightened, timid, fearful) before starting to write. Award up to 13 marks for content and up to 12 marks for style and accuracy (total of 25 marks). Possible points for inclusion:

- There's an eerie sound of the hooves before the Black Rider approaches.
- The hobbits stand in silence, listening.
- They quickly run into the shadows of the oak trees to see if it is a Black Rider.
- Pippin wants to go further back because of the sniffing; Frodo wants to be sure it's a Black Rider.
- The Black Rider approaches rapidly so there isn't enough time to find a better hiding place other than in the tree shadows.
- Sam and Pippin cower behind a large tree trunk.
- Frodo steps back further towards the small road.
- There is a line of dim light through the wood but no moon.
- The sound of the hooves stops where they are.
- Frodo sees darkness pass through the dim light between trees and then stop/
- It looks like the outline of a horse behind a smaller shadowy figure.
- The dark phantom stands where they were on the path, gently rocking.
- Frodo thought he heard sniffing as the phantom lowered itself and started creeping towards him.

"Shadowmancer"

Student Book, page 183; Recording 6

In this passage, G.P Taylor is telling readers what is happening and how the characters feel. In this regard, the narrative voice is omniscient. You could listen to the passage on **Recording 6**.

Alternatively, ask students to read the text in silence and refer back to page 183 of the Student Book to identify the narrative voice. They should do this before starting the **Writing task** on page 183, where they are asked to emulate Taylor's style as far as possible. Spend some time examining the author's use of similes, metaphors and personification; use of the senses and short sentences for effect. The content of their writing should make reference to details from the passage, such as: strange shapes (fantasy), creatures with green skin, helmets in the shape of serpents' heads, two large fangs at the front of their helmets, breast plates of armour, swords and jewelled shields, description of fear, personification of the night, the use of colour (red, black, silver), physiological symptoms (e.g. sweating, feeling faint), the elements (wind, fire), muscles aching from holding the gun, unable to pull the trigger.

Explain that Narrative Writing questions often give words to start with as in this task. Set a time limit of one hour for the task. Tell students they should use the first 5 minutes to plan and leave 10 minutes to edit and proofread before the end of the hour. Award up to 13 marks for content and up to 12 marks for style and accuracy (total of 25 marks).

Developing language appreciation: a poet's choice of words

Workbook, pages 65–6

This poetry task follows on from the task on Workbook pages 65–6 on the origins of a poem. However, it is perfectly suitable for doing with Core students who are not studying English Literature. You may want to end this unit with this poem or use it before students start the Literature extension on page 185 of the Student Book, perhaps for homework. If your students struggle with poetry, tell them the poem is about a real event in the poet's life, which answers question 1. Advise them to do a *wh-* analysis before they answer the questions. Conduct a lengthy feedback

session, encouraging students to explain their thoughts and feelings about the poem and why it was written. Focus on mood and atmosphere, and relate back to previous work on point of view, showing and telling in this unit.

Self-assessment

Student Book, page 184; Resource 7.5

A version of the Self-assessment panel on page 184 is available for students to fill out on **Resource 7.5**, which you can customise to give more space as necessary. Allow a minimum of 15 minutes or set this for homework to ensure that they are thinking independently without peer influence. Remind them that it is important to reflect on what they have achieved but also to identify their weaknesses so that they know what to focus on in future.

Literature extension

Student Book, page 185; Resource 7.6

Remind students about literary non-fiction, such as Chatwin's description of the Himalayas on pages 176–8 of the Student Book. Then ask them to do **The Great Frost task** on page 184. They should be able to identify words and phrases that are of a serious, non-fiction nature such as reference to trade in London; "the extremity of want" in the countryside; king's recent coronation, or how the Thames was frozen. They should also be able to identify and examine the use of figurative language and imagery in some of the more fictitious or "fantastic" images such as "birds fell like stones"; the woman turned "visibly to powder" or wayfarers who were "petrified" and turned into local landmarks or drinking troughs. The passage is from what is now known as "time travel" historical fiction, a novel written by Virginia Woolf. It is described in the *Oxford Companion to English Literature* as a "fantastic biography".

8 World famous

The focus on what constitutes fame in this unit gives students preparing for Speaking and Listening assessments ample practice in speaking for different purposes in front of an audience. Students will look at how a variety of people from very different walks of life achieved fame and discuss, give presentations on or debate what makes people or places famous. There are samples of autobiography and biography, and students can assess a written coursework assignment. The unit also provides more differentiated practice for Core and Extended Reading tasks and there are Directed Writing and Composition tasks which can be done as timed practice.

Unit starter

Student Book, page 187

Give students 2 minutes in pairs to read the **Talking point** at the top of page 187 of the Student Book and discuss the questions. Point out that the picture on the same page shows the Colossus and the photo on page 186 shows what Mandraki Harbour, site of the statue on the island of Rhodes, looks like now. Read the statue's inscription. Allow students to give educated guesses if they don't know the answers. (The statue was destroyed in an earthquake in 226 BC and the Statue of Liberty looks rather like it.) This talking point is fundamental to the unit; make sure students understand that the statue, which was once huge and a wonder of the world, no longer exists.

Move on to the **Talking points** near the bottom of page 187 of the Student Book. Write the nouns *fame, celebrity, success* and *greatness* on the board.

Before looking at dictionary definitions or the quotations from celebrities, ask students to think about their own views on whether the nouns mean the same thing. It will be interesting to see if any, or how many, link fame and celebrity with success and greatness. Be prepared for some surprising responses to how the nouns differ.

Now read the quotations as a class. Organise students into groups of four and ask them to do the **Speaking and listening task** on page 187 of the Student Book. Take feedback and, if necessary, lead discussion round to celebrity culture and their views of it.

Famous people and places

Student Book, pages 188–197; Resource 8.1

Ask students to read the quotation from *Twelfth Night* and think about the questions at the top of page 188 of the Student Book. Allow time for them to share their views with a partner before discussing it as a class. They could consider, for example, royal families, nature and nurture debates, pushy parents, child stars, reality TV shows, entrepreneurs, scientists, etc. Ask them to work in pairs on the activity in the **Fame box** on page 189, leaving it open to interpretation and interesting discussion. They could list their ideas on **Resource 8.1**.

As preliminary homework or at some point during this section, ask students to research one person each who has created or discovered something really important. Then they can introduce the rest of the class to their findings, perhaps as a formal speaking and listening exercise. There are guidelines for giving a presentation on page 201 of the Student Book.

Ask students to look at the pictures in the **Success box** on pages 188–9 of the Student Book and do the matching task in pairs. You could award a small prize or merits to the first two to get the right answers. Answers to part 1:

Marie Curie: A; Christopher Columbus: E; Alexander Fleming: D; Wolfgang Amadeus Mozart: C; Gregor Mendel: F; Leonardo da Vinci: B.

Then consider part 2. You could hold a debate, dividing the class into two groups and asking them to debate for/against the statement: "The world would not be the same without –." Allow 10 minutes for them to plan their arguments before starting the debate. Alternatively, you could monitor debate in smaller groups of six to eight.

Preparing for Reading Passages (Core)

Workbook, pages 67–9

Prepare Core students to do this activity on their own as homework. Award up to 10 marks for content and up to 5 marks for style and accuracy (total of 15 marks). Points for inclusion:

- dangers such as loose or falling rocks, blizzards and sudden bad weather
- danger of avalanches in summer
- avalanches provoked by climbers, hikers, skiers
- dangerous to climb unknown routes without a guide
- safety precautions should include appropriate clothing and helmets
- experts say helmets and safety equipment are essential
- many die due to not being prepared
- stupid to pretend / or be brave or adventurous
- absentmindedness kills
- taking foolish risks costs lives
- with 20,000 people reaching the summit each year know there will be loose rocks and potential for avalanches.

Students should include thoughts on why taking safety precautions seriously and being fully equipped is safer and wiser than setting out as if it were a summer holiday hike. The leaflet should also include students' own ideas and opinions inferred from the text.

Preparing for Reading Passages (Extended)

Workbook, pages 70–2

Award up to 15 marks for content and up to 5 marks for style and accuracy (total of 20 marks). Points for inclusion:

- heavy (summer) snowfall can leave loose snow on overhangs
- unexpected weather conditions/snow/storms are dangerous
- steep face of Mont Blanc (unimpeded / velocity of avalanche)
- high winds can displace snow and ice
- climbers take unnecessary risks because of the thrill factor
- alpine peaks are alluring partly because of the risks involved
- this avalanche may have been caused by someone breaking a piece of ice (which rolled unimpeded down the steep slope)
- heavy summer rain had fallen as snow at high altitude / near the summit
- unexpected summer storm / no weather bulletin warning of these conditions
- a slab or sheet of ice snapped off and hurtled down the mountain
- some climbers were able to get out of its path but as it gathered strength, it hit a large number of climbers from different nations
- some climbers were with a professional guide
- others were climbing independently (which is a risk)
- Chamonix is a very popular centre for climbing, but climbing is always dangerous
- deep, churned-up snow made rescue difficult / hard to find bodies.

Students' interviewees should add their thoughts and feelings, ideas and opinions about the event and their lucky escape. They should comment on the need to take safety seriously, including checking weather reports, wearing appropriate clothing, taking appropriate equipment and not taking foolish risks, as well as commenting on the rescue services.

"The Olympic Games"

Student Book, pages 190–1; Resources 8.2–8.3

Start this topic by asking students what they know about the first Olympic Games and why so many people are interested in the modern games. Link this back to the idea of fame or celebrity; talk about what makes sportsmen and women famous.

Ask students to do the **Writing task** on page 191 of the Student Book. This is good practice for Directed Writing assessments, where students need to extract information from one text and write it up in another style. You may want to give them time to discuss and plan their responses in pairs first or go straight into timed exam practice (45 minutes should be enough after students have read the text). If you want to have a peer-marking session, suggested points for inclusion are listed on **Resource 8.2**. Remind students that the style must be appropriate for a sports magazine, include a catchy title or main heading, subheading and possible by-line. Award up to 10 marks for content and up to 15 for style and accuracy (total of 25 marks).

Resource 8.3 presents a language awareness task that can be used as a time-filler, as an extra activity for students who finish class work early or as part of a lesson on idiomatic language.

Madame Tussauds

Student Book, pages 192–5

Suggested answers to the **Core Reading task** on page 194 of the Student Book:

1. a. Marie Tussaud was taught to make wax models by Dr Phillipe Curtius. She made models for an exhibition in Paris and later made face masks of guillotine victims in the French Revolution. (2)

    b. Nowadays waxwork models are made using modelling techniques originally created by Marie Tussaud; the components are chicken wire, newspapers and clay; the models take four months to create; each strand of hair is real. (4)

    c. Madame Tussaud created wax impressions of current affairs of the day, such as the French Revolution. In 1835 she opened a museum in Baker Street where people could view a "chamber of horrors" showing wax models of unlawful citizens. (3)

    d. Modern Tussauds exhibitions provide historical education by showing the life stories of famous people and a place of pilgrimage because, for some, celebrity fame is like a new religion. (2)

    e. It is perhaps unexpected that people should still want to motionless wax models in an age when everyone is more used to very interactive forms of electronic entertainment. (4)

2. The letter should contain clear information about how models are made and why the student enjoyed his/her visit, using material taken from the text only. The style should be appropriate for a family letter. Award up to 10 marks for content and up to 5 for style and accuracy (total of 15 marks).

Suggested answers to the **Extended Reading task** on page 194 of the Student Book:

1. a. Models are made using modelling techniques originally created by Marie Tussaud; the components are chicken wire, newspapers and clay; the models take four months to create; each strand of hair is real; they do not use wigs. Models presented in life-like poses or scenes; people can touch them.

    b. Famous figures were placed in "dramatic historical dioramas" to illustrate contemporary events (in the past); the exhibition features the famous (royalty and celebrities) and infamous (criminals) as a form of living history.

Award up to 15 marks for content and up to 5 for style and accuracy (total of 20 marks).

2. Award up to a total of 15 marks, as indicated below.

    a. It is surprising that people should still want to see motionless wax models in an age when everyone is more used to interactive forms of electronic entertainment. (1)

    b. Tussaud's original travelling exhibition brought visual news of events before the invention of photographs. (2)

    c. Visitors can see and touch life-size models of people and see what famous people from the past and present look like in detail. (2)

    d. Tussaud exhibitions in different cities now include Hollywood film stars, who are known the world over. Students should demonstrate an understanding of "the ubiquity of Madame Tussauds" (line 77). (2)

    e. Answers should demonstrate an understanding of the fickle (sometimes brief) nature of fame. (3)

Award up to 10 marks for content and up to 5 for style and accuracy (total of 15 marks) for the **Core summary task** on page 195 of the Student Book. Points for inclusion:

- Marie Tussaud studied model-making under Dr Philippe Curtius, a doctor who became highly skilled at making anatomical models from wax
- she created figures for a waxwork exhibition during the French Revolutionary period
- made face masks of guillotine victims
- Tussaud inherited Curtius's models and started a travelling exhibition of waxworks
- it was the touring newspaper of the day, providing information on contemporary events, particularly the French Revolution, in a time before photographs
- Tussaud settled in Britain and opened a museum in Baker Street in 1835
- her most popular exhibit was the "chamber of horrors" featuring criminals
- this tradition of what academics call "dark tourism" endures today
- she provided entertainment, artistic enlightenment, historical education and a place of pilgrimage
- the exhibition continued under Tussaud's sons and grandsons, who placed famous figures in dramatic historical dioramas
- the youth of today are still interested in wax models of real people
- Madame Tussauds is now found everywhere (from Bangkok to Berlin)
- continued popularity is surprising because now so many more sophisticated forms of entertainment are available
- continued popularity is surprising because wax models are old-fashioned
- success across three centuries is part of a long tradition of the tourism of replicas, simulations and spectacle
- the recent dramatic increase in popularity may reflect a society increasingly obsessed with celebrity
- the exhibition has moved with the times and now has Bollywood stars
- it now has interactive exhibits and has removed ropes and the "do not touch" signs
- Tussauds has always been 3D.

Award up to 15 marks for content and up to 5 for style and accuracy (total of 20 marks) for the **Extended summary task** on page 195 of the Student Book. Points for inclusion:

- Tussaud created figures for a waxwork exhibition during the French Revolution to satisfy people's morbid curiosity
- roots date back to the Paris of 1770
- made face masks of guillotine victims
- Tussaud inherited Curtius's models started a travelling exhibition of waxworks
- it was the touring newspaper of the day, providing information of contemporary events, particularly the French Revolution, in a time before photographs
- Tussaud came to Britain in early 19th century with her travelling exhibition of revolutionary relics and effigies of public heroes and rogues
- Tussaud's museum in Baker Street in 1835 had a "chamber of horrors" featuring criminals
- this tradition of what academics call "dark tourism" endures today
- she provided entertainment and historical education
- Tussauds in London became a place of pilgrimage to see models of famous people
- it provided insight into global/foreign/important events
- it brought ordinary public face to face with the people in the headlines
- artefacts from the French Revolution and Napoleonic Wars had a direct bearing on everyday lives
- figures of leading statesmen and notorious villains; put faces to the names everyone was talking about
- the exhibition continued under Tussaud's sons and grandsons, who placed famous figures in dramatic historical dioramas
- the youth of today are still interested in wax models of real people
- Madame Tussauds is now found everywhere (from Bangkok to Berlin)
- Washington DC has a gallery of all 44 US presidents
- Tussauds in London is the nearest thing to a British Walk of Fame

- the comings and goings of celebrity models mirror the fickle nature of fame

- success across three centuries is part of a long tradition of the tourism of replicas, simulations and spectacle

- recent dramatic increase in popularity may reflect how modern society is increasingly obsessed with celebrity

- the exhibition has moved with the times and now has Bollywood stars

- it now has interactive exhibits and has removed ropes and the "do not touch" signs.

Famous places

Student Book, pages 196–7; Resource 8.4

You could start by asking who can name all the places shown in the photographs. If students struggle, organise the class into pairs to do the **Famous places task** on pages 196–7. They may need to go to the library or use the Internet to find information. Alternatively, set the information finding task for homework.

Hand out **Resource 8.4** and ask students to discuss the places as outlined in the **Speaking and listening task** on page 197. Point out that they will probably know more about each place than they think due to the influence of mass media. Once they have made notes on their chosen site, encourage them to circulate the class to find information about the other places until they have notes on exactly where each place is, why it was built and why it is famous. Suggested responses:

- The Taj Mahal is in Agra, India. It was built by Mughal emperor Shah Jahan in memory of his third wife, Mumtaz Mahal.

- The Eiffel Tower is in the Champ de Mars, Paris, France. It was erected in 1889 as the entrance arch to the 1889 World's Fair.

- The Statue of Liberty is on Liberty Island, in New York harbour. It was a gift to the United States from the people of France in 1886.

- Sydney Opera House is in Sydney, Australia. It was a competition-winning design and opened in 1973.

- The Blue Mosque is in Istanbul, Turkey. It was built between 1609 and 1617 to surpass that of Hagia Sophia.

- The Parthenon is in Athens, Greece. It was built between 447 and 432 BC in dedication to the Greek goddess Athena, patron of the Athenian people.

- Machu Pichu is in the Cusco region of Peru. It was built as an estate for the Inca emperor Pachacuti between 1438 and 1472.

- The Coliseum is in Rome, Italy. It was built to honour the Flavian dynasty of three Roman emperors.

- The Tower of London is on the north bank of the River Thames in England. It was built in the 11th century by William the Conqueror to protect London and assert his power.

- The pyramids are on the west bank of the Nile in Egypt. The earliest were built in 2630 BC as tombs for the country's pharaohs.

Then discuss and identify which are the least or lesser known sites and why. Broaden discussion to the concept of cultural knowledge – what we know about because it is relevant to our lives, where we live, etc. You could then review what was covered in Unit 7 on media and how the media has created the 'global village'. This could lead into how people obtained information about foreign places in the 19th century and how they learned about international events (refer back to Madame Tussaud's travelling exhibition).

You could then prepare students for a discussion on the Victorian British Empire: how and why so many British men and women set up homes in foreign lands during Victoria's reign. Discuss the advantages and disadvantages of colonialism in a matter-of-fact way. (You could remind students that Britain was also once a colony. As an outpost of the Roman Empire for 600 years, Britain benefited from Roman building skills and sophistication, but once Romans left the island it returned to its primitive ways and clan conflicts during what are now called the Dark Ages.) Make a point of introducing students to David Livingstone and saying something about how he truly believed that developing trade on the African continent would stop the slavery trade. In the end, he and people like Stanley opened the way for massive exploitation, but that was never Livingstone's intention.

Biography

Student Book, pages 198–200; Resource 8.5

Do the marking task in the **Be a coursework examiner box** on page 198 before asking students to write their own biographies (page 200). Hand out **Resource 8.5** so they can annotate and make notes on their own copy. Supporting information and suggested answers:

1. The content should include:

- The subject is David Livingstone.
- He worked in a cotton mill from the age of 10 to 26, studied medicine and theology, married Mary Moffatt (paragraph 1).
- He had endurance, persistence, empathy (paragraph 1).
- He travelled in South Africa as a missionary in 1856, drew attention to the cruelty of slavery, discovered different peoples and cultures
- He died in Zambia in 1873.
- He is remembered for his descriptions of people, scenery and animal life, and for his stance on the immorality of slavery.
- His books served to educate readers about Africa and its people, and drew attention to the illegal slave trade that still continued there.

2. The organisation of the paragraphs could be improved: the final paragraph could go before the mention of Livingstone's funeral.

3. Points on the writing style include:

- There is some interesting diction, e.g. "avid", "endurance", "persistence" and "enlightening" but also some clumsy wording, e.g. "do good in the world".
- The syntax is dominated by simple and compound sentences, e.g. "Missionary Travels in South Africa was published in 1857" and "His family was very poor and they all worked in a cotton mill". It could be improved by using a wider variety of complex sentences and varied sentence openers.
- The punctuation is mainly accurate but simple. It could be improved by using more sophisticated punctuation such as semi-colons and colons.
- Paragraphs have topic sentences, although the final paragraph could move before the mention of Livingstone's funeral.

The essay is within the word count for written coursework.

Now students should feel more confident about writing their own biography in response to the **Writing task** on page 200 of the Student Book. You could either present them with a variety of texts and articles from which to make notes or take them to the library or computer room to research and make notes on a person they're interested in. After writing, ask students to read each other's work and check for the same criteria as in the previous task. If your students are not doing coursework, set the word limit between 350 and 450 words.

Using English: persuasive language

Workbook, pages 73–6

You could use this activity in class or set it for homework. The passages are speeches made by very different people in the same epoch: an uneducated female ex-slave and a highly educated statesman. Introduce students to the first speech by explaining that it was made by a woman with no formal education; it was given without preparation and subsequently written down by another woman because what Truth was saying was so important. Draw out that Truth's use of rhetorical questions and repetition drive home a significant message, made all the more powerful by the personal and direct manner of her delivery; the way she addresses her audience (e.g. "Well, children", "that little man in black there" and "That's it, honey") give a sense of a private conversation. However, she ends on a rousing and rallying note: "the men better let them".

In contrast, Lincoln uses an elevated tone and educated voice, but avoids empty hyperbole. Point out that the use of the first-person "we" gathers the audience to him and personalises his message. Lincoln uses tripling ("we cannot dedicate, cannot consecrate, cannot hallow this ground") to reinforce his argument. He ends on a resounding, memorable note: "that government of the people, by the people, for the people shall not perish from this earth".

Suggested answers (award up to 30 marks as shown below):

1. Truth uses imperatives such as "Look at me" and addresses her audience personally. (2)

2. This is significant because she was once a slave who had no voice, no right to speak her thoughts aloud. (2)

3. Lincoln uses the tripling technique to reinforce his argument, saying the same thing in three different (poetic) ways. (2)

4. He includes his audience by using "us" and "we". (2)

5. This is important because they are on a battlefield where enemies have been killed; he is trying to bring his listeners together. (2)

6. Truth uses "Ain't I a woman?" to underline the fact that, despite being a slave she is a woman; that she has raised children and "ploughed and planted"; but she is a woman who has never been treated as a lady ("Nobody ever helps me into carriages"). She is repeating the fact to show what women have suffered and what they are capable of. (3)

7. Students select two words or phrases from Truth's speech and explain how they may have affected listeners at the time. Encourage them to use the SQuEE technique. (4)

8. Students select two words or phrases from Lincoln's speech in the same manner as above to explain how they may have affected listeners at the time. (4)

9. Encourage students to pick a topic they feel strongly about. Look for the use of tripling, repetition, first person, alliteration and rhetorical devices. (9)

Balloon debate

Student Book, page 200

Having done the work on persuasive language, go to the **Speaking and listening task** on page 200. It is vital that students speak persuasively in order to present their case. You could make the task more challenging by randomly assigning a famous person to each student or letting them pull a name out of a hat. Alternatively you could let them choose who they want to be in advance. Either way, students may need some time for research to add interest to the debate. Go through the instructions with students before beginning the debate.

Making a presentation

Student Book, page 201

Prepare students to do the **Speaking and listening task** on page 201. Suggest local people and places if students are short of ideas. Encourage them to make notes on their topic before you review the **Speaking skills panel** on page 201 as a class. Then ask them to organise their notes on cards or as bullet points. Remind them they cannot read from a script because they need to make eye contact with their audience. This is very good preparation for students going on to do the IB Diploma programme where many subjects include presentations and oral assessments.

Autobiography

Student Book, pages 202–3

Ask: Should an autobiography be informative or entertaining? Draw out that it can be both, as with travel writing. Explain that the passage **"A fight with a lion"** is autobiographical, but could also fall into the travel writing genre because Livingstone is writing about his experiences in Africa. Direct students to the **Writer's craft task** on page 203 of the Student Book. There are examples to justify describing the tone as both exciting and matter-of-fact, although the latter is prevalent:

*   exciting: "Growling horribly close to my ear, he shook me as a terrier dog does a rat." (lines 56–7); "The men then called out, 'He is shot, he is shot!'" (lines 45–6)

*   matter-of-fact: "the lion immediately left me and, attacking Mebalwe, bit his thigh" (lines 76–8); "It was like what patients partially under the influence of chloroform describe, who see all the operation, but feel not the knife." (lines 62–5).

You may want to examine Livingstone's diction as an example of pre-20th century prose and how it differs to modern diction and syntax.

Fiction

Student Book, pages 204–5

Ask students to read the passage **"The Dragon of Pendor"** on page 204. Students could sketch the scene that they see, working from their own imaginations if possible, but otherwise drawing inspiration from the illustration on page 204. This is a useful exercise for all students but particularly visual learners. Then ask them to do the **Writer's craft task** on page 205. Answers:

1. Le Guin's description is far more dramatic and exciting, including: dynamic verb choices ("flurried", "tore", "flew"); onomatopoeic sounds ("snapped", "swooped"); short clauses and listed verbs and adjectives ("doubled, snapped, swooped, lunged").

2. The setting includes: tower, sea, island, fire, wind. There is a larger dragon with two smaller ones, with enormous wings and claws; Ged also becomes a dragon and at the end of the passage the Pendor Dragon rises up.

3. Verbs: "snapped", "striking", "pursued", "tore", "lunged".

4. She uses onomatopoeia ("snapped", "swooped"); the sound of the waves ("No creature moved nor voice spoke […] only the waves beat loudly on the shore") adds to the tension.

5. She writes "striking and bearing the other down by neck and flank" to increase the excitement and brutal danger of the battle.

Move on to the **Writing task** on page 205 of the Student Book. Before they start planning, ask students to list the techniques they have identified in the last few tasks and encourage them to use these in their own writing. Remind them that descriptive writing does not tell a story and there should be no dialogue, only reported speech. If you want to use this task as practice for Composition, give students 1 hour from start to finish, including planning time. Award up to 13 marks for content and up to 12 marks for style and accuracy (total of 25 marks).

Auld Lang Syne

Student Book, pages 206–11, Resource 8.6

There are numerous recordings of this song available on the Internet, from an Elvis Presley version to Brooklyn bands and piano solos. You may like to play a traditional version then a more modern interpretation before students begin the tasks; you could ask students to write the words they hear while listening. Then introduce the song more fully by explaining that Robert Burns wrote it down in old Scots dialect in 1788 (there is more information about Burns on page 207 of the Student Book). You could ask them to translate the words into modern English, along these lines:

Times Gone By

> Should old acquaintances be forgotten,
> And never brought to mind?
> Should old acquaintances be forgotten,
> And days of long ago!

Chorus:

> For times gone by, my dear
> For times gone by,
> We will take a cup of kindness yet
> For times gone by.
> We two have run about the hillsides
> And pulled the daisies fine,
> But we have wandered many a weary foot
> For times gone by.
> We two have paddled (waded) in the stream

> From noon until dinner time,
> But seas between us broad have roared
> Since times gone by.

Ask students to work in pairs on the **activity** at the bottom of page 206 of the Student Book. After writing, encourage them to prepare to perform their song for the class. You could take a class vote on the best song. Doing fun activities such as this helps students preparing for oral assessments to lose some of their self-consciousness and boosts confidence.

Move on to the **Writer's craft task** on page 207, for which students need to read the article on pages 208–9 of the Student Book. Award two marks for each question (total of 20 marks). Suggested answers:

1. One song brought in 2012 at New Year.

2. Many of us don't know the meaning of all the lyrics, but the song is still very popular.

3. It a worldwide song about memory and kinship.

4. It has become popular in countries around the world.

5. It's an adaptable lyric and tune.

6. Everyone agrees on that issue.

7. The tune, as with the words, has a complex past.

8. Burns rose to popularity and all New York's elite wanted copies of his poems and songs.

9. US businessmen revered Burns as he was viewed as someone who had forged his own success.

10. Times Gone By

Practising reading comprehension

Resource 8.6

Resource 8.6 presents a passage on the history of football for basic reading comprehension for Core students. Remind students to write their answers in full sentences and award up to 10 marks as shown below. Answers:

1. Montevideo, Uruguay (1)

2. Uruguay (1)

3. Thirteen (1)

4. Association football was the result of teams and trainers coming together in 1863 to establish standard rules to be used in all matches. (2)

5. Nike was the Greek goddess of victory. (1)

6. The cup was hidden for safety. (1)

7. Pelé is a legendary Brazilian footballer, one of the greatest players of all time. (1)

8. North American Soccer League (1)

9. television (1)

Nobel Prize for Literature

Student Book, pages 210–11

Some students may not know anything about the Nobel prizes so start this section with a brief introduction to Alfred Nobel and his bequest. He was a Swedish chemist, engineer, inventor and philanthropist. The extract from his will on page 210 of the Student Book explains how the Nobel prizes were established.

Remind students that official documents use a style of formal language that differs from everyday speech. Ask them to read the information on Alfred Nobel's will and make a list of the words and phrases that are unfamiliar to them. Encourage them to use a dictionary to find the meanings and a thesaurus to find more commonly used synonyms or colloquialisms.

The Press Release for the 1983 prize, on page 211 of the Student Book, ends with a very brief synopsis of Golding's novel *The Lord of the Flies*. You could add that it was Robert Burns who coined the phrase "man's inhumanity to man", which is one of the main themes in Golding's novel.

Explain that the novel was written over half a century ago and many of the characters' expressions are no longer in common use. Golding also uses the image "painted savages"; explain that this was an image that featured in the comics and adventure novels he would have read as a child. Many aspects of this novel are no longer considered "politically correct", but the theme and universal characters are still directly relevant to modern society.

"Lord of the Flies"

Student Book, pages 212–18

Explain that the first passage on pages 212–13 occurs early in the story. Ralph is natural leader whose main objective is to be rescued: Jack, the leader of a school choir, is his ambitious and uncaring rival who only wants to hunt and have fun. Piggy's down-to-earth views show him to be the voice of reason. The conch is a symbol of democracy and organised civilisation.

Ask students to do the **Writer's craft task** on page 213 of the Student Book. Suggested answers:

a. "He went on in the silence, borne on his triumph." Ralph is pleased by the younger boys' confidence in him and happy to be popular.

b. " 'What do they think they're going to do on that mountain?' He caressed the shell respectfully." Piggy is sensible and wise; he respects the authority that the conch symbolises.

c. "Come on! Follow me!" Jack is already used to having authority and keen to lead the boys, but there is no evidence that he thinks rationally or logically.

Introduce the passage on pages 214–15 of the Student Book: in it the older boys have been up the mountain to find "the beastie". Explain that the beastie represents the boys' fear of the unknown and underlines the fact that they are children alone on an uninhabited island. Point out where Piggy removes his broken glasses and polishes the one lens (line 19), and explain that this is a motif throughout the novel. At this point Piggy's glasses are broken and he cannot "see things clearly". Later, Jack steals the spectacles to make fire, suggesting that he has returned to primitive ways.

Suggested answers for the Writer's craft task on page 215 of the Student Book:

1. Ellipsis points and dashes reflect the spontaneity of the boys' dialogue; the interruptions show their nervous excitement.

2. Golding makes the dialogue sound natural with, e.g. Jack and Ralph's childish bickering ("The next thing […] And the next thing […] I never said that!")

3. Tension is building between Jack and Ralph as they vie for leadership. Jack is becoming increasingly more dominant and forthright with his opinions, deliberately turning the boys against Ralph ("Ralph thinks you're cowards […] He isn't a proper chief.")

4. a. "Boys armed with sticks." Ralph can see the hunters for what they really are, but this also serves as an insult to Jack. Ralph confidently stands up to Jack, stating his views but gives in to him, "Go on! Take it!", allowing Jack to address the boys.

   b. " 'Quiet!' shouted Jack. 'You, listen.' " Jack is rude and highly assertive; use of imperatives shows his commanding nature.

He dominates and controls the other boys; challenges Ralph's leadership; shows determination in belittling Ralph's leadership qualities ("He isn't a proper chief.").

   c. "Are you sure? Really?" Piggy's abundant questions illustrate his cautious, worried nature. He looks to Ralph for reassurance and comfort, and fears Jack, but his comments are mature and perceptive; "Now you done it. You been rude about his hunters."

Move on to the third passage on pages 216–17 of the Student Book. Ensure students realise that it is Roger, Jack's right hand man, who releases the rock that strikes Piggy and the conch. Explain that during the course of the novel readers see how Roger's vicious nature is released from socialised norms and the boundaries of decent behaviour; he becomes increasingly cruel. Jack's tribe are described as a "painted group" (line 4) with spears; there is no more tying of shoelaces, they now enjoy the freedom of licensed cruelty ("delirious abandonment", line 91) under the excuse of survival. Despite this, Piggy does his best to make them see sense and holds up the symbolic conch (line 51) to remind them of how they used to be a united group.

Ask students to tackle the **Core** or **Extended reading task** on page 218 of the Student Book as appropriate. Suggested answers for the Core task:

1. Award up to 10 marks as shown below.

   a. "A great clamour rose among the savages." (2)

   b. With the use of the imperative "Grab them!" Jack even repeats this "angrily". He is a threatening force. (2)

   c. Piggy is trying to show the boys that there is a better way to exist on the island; he is drawing attention to their savagery and attempting to restore order and civilisation. (4)

   d. This suggests an unbreakable force, threatening, terrifying. (2)

2. Good answers will include details that demonstrate how Piggy was trying to make Jack and his tribe to see reason and re-establish the norms of decent behaviour. Very good answers will also comment on Jack's cruelty or abuse of power, and perhaps speculate on how Ralph and Jack would have made a good team. Award up to 10 marks for content and up to 5 marks for style and accuracy (total of 15 marks).

Suggested answers for the Extended task:

1. Although students are directed to the third passage, they may also make reference to previous passages. They may paraphrase or quote from the text as need be. Answers should outline how Piggy tried to reason with Jack and his tribe; how he didn't give up or appear to be afraid. More sophisticated answers will interpret how the voice of reason was silenced by brute force and violence. Students should also comment on how Ralph felt about Jack. Excellent answers will speculate on how he, Piggy and Jack would have made a good team if Jack had been less selfish or ambitious to be leader. Award up to 15 marks for content and up to 5 marks for style and accuracy (total of 20 marks).

2. a. "A solid mass of menace" (lines 82–83) suggests the homogeneity and unthinking nature of Jack's tribe. Jack has backed up against them; it is as if they close round him and together as a mass "bristling" with sharpened spears, which is a frightening image; it is evidence that there a real potential for harm (award up to 5 marks).

   b. As you may have already talked about juxtaposition with the class, answers should be a full discussion of Golding's choice of words with suitable quotations to support interpretation. Students should refer to how the conch is used as a symbol for civilised behaviour and the spear represents aggressive or threatening behaviour. The two images are opposites in this context. (Award up to 5 marks.)

Self-assessment

Student Book, page 218; Resource 8.7

A version of the Self-assessment panel on page 218 is available for students to fill out on **Resource 8.7**. Allow a minimum of 15 minutes or set this for homework to ensure that they are thinking independently without peer influence. Remind them that it is important to reflect on what they have achieved but also to identify their weaknesses so that they know what to focus on in future.

Literature extension

Student Book, pages 219–21; Recording 7

You could play **Recording 7** before students read these passages from *Pride and Prejudice*. Point out the photograph on page 220 and ask: Why is a novel written by a quiet, single woman at the beginning of the 19th century still being made into films 200 years later? Discuss the idea of universal themes and character archetypes, relating back to what students did in Unit 4 on Greek theatre and soap operas. This text also extends students' study of dialogue in the *Lord of the Flies* passages and how writers convey characters' personalities through dialogue. Ask students to do the **Reading task** on page 220 independently and then take feedback.

Suggested answers:

a. Mrs Bennet seems to be impatient, a busy-body, domineering ("Do you want to know who's taken it?"); obsessed with getting her daughters married off ("I am thinking of his marrying one of them.")

b. Mr Bennet seems to have a calm, rational manner ("I have no objection to hearing it"); apathy and indifference to his daughters' marriages ("It's more than I engage for, I assure you.")

Ask students what they think Mrs Bennet is trying to do (arrange marriages for her daughters) and why. At this point you may want to discuss what happened to middle-class women in this epoch if they didn't marry and who would provide for them after their parents died. Many young people see Mrs Bennet as a blustering busybody, but she has an eye to the future and her daughters' best interests at heart. Discuss the differences in contemporary and modern readers' reactions to Mr Bennet's disinterest or reluctance to do what Mrs Bennet asks.

Suggested answers to the **Writer's craft task** on page 220 of the Student Book:

a. Austen uses narrative detail to show the physical differences between Bingley and Darcy: Mr Darcy "was much handsomer than Mr Bingley"; he was too "proud", whilst Mr Bingley was "lively and unreserved". She uses implied gossip to comment on their different characters: Darcy's "manners gave a disgust which turned the tide of his popularity" (lines 15–21).

b. Dialogue is used to contrast Bingley's affable, open character with Darcy's self-opinionated, critical remarks. Students need to comment on how Darcy is inward looking: each remark involves a comment on his personal preferences, as in "You know how I detest it, unless I am particularly acquainted with my partner" (lines 50–2). Perceptive students may speculate that Darcy is trying to cover shyness or embarrassment.

9 Endings

This unit focuses on inference and how readers interpret words and texts in different ways. It looks at how various forms of prose and drama end, and how readers might react to those endings. Encourage students to express their views and interpretations, and justify their feelings with reasons. Part of the unit examines the structure and ending of classical tragedy and popular comedy. There are two poems written during the First World War that present opposing points of view. Encourage Core and Extended students to identify tone and explore each poet's point of view as this will help their understanding of word choice and comprehension skills. There are also exam-style passages where students need to be actively aware of how they are using their reading and writing skills. The unit ends with a prose writing task related to a poem by Thomas Hardy for more able students.

Unit starter

Student Book, page 223

The starter revisits myths (see also Units 2 and 6), looking at the end of the world. You could introduce this with a few comments about the Mayan belief in the end of an epoch in 2012 and ask students to relate myths and stories they know about how the world will end. The Robert Frost poem uses fire and ice as metaphors. Read it to the class and ask students to read it again silently. Discuss the idioms and clichés relating to fire and ice: an icy stare, burning with fury, etc. Use the image on page 222

of the Student Book as stimulus for a 350-word single draft, Descriptive Writing task. This is good exam practice and shows students how they can be creative in a limited time, while still paying attention to detail.

You may want students to do the **Writer's craft task** on page 223 of the Student Book before you discuss the poem in detail. Answers:

1. Abstract nouns: desire and hate.

2. Students should try to explain how the poet relates fire and ice to desire (which can be interpreted in different ways) and hate.

Give students about 5 minutes in pairs to discuss the **Talking points** on page 223 of the Student Book. Then take feedback. Draw out the importance of how one interprets a writer's work. By now students should be very familiar with explaining the effects of words and phrases, but here encourage them to go further and examine their personal reaction to a text. Take the opportunity to examine Angela Carter's comment that we each bring something different to a reading in greater depth.

A story about endings

Student Book, pages 224–7

Ask students what they know about life in the 1950s. Those doing History may mention Cuba and the nuclear threat. Develop this discussion into what houses and domestic life were like in those days: televisions and refrigerators were luxury goods, families sat and listened to the radio for entertainment; not every home had a television; most women stayed at home and were called housewives, etc.

Point out that Bradbury's story, on pages 224–7 of the Student Book was written in this epoch and ask students to read it independently. Then ask if they found anything shocking or surprising. Re-read the story as a class, stopping to examine how Bradbury uses the sci-fi genre but makes the content of the story seem within the realms of possibility. Examine the ending in detail but avoid discussing to what extent Bradbury was writing a warning, as this is one of the questions on page 227.

Direct students to do the **Reading task** on page 227 and encourage them to think about exactly what the questions are asking: they have to give their interpretations and justify them.

Award marks as shown below (total of 15 marks). Suggested answers:

1. Examples include: "the rain tapped on the empty house, echoing" and "It quivered at each sound, the house did"; "The house tried to save itself". Even the rain knows not to disturb the house too much as it taps and the house is fearful of any noise. (4)

2. Students must explain the use of three of the following verbs used to personify fire: fed (upon)/ lay (in beds) / backed off / felt (the clothes); from lines 203 to 223 ("The fire crackled […] clothes hung there"). (6)

3. There is a certain irony as the technological voice chooses a favourite poem about the devastation of mankind and how the world will just continue. In the same way, in the story, the house is the only thing still standing and even that perishes in the end paralleling Teasdale's poem. (5)

Total: 15 marks.

Practising reading skills: the narrator's voice

Workbook, pages 77–80

Students should be able to do this Core reading activity for homework. The questions focus on narrative voice and point of view. Remind them to time themselves as advised in the rubric. Point out that there is no word limit but as the question says "a short report" students should use their summary skills. Award up to 10 marks for questions 1–5 (as shown below) and up to 15 marks

for question 6 (10 for content and 5 for style and accuracy). Suggested answers:

1. Laurie's point of view is evident throughout. Students could comment on his thoughts about his teacher or the girls in his class, how he mentions his father's books or how he is eager to answer questions but not do any writing. (2)

2. Miss Glennie "opens her eyes wide" and tells the class about the way sweeps lit fires to force boys higher up chimneys; she explains the past in a pitying manner. (2)

3. Laurie scoffs at the girls' reactions, demonstrating his age and/or personality. (2)

4. There are various possibilities but students should justify interpretation using evidence. (2)

5. Students need to decide whether Miss Glennie is "soft" (Laurie's belief) or whether she is trying to encourage him with positive reinforcement. (2)

Famous last words

Student Book, pages 228–9

Start this section by looking at the **Talking points** on page 228. Ask students to comment on endings they have read recently. Were they satisfying or disappointing? Ask what they expected to happen and what led them to expect this. Mention storyline and plot (see the Reminder box on page 228). Then read the endings A–J on the pages 228–9. Draw out that the following endings are positive: B, C, E, H; and the following endings suggest a new beginning: now B, C, G. Ask students which ending makes them want to read the whole book.

How to end a story

Student Book, pages 230–1

For this section you could ask students to bring a book into class so they can read the last page aloud for class discussion.

Ask if students know what a ghost-writer is (the actual, but not the official, author of a text). Point out that nowadays many bestsellers are actually written by ghost-writers. Ask: Do you think this is ethical? Explain that there are hundreds of websites dedicated to writing fiction because self-publishing has become easier and, in some cases, more profitable than being published traditionally, where paperback authors only receive about 5% royalty. Point out that when Laura College mentions

"How to end your novel with prose", it is likely that she means narrative.

You may prefer to use the **Reading task** on page 231 of the Student Book for class discussion rather than written answers. Suggested answers:

1. She mentions three ways: dialogue, narrative, cliffhanger.

2. A cliffhanger ending is an open ending where the reader's questions are left answered.

3. She suggests using a cliffhanger ending if a sequel is being planned.

4. Ending with dialogue might not be satisfactory if questions remain unanswered or the story ends with a question.

5. In the first paragraph she uses four rhetorical questions, knowing that these will be answered if the reader reads on. There are no other questions, thus satisfying the reader.

6. If the reader's questions are not answered, they may feel frustrated and annoyed.

7. This is open to a range of responses.

8. Listen to a number of ideas here, but insist students justify their preferences or ideas.

Practising comprehension skills: "Treasure Chest"

Workbook, pages 81–5

This comprehension task is more challenging than the previous Workbook passage because of the vocabulary. You may need to explain that the Loire is a river in France and talk about river currents. Students are required to infer answers about what Boise actually does.

The reading comes in two parts and should be set as two separate homework sessions. Alternatively, look at Passage A in class, where you can focus on the author's use of words and imagery, and set Passage B for homework. Passage B is Extended question length, but as the question is accessible and there is no specific time constraint, encourage Core students to do it as well.

Remind students to time themselves and answer the questions fully using the SQuEE method. Award up to 15 marks as shown below. Suggested answers for Passage A:

1. The treasure is in an old purse in a "treasure chest" tied to a standing stone or pillar in the middle of the River Loire. (2)

2. The purse contains a few coins, perhaps two francs at most. (1)

3. Boise's mother knows exactly how much money she has in her purse. (1)

4. There is a strong current and steep drop "into nothingness"; the pillar is surrounded by smooth water, "a sign that a strong current was at work". (4)

5. This reinforces how dangerous the river is at this point and the risk Boise is taking. (2)

6. She wants to go to the cinema with her older sister and brother, and it's the only way to get money for the ticket without taking from her mother's purse. (2)

7. The description of the river and the location of the treasure chest demonstrate how dangerous the river is, and Boise is still only a child. Students should quote from the passage to justify their ideas. (3)

Suggested answers for Passage B:

1. Award up to ten marks. Point for inclusion:

   • Boise swam between Standing Stones or pillars

   • the stones are about 12 feet apart at their widest stretch

   • she could make five feet with a good strong kick against each pillar, aiming upstream so the current would bring her back to the next pillar, like a small boat tacking against the wind

   • at the fourth pillar she made a final lunge but the current dragged her towards the Treasure Stone and she went too far

   • the current dragged her

   • she was almost crying with panic

   • she grabbed the chain (which tied the Treasure Chest to the pillar)

   • she pulled the treasure chest up while kicking her legs frantically to stay in position

   • the mud-covered tarpaulin caught at her feet

   • it was difficult to get the purse out its protective wrapping

   • she put the purse between her teeth to swim back to the river bank

   • on the way back she missed the last two pillars and drifted 200 yards downstream

   • the current was very strong.

2. Award up to 10 marks for content and up to 5 marks for style and accuracy. Students must use their own words as far as possible and write no more than 200 words.

Drama

Student Book, pages 231–7; Recording 9

If your class is not studying any form of drama, use the information on tragedy and comedy to discuss films or television programmes (see pages 86–9 of the Student Book). Help students to see that the structure of almost every fictional narrative, play or film contains rising and falling action. They should then apply this when writing the beginning, ending or an episode from a story.

Move on to the passage from *Macbeth* on page 233 of the Student Book. First ask students to read it independently and then play **Recording 9**. Re-read the passage as a class and discuss the questions in the **Reading task** on page 233. Encourage students to identify where Macbeth's mood changes and how Shakespeare varies pace in the dialogue. Point out that they can incorporate these techniques in their own writing. Ask how they would use these techniques for effect in a short narrative. Suggested answers:

1. Macbeth's mood changes from that of brazenness and absolute ambition ("I have almost forgot the taste of fears") to stark, sobering despair ("Out! Out brief candle.")

2. His final analysis of life is that nothing matters, nothing has any significance ("A tale […] Signifying nothing.")

You could ask students to read the passage from **"The Importance of Being Earnest"** on pages 234–7 of the Student Book for homework. They could also write brief character sketches based on how each character behaves and speaks in this scene. In the next lesson, select confident speakers for the different parts to read the scene to the class. Encourage them to enjoy the humour. More able students should be able to identify how Wilde is 'untying the knots' and bringing order out of chaos.

Explain that the skills needed for the **Writing task** on page 237 of the Student Book are directly applicable to questions where they are asked to read a passage, adopt a persona and write in the first person. Students will need to make notes on how Jack's identity was revealed and then write those notes in prose (not as a script) from the point of view of one of the characters. Remind them they should express their thoughts and feelings, and develop the material from their personal perspective as one of the characters. Award up to 10 marks for content and up to 15 marks for style and accuracy (total of 25 marks).

Preparing for Reading Passages

Student Book, pages 238–44; Resources 9.1–9.2

The more timed practice students do at this stage of the course the better. However, to avoid tedium or burn-out try to intersperse practice in answering Reading Passage questions with related but less demanding activities. Before students start this section, discuss what they expect to find in the Reading Passages and questions, and review strategies for timing, checking and editing.

As far as possible leave students to do exam-style questions under exam conditions. If your lessons are too short for the time required, collect students' scripts at the end of the lesson ready to hand out and be finished in the next. Specify which students should be doing the Core or Extended papers and direct them to the relevant pages. Remove dictionaries.

Mark schemes are available on **Resource 9.1** (Core) and **Resource 9.2** (Extended). It is useful at this stage for students to fully understand the distribution or weighting of marks.

Figurative language

Student Book, pages 245–48

Explain that in the First World War there was no public broadcasting service so any information about the war was obtained from the daily press, which was heavily censored between 1914 and 1918. This partly explains why Owen's poem was so shocking: many people had no idea about the reality of life in the trenches. If students are interested in this topic, encourage them to read the opening chapters of *All Quite on the Western Front* by Erich Maria Remarque, which gives a German perspective and describes how a group of students are recruited and what happens to them.

As a class, read and discuss the rubric on page 245 of the Student Book. Review figurative language and how the five senses are used in poetry and prose to create vivid imagery. Draw out how the onomatopoeic sounds in the example from

"Anthem for Doomed Youth" on page 245 imitate the noises of the battlefield.

Move on to the poem **"For the Fallen"** on page 246 of the Student Book. Binyon was already in his mid-40s when war broke out and too old for active service. Point out that the fourth stanza is read every year at Armistice services across Britain and the Commonwealth, and is used as an inscription on thousands of war memorials. Although not a soldier poet, Binyon is remembered as a war poet.

Organise students into pairs or small groups to do the **Writer's craft task** on page 246 of the Student Book. Lines 7–8 suggest a sense of optimism and pride amidst despair; lines 25–6 portray the alignment of the fallen soldiers to the stars, a romantic and idealised notion of the nobility of war; despite the sadness, there is an uplifting mood at the end of the poem. Students need to explain their choice of words and how they interpret their meaning when they discuss mood or tone.

They should also be able to say whether the word is a noun, abstract noun, verb, etc.

Read **"Anthem for Doomed Youth"** on page 247 of the Student Book and discuss the tone and mood. If you have a class of high-flyers, you could discuss the following points with your class.

- Binyon's poem presents war as a glorious endeavour; proud to serve their nation; a sense of optimism at being part of the war effort.

- Owen's poem challenges the perception of war as a noble thing; readers would not have read about this in the press but they could have witnessed it or heard about the horrors of the battlefield from friends or brothers; while this poem may have come as a shock or surprise, it would have resonated.

- Students should use their earlier discussion points on Binyon's poem; the theme of "Anthem for Doomed Youth" is the brutality and true nature of war.

- As opposed to the third stanza of Binyon's poem, in "Anthem for Doomed Youth" young men "die as cattle", a simile that brings to mind images of the slaughterhouse and how soldiers are killed en mass. The juxtaposition of "choirs" and "wailing shells" would have been horrifying for many readers in this epoch. Students should use their earlier discussion points on Binyon's poem; the tone of "Anthem for Doomed Youth" echoes the finality of death, bleakness of war and hopelessness.

Move on to the **Writing task** on page 248 of the Student Book. It's a fun activity with a serious purpose. Use it to help students preparing for the Composition assessment. Insist they to plan carefully and use only a few characters. You could set a time limit of 1 hour or ask students to prepare the composition in one lesson and write it out under exam conditions in the next lesson. This will help them to time themselves, making sure they leave at least 5 minutes to proofread and edit their composition before they hand it in.

Self-assessment

Student Book, page 249; Resource 9.3

A version of the Self-assessment panel on page 249 is available for students to fill out on **Resource 9.3**. Allow a minimum of 15 minutes or set this for homework to ensure that they are thinking independently without peer influence. Remind them that it is important to reflect on what they have achieved but also to identify their weaknesses so that they know what to focus on in future.

Literature extension

Student Book, page 249

Let students read **"The Voice"** on page 249 of the Student Book independently. Then ask for their interpretations. Ask: Who or what is the voice? Explain that Thomas Hardy wrote it between 1912 and 1913 after the death of his first wife, Emma. You could tell students that at the time of her death Hardy and his wife were living apart albeit in the same house. He greatly regretted that his wife died before they could resolve their differences, and this increased his suffering and sense of loss or guilt. It is important that students understand how Hardy creates atmosphere and describes his surroundings (pathetic fallacy).

Spend a few minutes looking at the imagery in the final verse before setting the **Writing task** on page 249. Remind students to use a range of descriptive writing techniques to create atmosphere: figurative language, use of the senses, diction for effect, a range of sentence structures, etc.

Move on to the **Writer's craft task** on page 249 of the Student Book. Explain that *listlessness* comes from Old English and is now used to describe a state of apathy or lack of energy. Encourage students to look at stanza 3 as a whole and identify how Hardy uses the elements to convey his personal feelings. Draw out that "wistlessness" could be connected to *listless* and *wistful* – a sense of being locked in the past and having no sense of purpose or hope of future happiness. The final stanza suggests the autumn or winter of life and "faltering" confirms what the previous stanza suggests with "listlessness". Discuss the idea of "wind oozing" through thorn trees from the north and how students could use this type of description in their own narratives.

Exam practice

This unit is includes practice for the written exam papers. Set the practice exam-style papers according to whether students will be sitting Core or Extended exams. For more guidance on marking, the skills tested and what examiners are looking for, go to www.cie.org.uk.

Explain that when you set exam-style papers in class, students will work under exam conditions to give them practice and confidence. Stress that timing themselves is a vital skill: they need to learn how long it takes to read a passage (twice if possible), how long they have to answer questions and how much time is left for checking answers. Explain that before every exam-style paper you will remind them to note down when they start and calculate when they must finish.

As a class, spend time working through exactly how to approach a Reading paper and a Writing paper so students are consciously aware of what is required. Insist they take notes. Explain that although some of the exam-style papers in the Student Book contain marginal notes, which will help them to answer the questions, students will need to add more information to their answers. Also remind them that these helpful notes will not appear in the actual exam.

After you have handed back marked scripts, dedicate at least half a lesson to a review session. Ask students to comment on what was easy or difficult; take feedback on timing strategies; recap on the importance of proofreading and checking answers.

Reading Passages (Core)

Student Book, pages 251–9; Workbook, pages 86–8

A total of 50 marks is available for Reading Passages (Core) questions. The time allowed for answering them is 1 hour 45 minutes.

Passage A: A Trading Post in Alaska

Student Book, pages 251–3

Set these exam-style questions to be done in class under exam conditions.

Question 1. Award up to a total of 20 marks, as indicated below. Suggested answers:

a. They are carried ashore from the boat by Daniel and George. (2)

b. She sees riotous colour(s); women in bright calico; bare feet; rainbow clothes; turbans; black and brown wool; wild colours. (3)

c. She hears the babble of sounds; unfamiliar words and sounds accosted her ears. Máire cannot make sense of what she hears; the sounds are loud and perhaps aggressive or frightening ("accosted"). (2)

d. She notices the pungent odours of smoke and fish; fish in the water around the boat. (2)

e. Daniel is bare-chested; bare-headed; he separates from the group and goes into water. (2)

f. Mrs Paxson tells people what to do and issues orders; she's authoritative, bossy, short-tempered. (3)

g. They have been expecting her ("Are you the school teacher?"); she looks very different to them; curiosity; they wonder if she is like Mrs Paxson (the only other foreign woman they know); they may have seen her reaction to Daniel; sense she is nervous or afraid. (6)

Question 2. Ideas must relate to the content of the passage but students may speculate on connected matters. They must not copy directly from the passage. They must write in the first person and the register can be informal (for a private journal). Award up to 10 marks for content and up to 5 marks for quality of writing (total of 15 marks). They should include and explain:

- first impressions of the trading post
- impressions of the people she is going to be living with
- thoughts about how different things seem from what she is used to
- concerns about working as a teacher at the trading post / how will she communicate / whether she be able to learn the local language / what do they need to know.

Passage B: An American in India

Student Book, pages 254–5

Set this exam-style question to be done in class under exam conditions. Award up to 10 marks for content and up to 5 marks for style and accuracy (total of 15 marks).

Question 3a. Answers should be written in short notes. Everything in India interests Gallagher because it is different to America so accept "different" or "interesting" within the context of students' notes. Points for inclusion:

- mundane experiences, such as walking down an ordinary street
- nothing is boring: everything is "colored" with the culture of surroundings
- bright colours
- (cryptic) languages seen on billboards
- towers of Hindu temples along the roadsides
- animals in the streets
- rickshaws
- old British-style taxis
- courtesy and/or dignity
- attitudes towards marriage and the family

- everyday things that are different to the USA
- the attitudes and aspirations of students
- his teacher's ideas / faculty at Manipal offered insight into the Indian character
- speaking with friends about Indian values and aspirations.

Question 3b. Students should use continuous writing in an appropriate summary style and write 100–150 words, in their own words as far as possible.

Preparing for Reading Passages (Core)

Workbook, pages 86–8

Set these exam-style tasks as homework to give Core students extra independent practice.

Question 1. Answers should be written in short notes. Award up to 10 marks for content (10 points). Points for inclusion:

- He encourages hundreds of young musicians aged as young as six.
- He was a global sensation at 28 but learned the hard way about the perils of parental coercion.
- At nine years old, his tyrannical father urged him to kill himself for missing two hours of practice.
- He believes parents need to strike a careful balance regarding how they encourage children to practise.
- He doesn't believe that putting children under a lot of pressure is a good policy or leads to success.
- He plans to raise his own children differently from his father's way, letting them decide what they want in life.
- Youngsters are included in Lang's Piano Orchestra; they include a 6-year-old who is one of 12 he has hand-picked from more than 500 hopefuls.
- Lang hopes to be able to mentor the most promising pianists.
- 50 or more Brazilians in the Youth Orchestra of Bahia also play with Lang.
- He regards himself as "something of a missionary" when it comes to inspiring others, regardless of their nationality.
- He says musicians are citizens of the world and need to share their passion with everyone.
- He says there no shortcuts to reaching the top.
- To be successful demands practice.

Question 2. Students should use continuous writing in an appropriate summary style and write 100–150 words, in their own words as far as possible. The summary should include all 10 points from question 3a. Award up to 5 marks for style and accuracy.

A total of 15 marks is available for Question 3.

Passage A: Escape from Málaga

Student Book, pages 256–8

Set these exam-style questions to be done in class under exam conditions. Point out that there are no hints or guidelines to help students. Ask them to note down where they encounter problems, but to continue as if in a real exam. After you have collected the papers, ask how they resolved any problems encountered and address these issues in your feedback session after marking.

Question 1. Award up to 20 marks, as indicated below. Suggested answers:

a. Most leave on foot / some children on donkeys. (2)

b. It will take three days and three nights. (1)

c. There are so many people it looks as if the whole population of Málaga is leaving. (2)

d. People have to ignore their children's "plaintive cries" and even abandon elderly relations to get to safety: "If they dawdled they would die; this was a race for their lives" (lines 9–10); "They had to reach Almeria and safety at all costs" (lines 13–14). (4)

e. Lines 18–22: "wrapped in coats and blankets"; "nothing more than a single garment"; "legs swollen with ulcers"; "sandals". (3)

f. Students need to describe the physical geography of the location: estuary; mountains; bare granite; wide flat valley; fertile plain of orange and avocado trees. In this area people are walking in a "column of black shapes along the valley floor", then a "second stream of refugees" join the "exodus". (4)

g. Students must examine the writer's use of emotive language in two phrases. Accept examples accompanied by explanation of the effect. Possibilities are: "plaintive cries"; "struggled to keep up"; "they walked on without her"; "weeping"; "blood running down into her sandals"; "terrified they would get lost"; "crying for food". (4)

Question 2. Students should write 200–300 words in the first person as Alex (he is male but this is not essential). The letter should start with the words given and include his thoughts, feelings and impressions of the people and landscape during the three-day walk. It should also include impressions of crowded Almeria and speculate on the situation (danger of being attacked) and where they may go or what they may do next. Award up to 10 marks for content and up to 5 marks for style and accuracy (total of 15 marks).

Passage B: Escape to Gibraltar

Student Book, pages 258–9

Set this exam-style question to be done in class under exam conditions. Award up to 10 marks for content and up to 5 marks for style and accuracy (total of 15 marks).

Question 3a. Answers should be written in short notes.

According to the passage people were afraid at the beginning of the Spanish Civil War because:

- soldiers are described as rough and merciless
- people were dragged out of their homes
- no one could tell the author and his mother what happened to the father
- they did not know where he had been taken
- there was chaos everywhere
- there was nowhere to flee except across the well-guarded isthmus or water to Gibraltar.

The author's family faced the following difficulties:

- no one wanted to risk trying to help them
- when they got a boat they had to evade "dreaded Moorish" troops and Spanish soldiers
- they couldn't risk using a light or torch to see where they were going
- they couldn't make a noise
- everything was dark
- they had to get to a beach, not come up against the vertical north face of the Rock.

Question 3b. Make sure students use continuous writing in an appropriate summary style and write, in their own words as far as possible, between 100 and 150 words. The summary should include all ten points from question 3a.

Exam practice for Reading Passages (Extended)

Student Book, pages 260–9; Workbook, pages 89–90

Draw attention to the **Writing skills panels** on page 262 and the **Summary skills panel** on page 265 of the Student Book, which are designed to help students work through the exam-style paper on their own. Ask them to note down where they encounter problems, but to continue as if in a real exam. After you have collected the papers, ask them how they resolved any problems encountered and address these issues in your feedback session after marking. Compare how students approached the questions with the advice in the Writing skills panels.

A total of 50 marks is available for Reading Passages (Extended) questions. The time allowed for answering them is 2 hours.

Passage A: A Street March

Student Book, page 260–2

Set this exam-style question to be done in class under exam conditions.

Question 1. Students should write 250–350 words in the first person. Award up to 15 marks for content and up to 5 marks for style and accuracy (total of 20 marks). The report should begin with the given words and be specifically about the demonstration and address:

- who was involved in the demonstration and what happened in the street

- Maguire's impressions of the people involved

- Maguire's thoughts and feelings about crowd behaviour.

Question 2. Students should write 200–300 words. Award up to 10 marks for content.

a. The description of the anti-fascist crowd in paragraph 2 may include how the crowd was "increasing in size and confidence" as if it were a homogenous mass or one body; how the "narrow line" of police "bulged and leaned dangerously" as it tried to contain this mass; "breaking point" and "explosive pressure" are set against the tensions caused by "belligerent drivers" who "bellowed abuse", "Blaring horns" and "revving engines". Students should explain how these words lead to the sense of noise, increasing tension and potential for the demonstration getting out of control. There is a "mounting clamour" and a "deafening din".

b. Paragraph 2 contains words and phrases relating to guns and bombs: "exploding"; "sharp retorts"; "sulphurous yellow smoke"; "gunfire". The reaction of the horse as it "shied violently" heightens the nervous excitement with its "hooves clattering and skidding". Also, the effect of the firecracker on one of the police horses: "its head, wild-eyed, snapping up and down".

Passage B: Crowd Behaviour during the French Revolution, 1789

Student Book, pages 263–4

Set this exam-style task to be done in class under exam conditions. Students may copy notes from the text (but not in the summary). Award up to 15 marks for content and up to 5 marks for style and accuracy (total of 20 marks).

Question 3a. Answers should be written in short notes. Points for inclusion:

- slanderous talk

- torrent of people in unison

- joining in with the chanting – contagious excitement

- a unison of purpose and/or emotion

- "feverish pitch" suggesting contagious hysteria or repeating slogans

- falling in with others ("who are flooding the streets") and being carried away by the crowd

- years of frustration and hatred for a government that ignores them

- people not originally out for blood merely trying to survive

- crowd formed to protest about rising food prices

- wages had been stagnant for years, but the price of bread kept rising

- the grain shortage became so bad in 1789 that the crowd besieged every baker's shop

- they received only a very small amount of bread

- always hearing warnings of shortages the next day

- people spent the whole day waiting at the baker's door without receiving anything

- food was snatched from the hand when they received paltry rations

- people were fighting over bad bread

- bread was "blackish, earthy and sour"

- swallowing it "scratched the throat, and digesting it caused stomach pains"

- injustice: the king and minister got fine quality fresh bread.

Question 3b. Make sure students use continuous writing in an appropriate summary style and write in their own words as far as possible. The summary should include all 15 points from question 3a.

Preparing for Reading Passages (Extended)

Workbook, pages 89–90

Set this exam-style task as homework to give Extended students extra independent practice. Students' letters should be 200–300 words long and persuasive in a formal to neutral register with an appropriate salutation. Award up to 15 marks for content and up to 5 marks for style and accuracy (total of 20 marks). Ideas should include the following points from the passage: how and why El Sistema started in Venezuela; how Sistema Scotland has benefited Raploch; views on how music can help young people; thoughts on starting an orchestra at their school. Points for inclusion:

- The fact that music is popular with young people is demonstrated in Raploch, a tough estate on the outskirts of Stirling in Scotland; the orchestra is playing in front of 8,000 people.

- Raploch has been notorious for poverty and crime for a long time.

- Four years ago only one child among the 3,000 people living there learned a musical instrument. Now it's 450.

- Sistema Scotland aims to transform a community by immersing it in music and appears to be working.

- El Sistema helps to build self-discipline and teamwork.

- In Venezuela 300,000 young people are enrolled.

- 80–90% of Venezuelan youth are from poorer backgrounds including shanty towns around Caracas.

- Music confers a huge range of cognitive, behavioural, emotional, therapeutic and social benefits.

- Music offers models of discipline and focused practice.

- It encourages aspiration.

- It needs teamwork and shared spirit.

- It benefits individuals, their families and society.

- Finland has an excellent education system that incorporates musical culture and produces lots of world-class talent.

- Virtually everyone has innate musical ability but that ability fades if not developed.

- Lessons and instruments cost money but music is for everyone not just the elite (fundraising will need to be solved).

- The annual cost will be less than 1% of the price of keeping a young person in secure accommodation.

Passage A: Travelling in the Desert

Student Book, pages 265–7

Set these exam-style tasks to be done in class under exam conditions. Point out that there are no hints or guidelines on the tasks, but remind them of the Writing skills panels on page 262 and the Summary skills panel on page 265. Ask them to note down where they encounter problems, but to continue as if in a real exam. After you have collected the papers, ask how they resolved any problems encountered and address these issues in your feedback session after marking.

Question 1. Award up to 15 marks for content and up to 5 marks for style and accuracy (total of 20 marks). Register may be informal and personal as suitable for a diary entry that will be use for a travel blog. Points for inclusion:

- plateau, the high dunes, the dry wadi beds and the verdant oases of the South Western desert

- pre-historic spear heads; arrow heads; crushing and cutting tools; shards of pottery; and even the eggshells of ostriches from pre-history; a Stone Age cutting tool lying at her feet

- engravings and delicate rock paintings demonstrating the artists' skill in drawing animals and the climate change

- ambling through wadis

- cracked, salt lakes

- strange, bulbous trees; white patches of gypsum; swathes of green plants with pale purple flowers, (a consequence of only three days rain two months before)

- Tuareg drivers vying with each other to be "there" first, but (you are) never sure where you are going

- driving over "impassable dunes whipped into geometric knife-edges by the ever-present desert wind"
- "blue-green slashes of still water, fringed with succulent date palms and stands of pampas grass"; "beautiful oases where turtle doves flutter through the air, tiny pink shrimps swirl in the water and, on one occasion, a solitary white camel was tethered on the shady bank"
- yellow colours of the sand
- the Tuareg are the people of the Sahara; their pride and honesty; generosity
- drivers', guides' and cooks' traditional songs
- herbs and cold water
- "Tuareg champagne" – strong green tea boiled over a driftwood fire, poured from a height to make cappuccino-like foam, reheated and poured into small glasses with plenty of sugar
- the romance of the desert.

Question 2. Award up to 10 marks for content.

a. Students may comment on the writer's use of the senses, especially sight, sound and taste; mention of colours; the shape of "strange bulbous trees" and "impossible, impassable" dunes; racing in the 4x4 contrasted with the stillness of the water; distance and solitary white camel.

b. They may mention the use of adjectives and positive nouns ("joy") to describe the Tuareg in lines 40–1; the element of tradition and culture; being in safe hands (in an unknown, potentially hostile environment).

Passage B: Travelling in the Desert in the 15th Century

Student Book, pages 267–9

Set this exam-style task to be done in class under exam conditions. Students may copy notes from the text (but not in the summary). Award up to 15 marks for content and up to 5 marks for style and accuracy (total of 20 marks).

Question 3a. Answers should be written in short notes. Points for inclusion:

- there are few wells in the Sahara
- the journey between wells depends on exact navigation by the stars (as used by sea captains)
- there is up to 200 miles between some wells
- the sand doesn't leave clear landmarks

- "winds blow, and dunes shift"
- marks left by previous caravan are "obliterated before the next"
- caravans can wander off course and perish
- have to walk by night to avoid the worst of the heat, stopping rarely
- sleep is brief and taken by day, when they lie with the camels and try to rest
- food spoils rapidly and is sparse; there is only maize and sour milk
- they are stung and bitten by "pests of the desert"
- the heat is unbearable and nights are "marginally cooler"
- only have bullock-skins of warm water to drink
- constantly stopping to adjust loads on camels
- camels kick and bite
- goats stray
- disputes break out among the people over trifles
- the danger of attack by armed Berbers
- sandstorms
- getting lost.

Question 3b. Make sure students use continuous writing in an appropriate summary style and write, in their own words as far as possible, between 200 and 250 words. The summary should include all 15 points from question 3a.

Directed Writing and Composition (Core and Extended)

Student Book, pages 269–75

Set this exam-style question to be done in class under exam conditions. The time allowed is 2 hours.

A total of 50 marks is available for Directed Writing and Composition (Core and Extended) questions.

Section 1: Directed Writing

Student Book, pages 269–71; Resources 10.9–10.10

Question 1. Point out that this first question is compulsory for Core and Extended questions students. Remind them that they are well prepared, have been doing Directed Writing tasks throughout the course and should use their summary skills to find relevant information for their answers. Draw attention to the guidelines on **Writing skills panel** on page 270 of the

Student Book. Hand out the text for the advertisement and web page on **Resources 10.9** and **10.10**.

The letter must begin with the words given and consist of between 250 and 350 words in a neutral to informal register. It should be persuasive (arguing that the student is responsible and old enough), explanatory (saying why *Not Alone Tours* is a good choice) and organised (a logical argument and why parents should not worry). Award up to 10 marks for content and up to 15 marks for style and accuracy (total of 25 marks). Suggested points for inclusion in the letter:

- long school vacation / I want to go abroad but parents cannot take time off
- have enough money saved to cover the cost of a trip abroad
- parents do not want me to travel alone
- seen *Not Alone Tours* advertisement in a magazine and printed off on-line brochure
- company has years of experience
- it provides and takes care of all accommodation and transport
- experienced tour managers organise trips, speak local languages and have information about history and culture of places visited
- I'll be with like-minded singles
- it's natural for parents to feel nervous but old enough now to manage on my own
- won't have to share a room in hotels with complete strangers
- chance to see exotic, interesting places
- parents/grandparents can use company website for advice and to post questions
- met at airport by tour leader who helps check in and answers any last minute questions
- emergency 24-hour phone service if there is a problem
- you can call the company or email for more information.

Section 2: Composition

Student Book page 272

Questions 2 and 3. Point out that students have to choose just one question from Section 2 and write in the appropriate style. Draw attention to the **Writing skills panel** and the **Reminder box** on page 272 of the Student Book.

Answers should be 350–450 words long in a descriptive or narrative style. This section specifically focuses on students' writing skills. Award up to 13 marks for content and up to 12 marks for style and accuracy (total of 25 marks). Look for how students:

- express what is thought, felt and imagined
- organise paragraphs; sequence facts; express ideas and opinions
- use vocabulary in an appropriate register for the chosen audience or context
- use a variety of sentence structures and correct spelling.

More Directed Writing and Composition exam-style questions

Student Book, pages 273–5; Resource 10.11

Give students extra practice using this exam-style questions. Remind students that they must answer Question 1 in Section 1 and then either Question 2 or Question 3 in Section 2. Hand out the text for the passage on **Resource 10.11**.

Question 1. The letter must begin with the words given and be 250–350 words long in a formal to neutral register. It should be persuasive and contain a sound, well-organised argument. Award up to 10 marks for content and up to 15 marks for style and accuracy (total of 25 marks). Suggested points for inclusion:

- plans to build a large hotel with a golf course on a small island of outstanding natural beauty
- Compton's largest resort is to be built among the hills of an idyllic little island
- Tabeira Cove; crystal clear waters and multi-coloured fish
- a large area of natural, undeveloped land will be transformed into a golf course
- extensive landscaping will destroy or change wildlife habitats
- sand dunes on the coast converted meaning sea birds and seals will be affected
- new ferry service from the mainland may have benefits but will pollute water
- luxury hotel resort means job prospects for hotel employees but they will come in from the mainland, not benefit small island population
- "floating lounge restaurant" in beautiful Tabeira Cove affect fishing and sea creatures

- Tanuca should be left as a natural island not become a business complex

- do the council believe "buildings will be integrated into the environment"?

- no plans to build a school or medical facilities

- Tanuca is possibly "last safe haven for wildlife and birds in the Mediterranean"

- ecologists and conservationists concerned native birds and mammals, including "very rare Spindling warbler and the minute Tanuca shrew, will be disrupted, if not destroyed"

- watering the golf course requires re-routing the only two streams on the island, where there is very little annual rainfall

- seal and sea lions use north coast of Tanacu as breeding grounds; they are already in decline from oil spills and mercury poisoning

- much development on the other islands around Tanuca.

Questions 2 and 3. Answers should be 350–450 words long in a descriptive or narrative style. This section specifically focuses on students' writing skills. Award up to 13 marks for content and up to 12 marks for style and accuracy (total of 25 marks). Look for how students:

- express what is thought, felt and imagined

- organise paragraphs; sequence facts; express ideas and opinions

- use vocabulary in an appropriate register for the chosen audience or context

- use a variety of sentence structures and correct spelling.

Preparing for Directed Writing and Composition (Core and Extended)

Workbook, pages 91–5

Give students extra practice using this exam-style paper. Remind students that they must answer Question 1 in Section 1 and then either Question 2 or Question 3 in Section 2.

Question 1. The letter must begin with the words given and be 250–350 words long in a neutral to informal register. It should be persuasive and explanatory. Award up to 10 marks for content and up to 15 marks for style and accuracy (total of 25 marks). Suggested points for inclusion in the letter:

- element of spectacle and excitement

- possibly first visit to a theatre for the children

- good will triumphs over evil

- explain something about tradition and stock characters

- tales children will know: Cinderella and Aladdin

- British humour

- *Commedia dell'arte.*

Questions 2 and 3. Answers should be 350–450 words long in a descriptive or narrative style. This section specifically focuses on students' writing skills. Award up to 13 marks for content and up to 12 marks for style and accuracy (total of 25 marks). Look for how students:

- express what is thought, felt and imagined

- organise paragraphs; sequence facts; express ideas and opinions

- use vocabulary in an appropriate register for the chosen audience or context

- use a variety of sentence structures and correct spelling.

11 Language reference

This unit is designed to help students improve and consolidate their skills for writing. Whether they originally learned English formally or informally, this unit offers a back-to-basics approach to the parts of speech, spelling, punctuation and grammar, explaining how to apply them appropriately.

The unit could be used on a regular basis with weaker students, for example, as a correctional device for recurring problems such as the misuse of the apostrophe. It will also help more able students understand how English works and why it is necessary to employ grammar rules, and spell and punctuate correctly. Also encourage students to dip into the unit for quick reference and as an aid to revision.

The colour-coding system (outlined on page 276 of the Student Book) for identifying nouns, verbs, adjectives and adverbs has many practical applications. It helps students understand the different parts of speech, improves their awareness of syntax and can also be applied in more advanced textual analysis for identifying and understanding an author's or poet's choice of words. It is a very useful tool for students going on to do 'A' level Literature and Language or the IB Diploma programme.

A short history of English

Resource 11.1

Resource 11.1 offers a very brief history of the English language, introduces students to its roots, how words came into use from different languages and how our vocabulary is constantly evolving to express new ideas. It can be introduced at any point in the course, but might be particularly relevant in Units 1 and 2 (see pages 24 and 25 in this Guide, where the answers for the activities on this Resource can also be found). Encourage students to keep a log of unfamiliar vocabulary they come across in pre-20th century novels, poems and plays, making a note of the source and a modern equivalent.

Make sure students are aware that they need to discuss parts of speech in Reading and Language questions in the final assessments.

Nouns

Student Book, pages 277–8; Resource 11.2

Answers to the activities on page 277:

1. **a.** toy boxes; **b.** baby-sitters; **c.** rooftops

2. **a.** jewel thieves; **b.** book shelves; **c.** bus drivers; **d.** film actresses; **e.** grand pianos

Answers to the activities on page 278:

1. **a.** coral reefs; **b.** baby teeth; **c.** field mice; **d.** ox carts; **e.** wolf cubs

2. **a.** brothers-in-law; **b.** mouse-traps; **c.** child protégés; **d.** passers-by; **e.** onlookers; **f.** step-children; **g.** housewives; **h.** Members of Parliament; **i.** Police constables; **j.** carving knives; **k.** dessert spoonsful; **l.** dove-cots

Use **Resource 11.2** to help students improve and consolidate their spelling of irregular plurals. Answers:

1. **a.** wives; **b.** ladies; **c.** echoes; **d.** pianos; **e.** brothers-in-law; **f.** children; **g.** cloths; **h.** leaves

2. **a.** fish; **b.** fox; **c.** sheep; **d.** goose

3. **a.** In the olden days, the royal men-at arms wore coats-of-mail.

   b. The prisoners were given packs of cards and chess sets.

   c. At English church weddings brides are followed up the aisle by their bridesmaids.

   d. The field mice were caught in the mousetraps.

   e. The sheep farmers left their farms to their sons-in-law.

   f. The onlookers watched as the policemen arrested the car thieves.

Noun phrases

Student Book, pages 278–9

Answers to the activities on page 278:

a. I saw lots of double-decker buses in London.

b. That blue pick-up truck is mine.

c. She is now an Oscar-winning film actress.

d. Purple-winged butterflies are rare in this part of the country.

Answers to the activity on page 279:

Youngest cousin Susan; private elementary school; class teacher; baggy green jumper; shiny cheap jewellery; Christmas tree.

Pronouns

Student Book, pages 279–80

Answers to the activities on page 279:

a. you; **b.** She; **c.** I; **d.** We; **e.** They.

Answers to the object pronoun activities on page 280:

a. me; **b.** her; **c.** them; **d.** you; **e.** you.

Answers to the possessive pronoun activities on page 280:

a. mine; **b.** yours; **c.** his; **d.** theirs; **e.** its.

Answers to the demonstrative pronoun activities on page 280:

a. This; **b.** that; **c.** These; **d.** Those.

Verbs

Student Book, pages 281–3, Resource 11.3

Answers to the activity on verbs tenses on page 281:

Growled; has eaten; trained, has trained; forgot, have forgotten; knew, have known.

Answers to the activity on past perfect verbs on page 281:

Lee said that we had been doing grammar lessons all week. He said that he had found them really useful.

Answers to the activities on active and passive verbs on page 282:

1. **a.** Poetry is written by poets. **b.** Newspaper reports are written by journalists. **c.** Plays are written by playwrights.

2. **a.** Coal miners discovered diamonds accidentally. **b.** A giant meteorite hit the Earth. **c.** Thousands of brilliant tiny stars blinded my eyes.

Answers to the activities on making deductions using modal verbs on page 282:

The incorrect sentence is *Joan said Paul must of gone*. It is a common mistake, especially in spoken English. It should be *Joan said Paul must have gone*.

Answers to the activity on expressing obligation using modal verbs on page 282:

From lowest to highest level of obligation: a. (*have to* is compulsory, legal or externally imposed obligation), e (must is personal obligation), c/d, b.

Answers to the activities on page 283:

Personal: a, e, f, g; legal/external obligation: b, c, d, h.

Answers to the activities on phrasal verbs and idiomatic expressions on page 283:

1. **a.** started to cry / or gave in to pressure in some way /admitted defeat

   b. was no longer discernible / stopped

   c. arrived unexpectedly / came without an invitation

3. A useful way to show students how many ways we can use words such as *get* or *put* is to write the word in a box centred on the board. Write prepositions such as *up, off, on,* etc. around the box with arrows leading to the formal equivalent of the phrasal verb. For example: to get off a bus = to alight; get on (well together) = to be compatible; to put off a meeting = to postpone; to put out a fire = to extinguish.

Use **Resource 11.3** to help students develop their understanding of the use of idiom in English. This resource focuses on idioms based on water and colours, but you could also ask students to look at idioms based on things in a similar way.

Adjectives

Student Book, pages 284–6

Answers to the activities on identifying adjectives on page 284:

a. hot/lazy; **b.** funny; **c.** sad/unhappy.

Answers to the activities on opposites on page 284:

Sad, poor, untidy, stupid, warm.

Answers to the activities on comparatives on page 284:

Glad/gladder; funny/funnier; obvious/more obvious; safe/safer; crazy/crazier; inconvenient/more inconvenient.

Answers to the activities on superlatives on page 285:

Sad/sadder/saddest; ugly/uglier/most ugly; fashionable/more fashionable/most fashionable.

Answers to the activities on absolute terms on page 285:

Each of these words is an absolute term. Students should explain why.

Answers to the activities on how much/many on page 286:

1. **a.** tall, two; **b.** second, first; **c.** freezing, both, bad; **d.** many, twenty-first.

Adverbs

Student Book, pages 286–7

Suggested answers to the activities on page 286:

1. **a.** rapidly; **b.** slowly, quickly; **c.** happily, noisily; **d.** recklessly, carefully; **e.** happily, silently.

Answers to the activities on identifying adverbial phrases on page 287:

1. **b.** last week / in their garden; **c.** earlier this morning; **d.** answered the questions carefully / before the end of the lesson; **e.** usually sleeps peacefully / on my bed throughout the day: **f.** going home soon; **g.** going directly / as soon as / do homework quickly.

4. The arrangement of the words should include where and when (in that order): I heard a pretty blue bird singing *in my garden this morning*.

Prefixes

Student Book, page 288

Answers to the activities on page 288:

1. **a.** uneducated; **b.** disembark; **c.** inefficient; **d.** unequal; e. inexpert.

2. **a.** inaudible; **b.** inconvenient; **c.** illegible; **d.** immortal; **e.** irregular; **f.** irresolute; **g.** impassive; **h.** inessential; **i.** insane; **j.** irreverent.

Suffixes

Student Book, pages 288–90; Resource 11.4

Answers to the activities on page 288:

1. **a.** capable; **b.** suitable; **c.** credible; **d.** sensible; **e.** durable.

2. **a.** attendance; **b.** dependence; **c.** observance; **d.** repentance; **e.** existence.

Read the poem **"Jabberwocky"** aloud to the class, making much of the events, adjectives (e.g. "frumious"), action verbs (e.g. "galumphing") and the manner in which the father speaks to his son. Ask students to read it again and then do the **Invented words task** on page 289 of the Student Book in pairs. They should identify and colour-code all the nouns, verbs, adjectives and adverbs. Take feedback, encouraging them to explain their reasoning.

Resource 11.4 will give students further practice in spelling words that end *ence/ance* and *ent/ant*. Answers:

1. appearance; confidence; **2.** performance; pleasant; **3.** inhabitant; governance; **4.** violent; innocent; incidence; **5.** intelligent; absence; **6.** dependent; assistance; **7.** conference; attendants; correspondents; **8.** distance; significance; **9.** descendents; existence.

Hand out dictionaries and leave students to work in pairs on the **Language work task** (on the suffix *-logy*) on page 290.

Answers to question 1:

- Biology – the study of life forms
- Archaeology – the study of historic and prehistoric peoples and their cultures
- Geology – the study of earth sciences

- Palaeontology – the study of fossils
- Criminology – the study of crime and criminals
- Pathology –the study of the origin, nature and cause of diseases
- Zoology –the study of biology dealing with animals
- Crypto-zoology –the study of evidence to substantiate the existence of creatures whose reported existence is unproved
- Graphology – the study of handwriting
- Psychology – the study of the science of the mind
- Genealogy – the study of family lineage
- Astrology – the study of star signs
- Sociology –the study of the origin, development and organisation of human society
- Ophthalmology –the study of the anatomy, functions and diseases of the eye
- Cardiology – the study of the heart and its functions

Questions 2–5 invite students to discuss some of the lesser known or more interesting subjects they could study after leaving school. It may generate quite a lot of noise, but it has a serious purpose – to open up future prospects and encourage students pass their exams! Allow plenty of time for discussion and then ask them to volunteer their choices, encouraging them to ponder about what is actually involved in their chosen fields.

Working with different types of sentence

Student Book, page 293

Answers:

1. Simple sentences: 1 and 4; compound sentences: 2 and 3; complex sentence: 5.

2. **a.** so; **b.** but; **c.** so/and.

3. **a.** As the students (had) worked hard in their lessons they did well in their exams.

   b. The tourist took prize-winning photographs when he climbed to the top of the hill. / After climbing / Having climbed to the top of the hill the tourist took prize-winning photographs.

   c. I fell down, cutting my hands and knees, as I ran along a stony path.

4. **a.** The boy had a hole in his pocket. He was (being) careless. He lost his ticket.

   b. I found an unusual ring in the grass. It looked valuable. I knew I couldn't (shouldn't) keep it. I took it to the police station.

Using sentence skills

Student Book, pages 295–6

Answers on *The Impressionist* on page 295:

1. So, the rain.

2. The last sentence is longest and has 8 clauses.

Answers on *Starting Out in Journalism* on page 295:

1. The second big advantage …

2. So what sort of people become freelance journalists?

3. The world is their oyster.

Suggested answers on *The Hound of the Baskervilles* on page 296:

1. I was at Holmes's elbow, and I glanced for an instant at his face.

2. It's coming!

3. Look out!

Answer on *Ice Cold in Alaska* on page 296:

Simple, compound, minor, complex, declarative.

Punctuation marks

Student Book, pages 297–300

Answers:

1. comma, full stop, apostrophe, speech marks, question mark, exclamation mark, dash.

2. The author has used a comma after each idea/phrase, which seems to emphasise the airlessness in the railway carriage and thoughts coming in short bursts.

3. **a.** It emphasises the number of children.

   b. The occupants of the carriage were a small girl, a smaller girl and a small boy.

4. The simple sentence acts like a statement that separates the bachelor from what is happening in the carriage. The children and aunt are speaking, but the bachelor remains silent.

5. **a.** The paragraph contains many narrative details; it is cramped and full (like the railway carriage).

b. The narrative details create a stifling, oppressive atmosphere.

6. The question mark occurs in various places as questions in direct speech; it is also used in the narrative on line 10.

7. The exclamation mark emphasises the aunt's feeble attempt to excite or entertain the child. There is an element of irony because there are many cows in many fields; it is neither new nor exciting.

8. a. She uses the Saxon genitive (possessive) apostrophe on "aunt's" (her remarks) and "children's" (their responses).

b. This is an apostrophe for omission to shorten 'do not'.

9. a. Reported speech would have the effect of telling not showing.

b. The effect of the direct speech is to reveal character or personality.

10. a. The author is quoting what the aunt and children say.

b. The author is creating effect; one can better appreciate the annoying children and ineffectual aunt this way.

Apostrophe *'s*

Student Book, pages 300–3

Answers to the activities on troublesome apostrophes on page 302:

1. a. There was a sign at the side of the road that said 'Strawberries for sale'.

b. Cherry's first name is really Cheri, but we call her Cherry. (correct)

c. The babies in the nursery were all crying.

d. The horse's hooves made a clip-clop noise as it trotted home.

e. The horses' hooves made a clip-clop noise as they trotted home.

2. a. Marcos plays for his school's football team.

b. Marcos' team's mascot is a goat called Gladys.

c. Gladys' ('s) owner takes her to every school match but Marcos doesn't like goats very much.

d. Most schools these days have sports teams for girls and boys; they play matches at weekends.

e. Sylvia's present was a puppy; its paws were all white so she called it Socks. (correct)

f. During the 1920s in New York, young people danced together at afternoon tea dances. (correct)

g. In the 1920s women's dresses were short with fancy frills and the men always wore hats.

h. Thousands of children's lives were ruined during the 1800s because they worked in factories.

i. Australia's rugby team beat New Zealand's then went on to play Wales.

j. Welsh rugby players are often good singers as well. (correct)

Answers the activities on abbreviation with apostrophes on pages 302–3:

1. "I can't do that, it ain't right. You mustn't do it either or I'll tell my dad, and my dad'll tell yours."

2. th' = the; 'tis = it is; Is't = Is it; night's (belonging to night); day's (belonging to day); tow'ring, hawk'd, kill'd (omitting 'e'). In Shakespeare's day, regular past tense words such as *killed* were pronounced as two syllables such as kill + ed. Hence the need to shorten the verb.

3. a. it was; **b.** against; **c.** whatever; **d.** never; **e.** murderous; **f.** whispering; **g.** whosoever; **h.** he had/would.

Dashes

Student Book, pages 303–4

Answers the activity on page 303:

The dashes show incomplete utterances where speakers do not finish what they start to say as in "This meeting –"; from line 14 on interrupted statements show the boys all speak at once. There is also a dash in line 8 instead of a colon.

Ellipsis points

Student Book, pages 304–5

Answers the activity on page 304:

2. b. The scene is told from the main character's point of view; he is only half-listening, so there are missing details. The ellipsis points show where he stops listening, indicating something has been left out of Mistress Hawkin's narration of events. The dash is used because she is not using formal, structured sentences and skips from point to point, interrupting herself.

Semi-colons

Student Book, pages 305–6

Answers the activity on page 305:

2. **a.** The information the child Pip learns in the churchyard crowds in on him; the details on the gravestones and the setting merge as one experience.

    b. Students need to use *wh-* clauses (*which was intersected by dykes* or *where there were cows*); they may also change the long complex sentence into shorter simple and compound sentences in a variety of ways.

Colons

Student Book, pages 306–7

Answers the activity on page 306:

2. **c.** The colon in line 2 serves to emphasise something new; the abruptness of Thornhill's realisation he is no longer a prisoner. The colon in line 14 emphasises what he has been used to and what he now encounters: the old and the new. The colons in lines 32 and 39 link two separate statements: what he feels or knows, plus an explanation of the feeling or how he knows it.

Test your punctuation skills

Student Book, pages 308

Suggested answer:

1. The stone wall was warm to the touch. Marcos Alonso Almendro, just eighteen, blond and bright as a new doubloon, stood in what had once been the doorway of a shepherd's hut, impatiently studying the road below. The two men staying in his mother's hostel would have to pass this way, but so far only two farm carts and an elderly peasant leading donkeys with laden panniers had passed by; no foreigners in carriages – nothing for what seemed hours. Time had passed: he now needed to shade his eyes. The view from the low hilltop was good, it would be impossible for anyone to get by without him knowing.

Identifying essential information

Read each of the following sentences carefully and consider what essential information it conveys.

> **A** For his 16th birthday the boy called Tom, who was very fond of music, was given a new guitar, a flute and a mouth organ. (25 words)

> **B** Our neighbours' dog, which is black and white, barks all the time and it will bite anyone that goes near it. (21 words)

1. Keeping the essential information, write a summary of sentence A in about ten words.

....

....

....

2. Keeping the essential information, write a summary of sentence B in about seven words.

....

....

....

Resource 1.2

Finding where texts agree and disagree

Where do Li and Bowes agree and disagree in their travel writing tips? Make one list for points on which they agree and another list for points on which they disagree.

Li and Bowes agree	Li and Bowes disagree

Resource 1.3

Recapping on writing criteria

Carefully read the criteria for writing below.

Put the criteria in an order of importance that makes sense to you. There are no correct answers, but be prepared to justify your decisions.

You can cut out the criteria to sort them if you wish or write a number in the first column. Use 1 for the most important through to 5 for the least important.

Order	Criteria
	Articulate experience and express what is thought, felt and imagined
	Order and present facts, ideas and opinions
	Understand and use a range of appropriate vocabulary
	Use language and register appropriate to audience and context
	Make accurate and effective use of paragraphs, grammatical structures, sentences, punctuation and spelling

Resource 1.4

Exploring 18th-century English

Read the following passage carefully.

According to the author, what did Selkirk take onto the island with him? See if you can work out what the unfamiliar items are.

The Story of Alexander Selkirk

The Person I speak of is Alexander Selkirk, whose Name is familiar to Men of Curiosity, from the Fame of his having lived four years and four Months alone in the Island of Juan Fernandez. I had the pleasure frequently to converse with the Man soon after his Arrival in England, in the Year 1711. It was matter of great Curiosity to hear him, as he is a Man of good Sense, give an Account of the different Revolutions in his own Mind in that long Solitude. When we consider how painful Absence from Company for the space 5 of but one Evening is to the generality of Mankind, we may have a sense how painful this necessary and constant Solitude was to a Man bred a Sailor, and ever accustomed to enjoy and suffer, eat, drink, and sleep, and perform all Offices of Life, in Fellowship and Company. He was put ashore from a leaky Vessel, with the Captain of which he had had an irreconcileable difference; and he chose rather to take his Fate in this place, than in a crazy Vessel, under a disagreeable Commander. His Portion were a Sea-Chest, his 10 wearing Cloaths and Bedding, a Fire-lock, a Pound of Gun-powder, a large quantity of Bullets, a Flint and Steel, a few Pounds of Tobacco, an Hatchet, a Knife, a Kettle, a Bible, and other Books of Devotion, together with Pieces that concerned Navigation, and his Mathematical Instruments. […] He had in Provisions for the Sustenance of Life but the quantity of two Meals, the Island abounding only with wild Goats, Cats and Rats. 15

From *The Englishman*, by Richard Steele (1672–1729)

....

....

....

....

....

....

Resource 1.5

Writing a leaflet

Eco-tourism is a form of tourism in exotic, uninhabited or inaccessible natural locations. This sort of holiday is organised so eco-tourists can observe wildlife or visit interesting geological sites without damaging the environment.

1. Read the following information about ecotourism from the International Ecotourism Society.

Do's and Don'ts While Traveling

By exploring alternative travel choices, you can have a unique trip and avoid leaving negative marks on cultures, economies, and the environment.

1. **At the hotel:** Ask about environmental policies and practices. Does the hotel support community projects?

2. **Language:** Learn a few words of the local language and use them.

3. **Dress:** Read up on local conventions and dress appropriately. In many countries modest dress is important.

4. **Behavior:** Be respectful of local citizens' privacy. Ask permission before entering sacred places, homes or private land.

5. **Photos:** Be sensitive to when and where you take photos or video of people. Always ask first.

6. **Environment:** Respect the natural environment. Never touch or harass animals. Always follow designated trails. Support conservation by paying entrance fees to parks and protected sites.

7. **Animal products:** Never buy crafts or products made from protected or endangered animals.

8. **Pay the fair price:** Don't engage in overly aggressive bargaining for souvenirs. Don't short-change on tips for services.

9. **Buy local:** Choose locally-owned lodges, hotels and B&Bs. Use local buses, car rental agencies and airlines. Eat in local restaurants, shop in local markets and attend local festivals/events.

10. **Hire local guides:** Enrich your experience and support the local economy. Ask guides if they are licensed and live locally. Are they recommended by tour operators?

2. Using the information above, write a leaflet for eco-tourists visiting an area of outstanding beauty. You can choose any area you know about.

Use your own words as far as possible and do not include illustrations.

Write between 250 and 350 words. Use a separate sheet of paper.

Resource 1.6

Dictogloss

1. Ask students to note down basic *wh-* points (who, what, where, when) while you read out the passage below.

2. Read the passage again and ask students to make notes on the five senses (what Lee saw, felt, heard, touched, smelled).

3. Organise students into pairs or small groups. Read the passage a third time and ask students to reconstruct the text from memory, within a set time limit. Ask students to exchange reconstructions with another group and to peer-mark by reading the passage themselves.

It took me two days to cross the Sierra Guadarrama, as through another season and another country, climbing a magnificent road of granite blocks to a point almost two miles high. Here were racing brooks, great shadowy forests, and fallen boulders covered with flowering creepers. It seemed already autumn here; clouds rolled down the summits, dropping cool intermittent showers, while shepherds scrambled about, followed by wolf-like dogs, and the air smelt freshly of resin and honey.   5

I spent the first night in a grove of oak trees, lying on leaves as wet as Wales, under a heavy dew and a cold sharp moon and surrounded by the continuous bells of sheep. In the morning I woke shivering to eat a breakfast of goat's cheese, which the night had soaked and softened, then watched the sunlight move slowly down the trunks of the pine trees, dark red, as though they bled from the top. Nearby was a waterfall pouring into a bowl of rock, where I stripped and took a short sharp bathe. It was snow-   10 cold, brutal, and revivifying, secluded among the trees, and when I'd finished I sat naked on a mossy stone, slowly drying in the rising sun. I seemed to be in a pocket of northern Europe, full of the cold splendour of Finnish gods. A green haze of pine-dust floated in shafts of sunlight and squirrels swung and chattered above me. Gulping the fine dry air and sniffing the pitch-pine mountain, I was perhaps never so alive and so alone again.   15

From *As I Walked Out One Midsummer Morning*,
by Laurie Lee

Creating a performance reading of a poem

Annotate this copy of the poem "Travel" ready for a performance reading. Remember to think about intonation, movement, facial expression and the rhythm of the reading. Note that the poem was written at the end of the 19th century, which is evident in some of the choices of vocabulary

I should like to rise and go
Where the golden apples grow;—
Where below another sky
Parrot islands anchored lie,
And, watched by cockatoos and goats,   5

Lonely Crusoes building boats;—
Where in sunshine reaching out
Eastern cities, miles about,
Are with mosque and minaret
Among sandy gardens set,   10

And the rich goods from near and far
Hang for sale in the bazaar,—
Where the Great Wall round China goes,
And on one side the desert blows,
And with bell and voice and drum   15

Cities on the other hum;—
Where are forests, hot as fire,
Wide as England, tall as a spire,
Full of apes and cocoa-nuts
And the negro hunters' huts;—   20

Where the knotty crocodile
Lies and blinks in the Nile,
And the red flamingo flies
Hunting fish before his eyes;—
Where in jungles, near and far,   25

Man-devouring tigers are,
Lying close and giving ear
Lest the hunt be drawing near,
Or a comer-by be seen
Swinging in a palanquin;—   30

Where among the desert sands
Some deserted city stands,
All its children, sweep and prince,
Grown to manhood ages since,
Not a foot in street or house,   35

Not a stir of child or mouse,
And when kindly falls the night,
In all the town no spark of light.
There I'll come when I'm a man
With a camel caravan;   40

Light a fire in the gloom
Of some dusty dining-room;
See the pictures on the walls,
Heroes, fights and festivals;
And in a corner find the toys   45
Of the old Egyptian boys.

By Robert Louis Stevenson (1885)

Resource 1.8

Writing descriptive compositions

Read the following points on how to write good descriptive compositions.

A descriptive composition is not a story; it does not need a beginning, middle and an end. Give your description a framework, such as a clear setting or location in time, to create a structure but do not create a storyline.

- Write about something you know well or have seen or felt in detail.

- Use interesting, unusual vocabulary and a variety of sentence structures. For example, be precise when you describe colour: red can be blood-red or bright scarlet; green can be sea-green, apple-green or the colour of new-mown grass. Don't repeat words: find synonyms or alternative ways to express what you are seeing, thinking or feeling.

- Try to use all five senses to give the reader a clear sense of the location, event and/or atmosphere. Include interesting, unusual or amusing details.

- Avoid using clichés or overused, childish vocabulary such as *nice, little, old, big, good, bad*. Find other ways to say *a lot of*. Descriptive writing gives you a chance to show off your vocabulary, so use it!

Self-assessment

Make notes about Unit 1.

The difference between skimming and scanning is:

....

....

....

To write a summary I need to follow these steps:

....

....

....

Two texts (poetry or prose) I remember in Unit 1 are:

....

Two new skills I learned are: ....

....

Two things I'm not sure about are: ....

....

I enjoyed doing: ....

I would like to .... *again because*

....

....

Resource 2.1

Taking notes

1. As a class, discuss Alfred Lord Tennyson's reference to "Nature, red in tooth and claw".

2. Make notes on the questions below, including points of view that are different from your own. Keep your notes neat as they might be needed for coursework later.

Question	My point of view	Alternative points of view
What do you think Tennyson was referring to?		
Is Nature, by nature, cruel? Note down reasons.		
What do we mean when we say "by nature"?		
Do you think people should try to tame or change Nature? Note down reasons.		
In what ways does Nature defeat humanity and constantly prove its power?		
List three ways people try to change the natural world for their personal benefit. (Examples of this are fish-farming, irrigation canals, training elephants to work in forests).		

Exploring poetry

In small groups, choose one of the questions below and have a discussion.

What do you think Tennyson was referring to?

Is Nature, by nature, cruel? Note down reasons.

What do we mean when we say "by nature"?

Do you think people should try to tame or change Nature? Note down reasons.

In what ways does Nature defeat humanity and constantly prove its power?

List three ways people try to change the natural world for their personal benefit. (Examples of this are fish-farming, irrigation canals, training elephants to work in forests).

Resource 2.3

Sorting facts

Cut these ten interesting facts about the history of salt into strips and arrange them into chronological order. Note that some items do not have dates, so you should put them in the order that you think makes most sense.

1. Marco Polo, a Venetian traveller to the court of Kublai Khan, who is said to have lived from 1254 to 1324, noted that in Tibet tiny cakes of salt were pressed with images of the Grand Khan and used as coins.

2. The belief that spilling salt brings bad luck dates back to the 16th century.

3. Greek slave traders often bartered salt for slaves, hence the expression someone "is not worth his/her salt".

4. To be "above (or below) the salt," refers to the seating arrangement at the long table in a manor house or palace in medieval times. Rank and honour were signified by where people sat in relation to the salt. A large salt-cellar was placed in the centre of the dining table and those who sat nearer to the host were "above the salt" with inferiors, seated further away, being "below the salt".

5. The expression to take something "with a pinch of salt" has been in use since the 17th century.

6. Protesting against British rule in 1930, Mahatma Gandhi led a 200-mile march to the Arabian Ocean to collect untaxed salt for India's poor.

7. The word *salary*, which we use to refer to what a person earns, was derived from the word "salt". Roman legionnaires were paid in *salarium* – meaning "salt" – the Latin origin of the word *salary*.

8. Salt is still used as money among the nomads of Ethiopia's Danakil Plains.

9. It is said that the first ever recorded war, in Essalt on the Jordan River, was fought over precious salt supplies.

10. In 2200 BC, the Chinese emperor Hsia Yu levied one of the first known taxes. He taxed salt.

Telling stories aloud

Read the story below and then answer the questions that follow.

The Drought

Once, in a faraway country there was a drought. There had been no rain for days. No rain for weeks. No rain for months. And the land was dry, dry, dry. And hard and cracked and brown and dusty. And the sun beat down relentlessly. And the heat was unbearable. Like living in an oven. Impossible to breathe. And everywhere the dust. On the ground. In the air. On your skin. In your eyes. In your throat. Suffocating dust. 5

And the plants were dying. Changing from green through yellow to brown, they withered and died. And the animals were starving [...] getting thinner and thinner and thinner ... and dying. And the people were starving too, for there was nothing to eat.

And the drought went on and on and on.

So one day, all the men went into the temple to pray for rain. In the sweltering heat, they got 10 down on their knees on the hard, dusty ground and they prayed and they prayed and they prayed for rain. But still there was no rain.

And so another day, all the women went into the temple to pray for rain. In the sweltering heat, they got down on their knees on the hard, dusty ground and they prayed and they prayed and they prayed for rain. But still there was no rain. 15

And then one day, a little girl went up the steps to the temple. She was about nine and she was wearing a dirty yellow dress that was torn. Her feet were bare and her legs and arms were dusty. Her long hair was tangled and in a mess. There was dirt on her face. And up she went, up the steps of the temple, to pray for rain. But do you know what she had with her? She had with her an umbrella. Not a posh umbrella. A scruffy old broken umbrella. But an umbrella just the same. And she skipped into 20 the temple and got down on her knees and put her umbrella on the ground beside her and she prayed and she prayed and she prayed for rain.

And do you know what? When she came out of the temple, it was raining.

From *In Your Hands*,
by Jane Revell and Susan Norman

1. Look at the different types of sentence in the passage. Find:

   a. a minor sentence (with no verb)

   b. a simple sentence (with one verb)

   c. a compound sentence (with two verbs and a conjunction)

   d. a complex sentence (with a few verbs)

   e. a rhetorical question.

2. The story was written to be read aloud. The language it uses is very simple, but how has the author used sentences to create effect?

3. Using this story as a model, write a descriptive passage or tale of your own in the same style. Start like this: *Once, in a faraway country* ...

Resource 2.5

Writing an informative text on training elephants

After you have written your informative text, swap with a partner and mark their work.

Award up to 10 marks: 1 mark for any of the points below. Then award a maximum of 5 marks for style and accurate use of grammar and punctuation. There are a total of 15 marks.

1. Training elephants can begin at the Center for Training Baby Elephants once they have been separated from their mothers.

2. At three years old, the baby elephant is put in a corral with other babies to wean it from its mother.

3. The elephants must be accustomed to wearing leg chains (hobbled).

4. They must learn to walk alongside mahouts.

5. They must learn the meaning of different prods (from the mahouts' stick or 'prod').

6. They must learn to wear tack (ropes/harness).

7. First, they are taught to pick up objects with the trunk (not tusks).

8. Then they are taught to pass objects to their mahout.

9. They are given sugar cane and then trained to pass this to the mahout.

10. They must learn to recognise/accept the mahout's leg and feet commands.

11. They learn to go left and right.

12. Then starts 4–5 years' training in log handling/dragging.

13. They learn to push logs with their tusks.

14. They must become accustomed to machinery and noise.

15. The elephants are in their prime at 20 years old.

16. They are expected to work for 35 years.

17. They retire at 60 years old.

Self-assessment

Make notes about Unit 2.

Two text forms in which writing to inform can be used are:

....

When writing or speaking to argue and persuade, I need to consider:

....

....

Two texts (poetry or prose) I remember in Unit 2 are:

....

Two new skills I learned are: ....

....

Two things I'm not sure about are: ....

....

I enjoyed doing: ....

I would like to .... *again because*

....

....

Resource 3.1

Writing summaries

1. Read the text twice.	**2.** Keyword the question.	**3.** Identify and underline relevant information.
4. Make notes. Write relevant details out as bullet point notes.	**5. Summarise.** Organise the notes according to the summary question. Write your summary. Count the words and put the number at the end in brackets.	**6. Proofread.** Read the summary; edit and correct spelling and punctuation mistakes.

Resource 3.2

Writing an interview script

Introduction by interviewer (I)
I'd like to welcome the author Mr Michael Ondaatje to our programme this evening.
Response by interviewee (M.O.)
Thank you, it is a pleasure to be here.
I: Topic 1
Mr Ondaatje, I believe your family is from Sri Lanka and you spent a lot of time there. Tell us about your childhood. Do you have any special memories about anything in particular?
M.O. (Number points for what M.O. will say)
1.   2.   3.
I: Second question to encourage Michael Ondaatje to say more about his memories
M.O. (use your reading skills to interpret Ondaatje's thoughts and feelings from the passage.)
I: (bring interview to an end and thank guest.)
M.O.

Resource 3.3

Exploring word choices

black drizzle
mourning
death of the sun
general infection of ill-temper
crust upon crust of mud sticking
Fog everywhere

Exploring mood and tone in prose and poetry

Re-read Passage B from *Bleak House* by Dickens and "Composed Upon Westminster Bridge" by Wordsworth, both on page 63.

Add to the table, by writing examples of nouns, adjectives and images in the appropriate boxes. Try to find three to five examples in each category.

	Dickens	Wordsworth
Nouns	*smoke*	*splendour*
Adjectives	*defiled*	*fair*
Images	*waterside pollutions of a great (and dirty) city*	*The river glideth at his own sweet will*

Resource 3.5

Analysing "Little Boy Crying"

Use this copy of the poem to analyse it as outlined in the Speaking and listening task on page 73.

Little Boy Crying

Your mouth contorting in brief spite and

Hurt, your laughter metamorphosed into howls,

Your frame so recently relaxed now tight

With three-year-old frustration, your bright eyes

Swimming tears, splashing your bare feet,   5

You stand there angling for a moment's hint

Of guilt or sorrow for the quick slap struck.

The ogre towers above you, that grim giant,

Empty of feeling, a colossal cruel,

Soon victim of the tale's conclusion, dead   10

At last. You hate him, you imagine

Chopping clean the tree he's scrambling down

Or plotting deeper pits to trap him in.

You cannot understand, not yet,

The hurt your easy tears can scald him with,   15

Nor guess the wavering hidden behind that mask.

This fierce man longs to lift you, curb your sadness

With piggy-back or bull-fight, anything,

But dare not ruin the lessons you should learn.

You must not make a plaything of the rain.   20

by Mervyn Morris

Resource 3.6

Analysing "Before the Sun"

Use this copy of the poem to analyse it as outlined in the Reading task on page 74.

Before the Sun

Intense blue morning
promising early heat
and later in the afternoon,
heavy rain.

The bright chips   5
fly from the sharp axe
for some distance through the air,
arc,
and eternities later;
settle down in showers   10
on the dewy grass.

It is a big log:
but when you are fourteen
big logs
are what you want.   15

The wood gives off
a sweet nose-cleansing odour
which (unlike sawdust)
doesn't make one sneeze.

It sends up a thin spiral   20
of smoke which later straightens
and flutes out
to the distant sky: a signal
of some sort,
or a sacrificial prayer.   25

The wood hisses,
The sparks fly.

And when the sun
finally shows up
in the East like some   30
latecomer to a feast
I have got two cobs of maize
ready for it.

I tell the sun to come share
with me the roasted maize   35
and the sun just winks
like a grown-up.

So I go ahead, taking big
alternate bites:
one for the sun,   40
one for me.
This one for the sun,
this one for me:
till the cobs
are just two little skeletons   45
in the sun.

by Charles Mungoshi

Resource 3.7

Self-assessment

Make notes about Unit 3.

Two ways in which writing to inform, describe and entertain can be used are:

....

What I remember about:

- *metaphors*..

- *similes*..

- *point of view*..

- *narrative voice*..

- *simple sentences*...

Two texts (poetry or prose) I remember in Unit 3 are:

....

Two new skills I learned are: ....

....

Two things I'm not sure about are: ....

....

I enjoyed doing: ....

I would like to .... *again because*

....

....

Using Shakespearean insults

Your abilities are too infant-like for doing much alone. *Coriolanus* (Act 2 scene 1)	I scorn you, scurvy companion. *Henry IV, Part 2* (Act 2 scene 4)
More of your conversation would infect my brain. *Coriolanus* (Act 2 scene 1)	Away, you mouldy rogue, away! *Henry IV, Part 2* (Act 2 scene 4)
The tartness of his face sours ripe grapes. *Coriolanus* (Act 5 scene 4)	Away, you cut-purse rascal! you filthy bung, away! *Henry IV, Part 2* (Act 2 scene 4)
There is no more mercy in him than there is milk in a male tiger. *Coriolanus* (Act 5 scene 4)	O braggart vile and damned furious wight! *Henry V* (Act 2 scene 1)
Away! Thou'rt poison to my blood. *Cymbeline* (Act 1 scene 1)	Avaunt, you cullions! *Henry V* (Act 3 scene 2)
O thou vile one! *Cymbeline* (Act 1 scene 1)	Such antics do not amount to a man. *Henry V* (Act 3 scene 2)
Frailty, thy name is woman! *Hamlet* (Act 1 scene 2)	He is white-livered and red-faced. *Henry V* (Act 3 scene 2)
They have a plentiful lack of wit. *Hamlet* (Act 2 scene 2)	They were devils incarnate. *Henry V* (Act 3 scene 2)
'Sblood, you starveling, you elf-skin, you dried neat's tongue, you bull's pizzle, you stock-fish! *Henry IV, Part 1* (Act 2 scene 4)	They are hare-brain'd slaves. *Henry VI, Part 1* (Act 1 scene 2)
There's no more faith in thee than in a stewed prune. *Henry IV, Part 1* (Act 3 scene 3)	Hag of all despite! *Henry VI, Part 1* (Act 3 scene 2)

Resource 4.2

Comparing Jaques' account of life with yours

Read the speech below and compare Jaques' account with the different stages of life with your own.

JAQUES:

All the world's a stage,

And all the men and women merely players:

They have their exits and their entrances;

And one man in his time plays many parts,

His acts being seven ages. At first the infant,   5

Mewling and puking in the nurse's arms.

And then the whining school-boy, with his satchel

And shining morning face, creeping like snail

Unwillingly to school. And then the lover,

Sighing like furnace, with a woeful ballad   10

Made to his mistress' eyebrow. Then a soldier,

Full of strange oaths and bearded like the pard,

Jealous in honour, sudden and quick in quarrel,

Seeking the bubble reputation

Even in the cannon's mouth. And then the justice,   15

In fair round belly with good capon lined,

With eyes severe and beard of formal cut,

Full of wise saws and modern instances;

And so he plays his part. The sixth age shifts

Into the lean and slipper'd pantaloon,   20

With spectacles on nose and pouch on side,

His youthful hose, well saved, a world too wide

For his shrunk shank; and his big manly voice,

Turning again toward childish treble, pipes

And whistles in his sound. Last scene of all,   25

That ends this strange eventful history,

Is second childishness and mere oblivion,

Sans teeth, sans eyes, sans taste, sans everything.

From *As You Like It*, by William Shakespeare (1599)

Defining theatre language

Mark your partner's answers to the Theatre language task on page 81. Give 1 mark for each correct answer, using the definitions below.

1. Scenery = props/items used to set the scene of a theatrical production

2. Proscenium arch = the arch that frames a stage

3. Backdrop = the background to a particular scene or situation

4. Prompt = to supply an actor/singer with a missing cue/line from offstage

5. Auditorium = a room built to enable an audience to hear and watch performances

6. Soliloquy = the act of talking while or as if alone

7. Monologue = the part of a drama in which a single actor speaks for some time

8. Stage left/stage right = the sides of the stage that are on the actor's left and right when facing the audience

9. Orchestra pit = the lowered area in front of the stage where the musicians perform

10. Dénouement = the final resolution of the intricacies of a plot

Resource 4.4

Making comparisons

Using information from your research and reading pages 82–4, complete the grid.

	Kathakali	Noh	Kabuki
Origin: where, when, why and how the dance-dramas began			
Audience and popularity: past and present			
Spectacle: costumes, make-up, special effects and music			
Performers: who performs and how they are trained			
Style of acting: how performers convey the stories			
Other points			

Making comparisons

Use this grid to mark your partner's work.

	Kathakali	Noh	Kabuki
Origin: where, when, why and how the dance-dramas began	Began in Kerala in 17th century as a ritual dance in temples during religious ceremonies	Began in Japan in 14th century; developed from Chinese performing arts and Japanese dance; performed to convey moral values	Began in Japan at end of 16th century; developed from Noh as more popular entertainment
Audience and popularity: past and present	Originally seen in temples and palaces; now reaches a broad audience as popular entertainment	Originally for aristocracy in temples and shrines; by end of 19th century more popular with working people	Originally for townspeople
Spectacle: costumes, make-up, special effects and music	Specific costumes, headgear and make-up for different characters; masks, flowing scarves, padded jackets, wide skirts; all is larger than life; vocal music and drums	Masks and elaborate costumes; 6-8 singers and 4 musicians; larger than life effects; no scenery	Heavily conventionalised make-up; now with revolving platform and stage devices such as trap doors
Performers: who performs and how they are trained	Professional actors; training starts aged 10 and takes 8-10 years, based on martial art of Kerala	All male cast	All male cast
Style of acting: how performers convey the stories	Hand signals, facial expressions, and body and eye movements act as sign language to convey emotions and attitudes	Principal actor acts the story; another is storyteller; others suggest aspects of the story with visual appearance and body movement	Formal stylised drama; supposed to be no audience interaction
Other points	Reflects on what is important in life	Reflects on human values	Based on popular myths and legends

Resource 4.6

Self-assessment

Make notes about Unit 4.

The differences between plot and theme are:

....

Stage directions are:

....

What I remember about:

• *Kathakali* ....

• *Noh* ....

• *Kabuki* ....

• *Commedia dell'Arte* ....

• *Greek theatre* ....

• *monologue* ....

• *the way different characters speak in Macbeth* ....

....

Two plays I remember in Unit 4 are:
....

Two new skills I learned are: ....

....

Two things I'm not sure about are: ....

....

I enjoyed doing: ....

I would like to .... *again because*

....

Identifying key words

s	p	o	t	l	i	g	h	t	s	o	v	m	d	s	t
l	k	r	h	t	o	p	s	y	n	c	i	o	i	t	r
p	s	c	e	n	e	r	y	u	i	o	l	n	a	a	k
f	t	s	r	s	j	o	h	o	w	s	l	o	l	g	a
y	a	u	d	i	e	n	c	e	m	t	a	l	o	e	c
s	w	b	e	x	g	s	x	p	k	u	i	o	g	d	t
o	o	p	y	q	s	t	y	w	b	m	n	g	u	i	s
l	t	l	h	r	n	a	f	b	s	e	b	u	e	r	j
i	r	o	t	r	a	g	e	d	y	s	i	e	t	e	k
l	d	t	q	t	c	e	s	c	v	m	r	n	m	c	d
o	h	k	b	h	m	d	c	o	m	e	d	y	o	t	c
q	j	l	o	b	l	a	n	k	v	e	r	s	e	i	x
u	q	r	d	q	k	b	e	r	e	v	i	e	w	o	e
y	u	u	h	e	r	o	j	s	c	r	i	p	t	n	t
s	v	a	c	s	s	o	p	h	o	c	l	e	s	s	q
a	f	t	d	v	a	p	r	o	n	s	t	a	g	e	w

Find the key words in the wordsearch using the definitions below. Most of the words appear across or down the grid, but a few are diagonal.

1. A type of stage
2. A Greek playwright
3. What the playwright writes
4. Instruction for the actors on stage
5. The people watching
6. When an actor speaks his thoughts just to the audience
7. Script written for one actor
8. The type of poetry Shakespeare used in his plays
9. How stage managers set the scene
10. What actors wear on stage
11. A play that ends unhappily
12. A play that makes people laugh
13. What a theatre critic writes for a newspaper or magazine
14. How the scenes in a play are organised
15. The best man in the play
16. The baddie
17. The actor who comments on the action in Greek plays
18. Used to focus attention on a character
19. What the actors say to each other
20. The second story running through the play

Resource 4.8

Identifying key words (answers)

Here are the answers to the wordsearch on Resource 4.7.

s	p	o	t	l	i	g	h	t	s	o	v	m	d	s	t
l	k	r	h	t	o	p	s	y	n	c	i	o	i	t	r
p	s	c	e	n	e	r	y	u	i	o	l	n	a	a	k
f	t	s	r	s	j	o	h	o	w	s	l	o	l	g	a
y	a	u	d	i	e	n	c	e	m	t	a	l	o	e	c
s	w	b	e	x	g	s	x	p	k	u	i	o	g	d	t
o	o	p	y	q	s	t	y	w	b	m	n	g	u	i	s
l	t	l	h	r	n	a	f	b	s	e	b	u	e	r	j
i	r	o	t	r	a	g	e	d	y	s	i	e	t	e	k
l	d	t	q	t	c	e	s	c	v	m	r	n	m	c	d
o	h	k	b	h	m	d	c	o	m	e	d	y	o	t	c
q	j	l	o	b	l	a	n	k	v	e	r	s	e	i	x
u	q	r	d	q	k	b	e	r	e	v	i	e	w	o	e
y	u	u	h	e	r	o	j	s	c	r	i	p	t	n	t
s	v	a	c	s	s	o	p	h	o	c	l	e	s	s	q
a	f	t	d	v	a	p	r	o	n	s	t	a	g	e	w

Topic sentences

A topic sentence contains the key information in a paragraph. You should include a topic sentence in each of your paragraphs in all forms of writing. Although topic sentences may appear anywhere, in non-fiction writing they often appear at the beginning of the paragraph.

Paragraphs are a series of sentences (technically a minimum of two) organised into related topics that lead towards the conclusion of your argument, discussion, description, narrative or account. Almost every piece of writing you do will be arranged in paragraphs. A reader should be able to clearly identify your line of thought by the arrangement of your paragraphs.

If a reader underlines or copies down your topic sentences they should be able to see how you planned and arranged your essay. In discursive writing, reports and accounts, topic sentences carry the main points of an argument and should progress towards your conclusion. In narrative writing, topic sentences move the story line. In descriptive writing, topic sentences tell the reader the different stages of your experience or the focus of your attention.

These key sentences work in two ways: they relate each paragraph to your main subject or thesis statement, acting as signposts that show how your writing has been structured and organised; they also define the content of each paragraph in itself.

Remember the following key points about paragraphing and topic sentences:

- a well-organised paragraph supports or develops a single idea (expressed in the topic sentence)
- a topic sentence can be used to substantiate or support an argument
- a topic sentence unifies the content of a paragraph and directs the order of the sentences
- it advises the reader what is being discussed
- readers usually glance at the first sentence in a paragraph to get the gist of what is being said
- placing a sentence before the topic sentence in a paragraph can make a clear link from what you have said earlier.

Resource 5.2

Identifying topic sentences

Read the passage below about Anahareo, a Canadian First Nations woman who became a national heroine.

1. Identify the writer's topic sentences (the first one is underlined).

2. Write a subheading for each paragraph.

Anahareo and Grey Owl

<u>Gertrude Bernard was born in 1906, the daughter of a Mohawk and Algonquin parents who raised her in Mattawa, a small Ontario town in Canada.</u> In this time period most First Nations people lived difficult and restricted lives on reservations (called reserves in Canada) but Gertrude's family were among a small number who lived in a town. Though her family escaped the hard life of the reserve, they still endured prejudice and restrictions in Mattawa. Gertrude, a high-spirited tomboy, found 5 such restrictions difficult. She liked to climb trees, paddle canoes or swim in the river, at a time when the approved activities for girls, especially First Nations girls, were playing with dolls and learning to cook and sew.

When she was nineteen Gertrude went north and took a job as a waitress at Camp Wabikon on Lake Temagami, a holiday spot for wealthy people from New York City who yearned for wilderness 10 surroundings while they enjoyed canoe trips, swimming and hiking. During her stay Gertrude noticed and fell in love with one of the canoe guides, Archie Belaney whose shoulder-length hair, buckskin trousers and moccasins made him seem like her romantic heroes, Jesse James and Robin Hood. He told her he was half Apache and courted her energetically, eventually convincing her to join him in the wilderness where he earned his living trapping, though she knew people would condemn such 15 behaviour.

With Archie's help she honed her bush skills and learned to trap, but then found its practice too cruel to continue. It was when she and Archie discovered two motherless beaver kits and she convinced him to raise the kits and give up trapping that a new life promoting wilderness preservation emerged. With trapping no longer a means of income Archie turned to writing, and through his hugely popular 20 books, their pioneer work in wilderness preservation caught the public's attention. Archie authored the books as Grey Owl and gave Gertrude the name, Anahareo, a modified form of the name of one of her ancestors. Eventually, the Canadian Parks Department asked Grey Owl and Anahareo to raise beavers in one of their newly opened parks. The couple agreed and lived for a brief time at Riding Mountain National Park, Manitoba before moving to Beaver Lodge at Ajaawan Lake in Prince Albert 25 National Park, Alberta. There thousands of visitors came to the wilderness see Anahareo and Grey Owl with the beavers and later, their daughter, Dawn.

Anahareo's passion for the wilderness was always strong, and despite the racism she faced, she carved out an independent life as a prospector and dog musher while Grey Owl wrote his books. As a celebrity, she challenged the negative stereotypes of First Nations women by her dynamic presence, unconventional breeches, boots and jacket and her stylishly bobbed hair. She could, in Grey Owl's words, "swing an axe as well as she could a lipstick." When Grey Owl died in 1938 the news media revealed that Grey Owl was an Englishman from Hastings and had no trace of Apache or any other First Nations heritage. Anahareo denied any knowledge of Grey Owl's real background to the media, but in view of the public's anger at Grey Owl for what they considered a betrayal of trust, the media's interest in her faded. 30

35

Anahareo married again a year later and had two more daughters, but she never again returned to live in the wilderness. Later in life she advocated for animal rights and other conservation issues and for her efforts the International League of Human Rights awarded her the Order of Nature in 1979 and Canada selected her for their highest honour, The Order of Canada in 1983. She died three years later at the age of eighty. 40

From *Anahareo: A Wilderness Spirit*,
by Kristin Gleeson

Resource 5.3

Writing a summary – Core

1. Using the information in the passage on page 110, make notes on when a boy from a humble family could marry in Ancient Egypt. Although the passage is longer than you will encounter in assessments, you do not need to use it all. Find the paragraphs you need before you start to annotate the text. In your notes, include:

   a. his age and circumstances

   b. how his bride was chosen

   c. what arrangements he was expected to make for his bride.

   Write your notes out as a summary.

   Write between 100 and 150 words.

2. After you have written you notes, check that you have included at least ten of the following points.

   - The bridegroom would be aged 17 to 20, or older if he had been married before or was a widower.
   - A man was able to marry when he was considered old enough or able to support his spouse and any future children.
   - Marriage depended on parental consent.
   - Some couples chose their partners or made love matches.
   - Couples married within their social class or same economic status, but Egyptian men sometimes married foreigners.
   - Females were important in organising the marriage.
   - A woman could be used as a go-between to speak to the girl's mother, instead of her father.
   - The bridegroom had to have a home so that the young woman could move her belongings into his house on the day of the marriage.
   - A contractual agreement was made in the majority of marriages.
   - The marriage contract was made between the bride's father and the husband-to-be.
   - The bridegroom had to provide for his new wife as part of the agreement.
   - The agreement set out property entitlements and financial arrangements between both partners during the marriage and after possible separation.
   - The agreement set out what a wife and her children should have if there was a divorce.
   - The man was expected to give his wife money if he divorced her.

Writing a summary – Extended

1. Using information from the passage on page 110, make notes on how marriages were arranged and ended in Ancient Egypt. Include:

   - when young people married

   - how marriages were arranged

   - what was included in a marriage contract.

   Write your notes out as a summary.

   Write about 200 words.

2. After you have written you notes, check that you have included at least 15 of the following points.

   - Brides were aged between 14 and 15.

   - Bridegrooms were 17–20 years old.

   - Boys could marry when considered physically mature.

   - Men could marry when considered old enough to support a spouse and children.

   - The boy was expected to have a home ready for his new wife to move into.

   - Marriages were usually arranged by parents or with parental permission.

   - Many couples chose their partners or made love matches.

   - A male suitor could use a female go-between to approach the girl's mother.

   - Women were important in organising marriages.

   - A contract was drawn up between girl's father and the bridegroom.

   - Often, the bride-to-be was part of the contract.

   - The contract established rights to maintenance and possessions during the marriage.

   - The contract safeguarded material rights of the wife and her future children if there was a divorce.

   - A marriage was terminated by telling the wife she was no longer required.

   - The husband had to give his wife money and possessions as agreed in the contract to end their marriage.

Resource 5.5

Identifying different forms of love

Different forms of love

Romantic love is just one form of love. Copy the chart below and add to it where you can.

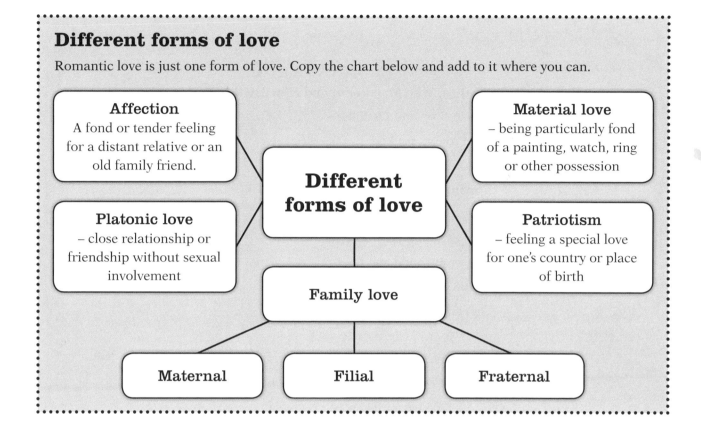

© Oxford University Press 2013: this may be reproduced for class use solely for the purchaser's institute

Annotating poems (1)

Annotate this poem to find out who is loved by whom and why.

To Anthea, Who May Command Him Anything

Bid me to live, and I will live
    Thy Protestant to be,
Or bid me love, and I will give
    A loving heart to thee.

A heart as soft, a heart as kind,   5
    A heart as sound and free
As in the whole world thou canst find,
    That heart I'll give to thee.

Bid that heart stay, and it will stay
    To honour thy decree: 10
Or bid it languish quite away,
    And 't shall do so for thee.

Bid me to weep and I will weep
    While I have eyes to see:
And having none, yet will I keep   15
    A heart to weep for thee.

Bid me despair, and I'll despair
    Under that cypress tree.
Or bid me die, and I will dare
    E'en death to die for thee.   20

Thou art my life, my love, my heart,
    The very eyes of me,
And hast command of every part,
    To live and die for thee.

By Robert Herrick 1591–1674

Resource 5.7

Annotating poems (2)

Annotate this poem to find out who is loved by whom and why.

A Poison Tree

I was angry with my friend:

I told my wrath, my wrath did end.

I was angry with my foe:

I told it not, my wrath did grow.

And I watered it in fears,   5

Night and morning with my tears;

And I sunned it with smiles,

And with soft deceitful wiles.

And it grew both day and night,

Till it bore an apple bright.   10

And my foe beheld it shine.

And he knew that it was mine,

And into my garden stole

When the night had veiled the pole;

In the morning glad I see   15

My foe outstretched beneath the tree.

By William Blake (1757–1827)

Annotating poems (3)

Annotate this poem to find out who is loved by whom and why.

Full Moon and Little Frieda

A cool small evening shrunk to a dog bark and the clank of a bucket –

And you listening.

A spider's web, tense for the dew's touch.

A pail lifted, still and brimming – mirror

To tempt a first star to a tremor.   5

Cows are going home in the lane there, looping the hedges

  with their warm wreaths of breath –

A dark river of blood, many boulders,

Balancing unspilled milk.

"Moon!" you cry suddenly, "Moon! Moon!"

The moon has stepped back like an artist gazing amazed at a work   10

That points at him amazed.

By Ted Hughes (1930–98)

Resource 5.9

Finding synonyms for love and hate

Add your own synonyms for the words love and hate to the diagram.

Synonyms for love and hate

Using a thesaurus, write down nouns for *love* and for *hate*.

Put the nouns in the appropriate triangle according to the strength of the emotion: stronger emotions go in the wider parts of the triangles; weaker emotions go in the narrower parts. Write the nouns in red.

Adoration

Fondness

Indifference

Dislike

Abhorrence

Writing a discursive essay

Introduction: the topic to be discussed
Thesis statement: the principal aspect of the topic you are discussing and your opinion
Give a general overview and define your terms.
Objective outline of what the topic involves: who, what, where, when, why …
Example 1 – advantages
Example 2 – disadvantages
Transition
A different aspect of the subject: looking at same topic from another perspective
Example 1 – positive outcome
Example 2 – negative outcome
Transition
Other thoughts on the topic and/or people involved (individuals and/or community)
Example 1 – evidence with example(s)
Example 2 – opposing evidence with example(s)
Conclusion – brief summary of points made and your views based on the evidence above

Resource 5.11

Sinister words (answers)

Here are the answers to the wordsearch on pages 46–7 of the Workbook.

a	e	q	t	n	i	p	h	a	s	f	b
w	m	a	l	a	d	r	o	i	t	r	g
k	p	b	y	c	z	b	m	k	u	f	a
w	m	s	i	n	i	s	t	e	r	h	u
a	t	n	u	d	o	i	s	v	m	k	c
r	i	g	h	t	e	o	u	s	o	e	h
d	w	t	k	m	v	x	w	z	o	p	e
o	a	a	d	r	o	i	t	e	g	n	k
h	p	r	g	j	e	o	p	r	n	r	t
t	w	m	o	d	t	j	a	s	o	a	i
k	a	r	d	e	x	t	e	r	o	u	s
m	y	a	k	b	e	i	d	m	j	o	s

Resource 5.12

Self-assessment

Make notes about Unit 5.

Style means ....

....

Tone means ....

....

Register means ....

....

Writers use the past tenses and present tenses to ....

....

....

Two texts I remember in Unit 5 are:

....

Two new skills I learned are: ....

....

Two things I'm not sure about are: ....

....

I enjoyed doing: ....

I would like to .... again because

....

Resource 6.1

Marking a summary

Use the list below to help you mark the content of the summary on "The Devastating Costs of the Amazon Gold Rush" on pages 142–4. Award 1 mark for each of the points in the list for a maximum of 15 points.

- I'm a poor man earning just $30 a month at home.
- Now I work on the Madre de Dios River.
- I own a dredge barge on the river.
- I live on the barge with my family.
- We sleep in handmade beds on deck.
- I eat from a galley kitchen run by my mother.
- If I get two grams of gold a day, I can earn a lot more than $30.
- The dredging engine is deafening.
- The rock falling into the sluice is very noisy.
- Stones dredged up from the river are always falling down and crashing onto the banks.
- There is a danger of stripping the forest up to 50ft down.
- I have to start work very early in the morning.
- I have to work very long hours.
- I have to work standing waist-deep in muddy water.
- Anything else about the working conditions.

Practising reading comprehension

Read the passage and then answer the questions that follow on a separate sheet of paper.

Rain forests

Rain forests are structured in layers. The main canopy is between 30–40m high. Above, a few taller trees irregularly protrude. These are the giants of the forest, often 60m tall, with huge crowns of branches spreading out over the others. Below are shorter trees between 15–25m high; some are young emergents which will eventually reach the main canopy or beyond. The upper levels receive much more rain, wind and sun; the lower are stiller, shadowed and humid. In effect, the various canopies act like filters or giant   5 umbrellas, allowing just 2% of the sunlight to reach the forest floor and breaking the force of even the fiercest tropical storm to a fine spray by the time it reaches the ground. […]

While the forest floor is often free from plant litter, save for a thick mat of interconnecting roots, lianas (climbing vines) and epiphytes (most commonly plants like orchids) grow on, up, around and through the main tree growths, binding everything together. The leaves of tropical trees are often thick (to store   10 nutrients from rain water), tough and glossy (to reduce leaching of valuable minerals and evaporation of water, both needed for growth). The bases of many tree species are surrounded by buttresses; sheets of wood which flare out from the trunk acting as extra supports.

Each layer of the forest is a world of its own, with distinctive populations of mammals, birds and insects. These adapt to take advantage of the special conditions characterising each "zone", and rarely pass   15 between. Ornithologists estimate that perhaps as many as 95% of birds used to the darkness of the inner forest will not cross clearings, even to breed or feed. More animals live in the canopies than any other parts of the forest – up to half of all mammals in the Malay Peninsula, for instance. (In temperate forests the average is 15%).

Generally rain forest soils are poor and barren; in part because they are so old. Almost two-thirds are acidic   20 and low in nutrients, and unsuitable for conventional agricultural systems. Because they often contain high concentrations of iron and aluminium, valuable nutrients are either immobilised (phosphorous) or simply pass through before they can be absorbed (calcium, magnesium and potassium).

The humid tropics of Latin America have the worst soils: 82% are acidic and barren (African humid tropics 56%, Asia 38%). 40% of humid tropical Asia has somewhat fertile soil, 24% of Africa and 13% of Latin   25 America. In the Amazon Basin only 6% of the soils can be considered suitable for agriculture, and they are scattered along the river's flood plains.

The volcanic regions of countries like the Philippines, Indonesia, Papua, New Guinea, Cameroon, and along the flood plains of the Amazon and Congo river systems, have more fertile soils. Accounting for perhaps 18% of the total rain forest, these areas already support tens of millions of people.   30

One of the great biological ironies of tropical moist ecosystems is that they support such tremendous concentrations of plants, birds, insects and other animals on such barren ground. The secret lies in the fact that these forests are virtual closed systems in which nutrients are perpetually recycled. They are highly efficient – studies have revealed that less than 1% of nutrients are lost through leaching. Whereas in temperate forests the great bulk of nutrient matter is found in the soil, the reverse is true in the rain forests.   35 Here, as soon as any organism dies, it begins to break down and is absorbed by living organisms. Leaves, roots, trunks, insects, birds, and other animals all benefit. As Woody Allen once said about nature – "it's one giant restaurant, everything eating everything else".

From *Tropical Forest Expeditions*, by Clive Jeremy and Roger Chapman, *et al*.

Ornithologist (n.): someone who studies birds.
Leaching: draining away.

1. In what way(s) does the rain forest canopy act like a giant umbrella? (1 mark)

2. What are the leaves of many tropical rain forest trees like, and why? (2 marks)

3. Explain what epiphytes are and how they grow. (2 marks)

4. Explain in your own words why such a high proportion of birds stay in their own specific areas of the rain forests. (2 marks)

5. Explain in your own words why rain forests are generally unsuitable for conventional agriculture. (3 marks)

6. Name two types of region that have more fertile soils and can support human life. (2 marks)

7. Explain what the authors mean by "One of the greatest biological ironies". (2 marks)

8. Explain in your own words what Woody Allen means by "one giant restaurant". (2 marks)

9. Using the information in this text only, describe what an explorer would see in a tropical rain forest. (9 marks)

(25 marks)

Identifying features of persuasive writing

Read part of Martin Luther King's famous speech, given at the Lincoln Memorial in Washington DC, USA, in 1963.

Identify the features of persuasive writing.

"I have a dream"

… I say to you today, my friends, that in spite of the difficulties and frustrations of the moment, I still have a dream. It is a dream deeply rooted in the American dream.

I have a dream that one day this nation will rise up and live out the true meaning of its creed: "We hold these truths to be self-evident: that all men are created equal."

I have a dream that one day on the red hills of Georgia the sons of former slaves and the sons of former slave owners will be able to sit down together at a table of brotherhood.   5

I have a dream that one day even the state of Mississippi, a desert state, sweltering with the heat of injustice and oppression, will be transformed into an oasis of freedom and justice.

I have a dream that my four children will one day live in a nation where they will not be judged by the color of their skin but by the content of their character.   10

I have a dream today …

I have a dream that one day every valley shall be exalted, every hill and mountain shall be made low, the rough places will be made plain, and the crooked places will be made straight, and the glory of the Lord shall be revealed, and all flesh shall see it together.

This is our hope. This is the faith with which I return to the South. With this faith we   15
will be able to hew out of the mountain of despair a stone of hope. With this faith we will be able to transform the jangling discords of our nation into a beautiful symphony of brotherhood. With this faith we will be able to work together, to pray together, to struggle together, to go to jail together, to stand up for freedom together, knowing that we will be free one day.

This will be the day when all of God's children will be able to sing with a new meaning,   20
"My country, 'tis of thee, sweet land of liberty, of thee I sing. Land where my fathers died, land of the pilgrim's pride, from every mountainside, let freedom ring."

By Martin Luther King (28 August 1963)

Resource 6.4

Self-assessment

Make notes about Unit 6.

What I remember about the writing skills of the following:

• *writing to complain* ....

....

• *writing a press release* ....

....

• *writing a business report* ....

....

• *writing a persuasive speech* ....

....

Three useful things I remember about giving a speech are: ....

....

....

Two texts I remember in Unit 6 are:

....

Two new skills I learned are: ....

....

Two things I'm not sure about are: ....

....

I enjoyed doing: ....

I would like to .... *again because*

....

Resource 7.1

Exploring new media

- Why do people want to know the daily news?

- How many different ways can people find out what is happening in the news?

- How many of you read a print newspaper?

- Is there any difference between an online newspaper and a printed newspaper?

- How might headlines differ between online and printed newspapers?

Resource 7.2

Writing a newspaper report

The following notes were written by a journalist about the earthquake in Mexico. Include the same details in your own report.

Mexico earthquake notes

- 7.4 tremor shook Mexico City

- Lasted for more than one minute

- 11 people were injured.

- No deaths

- In the southwestern state of Guerro, an estimated 800 houses were destroyed.

- One of the most powerful quakes to strike Mexico since 8.1 magnitude quake of 1985

- 18 aftershocks

- Acapulco is undamaged.

- Malia Obama, the President's daughter is unharmed.

- Ana Fernandez, who works in an office in the Central Roma area, reported "I stood up when I saw the lights moving."

- She was "really scared" but remained calm.

- Mexico City Mayor, Marcelo Ebrand, commented that there was no destruction according to air inspection

- Local radio, Formato 21, commented that one person was wounded as a pedestrian bridge crumpled onto a bus, with no passengers.

- Francisco Bernal, another bureau worker, was told to "evacuate around 50 people."

- The earthquake's epicentre was 12.4 miles deep and 100 miles from Oaxaca, as stated by USGS.

Comparing content, style and diction (1)

Complete the grid by filling in details to show what the news reports on pages 170–1 have in common and how they differ.

Look closely at the content, style and diction of each report before you start.

Style and diction – how they are written	Content – what is in the articles
Discovery News	
Daily Mail (8 February)	
The Sun	
Daily Mail (11 October)	

Resource 7.4

Comparing content, style and diction (2)

Use this grid to check your answers to the Writer's craft task on page 171.

Style and diction – how they are written	Content – what is in the articles
Discovery News	
"alleged sea serpent" (tabloid language); sensationalist "sea serpent"; "believe" and "been reported for years" suggests heresy.	A monster, similar to the Loch Ness Monster, is sighted in Alaska.
Daily Mail (8 February)	
"notorious 'snake-like' creature" (sensational wording); "subject of many a supposed sighting" suggests heresy.	Sighting of Iceland's Loch Ness monster
The Sun	
"Scientists could be … " uses modal verb to suggest uncertainty; "claiming" is a verb of alleged information.	Scientists are close to finding that the Yeti actually exists.
Daily Mail (11 October)	
'Is this … ?' question form shows the possibility of Yeti existence; includes indirect and direct eye-witness accounts, e.g. "villagers say … ".	Possible evidence to prove Yeti existence

Resource 7.5

Self-assessment

Make notes about Unit 7.

The difference between show and tell is:

....

Journalists use emotive language in news articles ....

....

Journalists use human interest to make stories more personal ....

....

Two texts (media, non-media or fiction) I remember in Unit 7 are:

....

Two new skills I learned are: ....

....

Two things I'm not sure about are: ....

....

I enjoyed doing: ....

I would like to .... *again because*

....

....

Resource 7.6

Fiction or non-fiction?

Use this copy of the poem for annotation.

The Great Frost

THE Great Frost was, historians tell us, the most severe that has ever visited these islands. Birds froze in mid-air and fell like stones to the ground. At Norwich a young countrywoman started to cross the road in her usual robust health and was seen by the onlookers to turn visibly to powder and be blown in a puff of dust over the roofs as the icy blast struck her at the street corner. The mortality among sheep and cattle was enormous. Corpses froze and could not be drawn from the sheets. It was   5 no uncommon sight to come upon a whole herd frozen immovable upon the road. The fields were full of shepherds, ploughmen, teams of horses, and little bird-scaring boys all struck stark in the act of the moment, one with his hand to his nose, another with the bottle to his lips, a third with a stone raised to throw at the raven who sat, as if stuffed, upon the hedge within a yard of him. The severity of the frost was so extraordinary that a kind of petrifaction sometimes ensued; and it was commonly   10 supposed that the great increase of rocks in some parts of Derbyshire was due to no eruption, for there was none, but to the solidification of unfortunate wayfarers who had been turned literally to stone where they stood. The Church could give little help in the matter, and though some landowners had these relics blessed, the most part preferred to use them either as landmarks, scratching-posts for sheep, or, when the form of the stone allowed, drinking troughs for cattle, which purposes they   15 serve, admirably for the most part, to this day.

But while country people suffered the extremity of want, and the trade of the country was at a standstill, London enjoyed a carnival of the utmost brilliancy. The Court was at Greenwich, and the new King seized the opportunity to that his coronation gave him to curry favour with the citizens. He directed that the river, which was frozen to a depth of twenty feet and more for about six or seven   20 miles on either side, should be swept, decorated and given all the semblance of a park or pleasure ground with arbours, mazes, alleys and drinking booths etc. at his expense.

From *Orlando* by Virginia Woolf (1928)

Categorising famous people

1. Make a list of 12 famous people that you know about. You can name people from the past or the present. Here are a few suggestions to get you started:

   - Mahatma Gandhi
   - Charlie Chaplin
   - Nelson Mandela
   - Edwin Hubble
   - Albert Schweitzer
   - Martin Luther King
   - Maria Montessori
   - Walt Disney
   - Bill Gates
   - Steve Jobs
   - Mother Teresa
   - Amelia Earhart

2. Complete the table by writing these famous people's names in the correct column.

Those who were born great	Those who have achieved greatness	Those who have had greatness thrust upon them

Resource 8.2

Writing about the Olympic Games

Award 1 mark for each of the points listed below, or for any other valid point, up to a total of 15 points/marks.

- Astylos of Croton competed in three Olympiads, winning six olive wreaths in one diaulus and two stade events.

- He competed for Croton in the first games and this won him great fame.

- In the latter two games, he represented Syracuse and the citizens of Croton took revenge.

- Milon of Croton won the wrestling event six times.

- He began his succession of wins in 540 BC as an adolescent before going on to win five more times.

- He won 26 more titles at other major sporting events, including the Pythian and Nemean games.

- Leonidas of Rhodes won 12 running events in the stade, diaulus and armour competitions.

- These victories were in four consecutive Olympic Games.

- Leonidas was one of the most famous runners in Ancient Greece.

- In 49 BC, Melankomas of Caria won the boxing event as well as other titles.

- He achieved great fame through his boxing stratagem and interesting style.

- Victory was achieved without Melankomas being struck or having to lash out himself.

- The earliest female winning athlete to be recorded was Kyniska from Sparta.

- She achieved victory in the chariot race in both 396 and 392 BC.

- In the Olympiads, women were not allowed to attend and Kyniska was the first to do something different and compete.

Using sports idioms

1. Read the following expressions taken from sports and write down what they have come to mean. The first few have been done for you.

Expression	Sport	Popular use
The ball is in your court	Tennis	*It's your decision or responsibility to do something now.*
Call the shots	Billiards	*The person who calls the shots is the person who makes the decisions.*
Front runner	Horse racing	*The person most likely to win.*
Off the hook	Fishing	
Give it your best shot	Tennis	
Jump the gun	Track	
A level playing field	Any sport	
To move the goal posts	Football	
Neck and neck	Horse racing	
Not up to par or below par	Golf	
Throw in the towel	Boxing	

2. Write down other idioms or expressions from sport.

....

....

....

Resource 8.4

Exploring famous places

1. In pairs, choose one of the places on pages 196–7. Complete the row for your place in the grid below.

2. Circulate, and exchange information with other pairs to complete the rest of the grid.

Place	Where it is	Why it was built	Why is it famous
Taj Mahal			
Eiffel Tower			
Statue of Liberty			
Sydney Opera House			
Blue Mosque			
Parthenon			
Machu Picchu			
Colosseum			
Tower of London			
Pyramids			

Being a coursework examiner

Use this copy to annotate the student's biography.

"Dr Livingstone, I presume."

David Livingstone was born in Lanarkshire Scotland in 1813. His family was very poor and they all worked in a cotton mill. David Livingstone started at the cotton mill when he was ten years old. It was hard, boring work. He continued with his school lessons after his long working day. He was an avid reader and after reading many books about religion and philosophy he decided he could do good in the world by studying medicine. Working in the mill until he was 26 taught him endurance and persistence and helped him to empathise with people who had no choice in life but to live and work in the worst of conditions. Qualities that helped him in his travels in Africa. In 1836 he began studying medicine and theology on Glasgow and then joined the London Missionary Society. He wanted to go to China. But in 1841 he was posted to the edge of the Kalahari Desert in Africa instead. In 1822 Livingstone married Mary Moffatt. They had six children, but Livingstone rarely saw his family because he was travelling all the time. In the last year of her life his wife joined Livingstone on his travels but she died of malaria in 1862. This saddened him and he always regretted not seeing more of his children who had to grow up without him.

Dr Livingstone was appalled by the slave trade that still flourished in Africa. In 1856 he returned to England to publish his books, intending to show slavery was cruel and immoral. The British had stopped their involvement in slavery, but an illegal trade continued and America was still importing slave labour for her plantations.

Missionary Travels in South Africa was published in 1857. It caused a sensation, forcing British readers to examine their ideas about the African continent. Up until then, central Africa was thought to be a dry, mountainous region. Livingstone's book demonstrated it was in fact fertile grassland supporting a very wide range of animal life. Readers learned for the first time about great rivers such as the Zambesi and the people living in different regions, who like any native group in the world, were sometimes suspicious, but could be welcoming to outsiders.

Livingstone had a remarkable life but Livingstone wrote about his travels modestly without exaggeration. He walked from Cape Town, South Africa through the Kalahari Desert to the coastal town of Loanda which is now called Luanda in Angola then followed the Zambesi to the east coast of Mozambique, accompanied only by members of the Makololo tribe, with whom he was friends. He met a wide variety of people during his travels, including nomadic Bushmen and Bakalahari herdsmen and describes people, scenery and animal life accurately without romanticizing them. Livingstone died in Chitambo, Zambia in 1873. His body was returned to England and he was buried in Westminster Abbey. Unfortunately, the books Livingstone wrote about his travels with the intention of enlightening the British about real life in Africa encouraged people to go to Africa to exploit its natural resources.

The famous words, "Dr Livingstone, I presume" were spoken by Henry Morton Stanley, a young, ambitious American journalist. Stanley set out to find Dr Livingstone for the New York Herald newspaper. Other expeditions had already been sent to Africa to find Dr Livingstone for the same reason – to either find Livingstone alive or find evidence of his death. Stanley picked up Livingstone's trail at Lake Tanganyika and the two men finally met on 10th November 1871 in Ujiji present-day Tanzania. According to the story, Stanley's first words on approaching the only other white man in this part of Africa, was, "Dr. Livingstone, I presume?"

From very humble beginnings Dr David Livingstone became world famous. (624 words)

Resource 8.6

Practising reading comprehension

Read the passage and then answer the questions that follow.

The World Cup

Football, or soccer as it is known in the USA, has been popular as a spectator sport for over a hundred years. Prior to that, football was played in most villages and towns throughout Britain as a particularly brutal sport. In medieval times youths simply formed two teams and kicked a leather ball from one end of their hamlet or village to the other – the two entrances to the village forming the goals. Play was extremely rough; there were no rules and a lot of injuries.   5

In the 1860s, different, less aggressive versions of football were being played in Britain's major public (private) schools. Rugby football was played at Rugby School; Eton, Harrow and Winchester played other types of football, some of which included the rule stating a player must not touch the ball with his hands. On October 26th, 1863, teams and their trainers came together to create a standard set of rules to be used at all their matches. Eventually they agreed on a set of rules and wrote them down as   10 the rules for the game of "Association Football".

The Football World Cup was first played in Montevideo, Uruguay, in 1930. At the time only thirteen countries participated, eight of them being from South America. Uruguay won. In 1934 the World Cup was held in Europe. More than thirty teams played a series of elimination matches until Italy won. Italy won again in 1938. No matches were played in 1942 and 1948 because of the Second World War   15 and the cup itself was hidden to keep it safe. The Football World Cup trophy is a statuette of Nike, the Greek goddess of victory.

When the World Cup was reinstated after the war it was like 1928 all over again: only thirteen teams played, the matches were held in Brazil, and Uruguay won. Interest in football however, was reignited, and by the time West Germany won the Cup in 1954, millions of people were watching matches in their   20 home towns on a regular basis.

In 1958, fifty-three teams played in Sweden, and matches were televised. This was the first time the world saw the legendary Pelé play for Brazil. Pelé's team won that year, and Pelé became one of the greatest footballers of all time. In the 1970s, Pelé moved to the USA, where he played for a New York team. Soccer, as football is known in the USA, wasn't very popular there at the time. There was little   25 money to pay professional teams and few ordinary people knew about the fast moving spectator sport so popular in Europe and South America. After Pelé and some other international stars started playing though, people began to see how fascinating and exciting soccer could be and soon there was a professional league called the North American Soccer League (NASL). Nowadays soccer games are attended by up to sixty thousand spectators in the USA – whatever the weather.   30

Champion league football is now played on every continent. Apart from the World Cup, which is held every four years, there is also the European Cup, the FIFA Cup, the European Champions Cup, the African Cup and Asian Cups. It is estimated that one-quarter of the population of the world watches the final elimination rounds of the Football World Cup on television every four years.

1. Where was the first Football World Cup held?

....

2. Who won the first game?

....

3. How many teams participated in the first World Cup?

....

4. When and why was Association Football created?

....

5. Who or what is Nike?

....

6. What happened to the World Cup trophy during the Second World War?

....

7. Who is Pelé?

....

8. What is NASL?

....

9. What enabled so many people to watch the World Cup after 1950?

....

Resource 8.7
Self-assessment

Make notes about Unit 8.

The speaking skills for giving a presentation are:

....

....

....

The speaking skills for leading a debate are:

....

....

....

Two texts (fiction or non-fiction) I remember in Unit 8 are:

....

Two new skills I learned are: ....

....

Two things I'm not sure about are: ....

....

I enjoyed doing: ....

I would like to .... *again because*

....

....

Markscheme for Reading Passages – Core

Part 1

1. Award up to a total of 20 marks, as shown below.

   a. Give four examples of why Bryson thinks Istanbul is a noisy city. (4)

   For example: "car horns tooting"; "sirens shrilling"; "people shouting"; "muezzins wailing"; ferries "sounding booming horns".

   b. Explain why the Galata Bridge seemed crowded. (2)

   Bryson says the Galata Bridge is "swarming" with people and lists "pedestrians, beggars, load bearers, amateur fishermen".

   c. Why does Bryson say Istanbul is "one of those great and exhilarating cities where almost anything seems possible"? (2)

   In paragraph 2 Bryson lists different types of people in the street and what they are doing: fishermen are catching "poisoned-looking fish" and two men are leading brown bears on leashes through the traffic. No one pays any attention to them so anything seems possible.

   d. Explain in your own words: "I walked past the Blue Mosque and Aya Sofia, peeling postcard salesmen from my sleeve as I went". (2)

   Bryson walks past these two famous buildings trying to avoid or side-step postcard salesmen who get far too close to him or grab his arm.

   e. Describe in your own words why Bryson found the Gülhane Park "inviting and miraculously tranquil". (4)

   Bryson finds the park pleasant and peaceful because it is quieter than the noisy streets, it is spacious, cool and shady; contented families are there and children are visiting a zoo. A café is playing the sort of music Bryson doesn't like, but not loudly so he can tolerate it.

   f. Describe in your own words what Bryson sees when he takes a seat in an open-air taverna in the final paragraph. (6)

   Bryson sits and looks at the view. He sees white houses on a brown hillside two miles across the strait (Bosphorus). In the distance he can make out cars from the way their metal glints in the sun. Ferries are going to and fro across the water and out as far as Princes' Islands.

2. The article should be written in an appropriate popular newspaper style and register. It may make mention of Bryson by name and include what he was doing. The article must include reference to the people and places he mentions; the Galata Bridge, noisy streets, tranquil park and the view across the Bosphorus. Students must describe the city and its atmosphere in their own words as far as possible, writing 200–300 words. Award up to 10 marks for content and up to 5 marks for style and accuracy (Total of 15 marks).

Part 2

3. **a.** Students' notes should include ten of the following points. Award up to 10 marks. Points for inclusion:

   - Istanbul is defined by Eastern and Western influences.

   - It was founded in the 7th century BC and once known as Constantinople.

   - Istanbul was the most important city of the Byzantine and Ottoman empires.

   - There are spectacular historical sites and monuments from these two great empires in the Old City, Sultanahmet, a UNESCO World Heritage Site.

- Aya Sofya museum is considered to be one of the world's greatest architectural achievements. Aya Sofia was the cathedral of Constantinople, until the city was conquered in 1453 by the Ottoman Turks.

- At Meydani, the Square of the Horses, is a public garden that used to be the Hippodrome, huge crowds went there to see races, athletics, celebrations and executions.

- The Great Palace in Sultanahmet has royal apartments, staterooms, gardens and courtyards reaching down to the shores of the Sea of Marmara. It was built by Constantine in the 4th century.

- Also in the Old City is the Topkapi Palace, built between 1459 and 1465.

- The famous Blue Mosque, the Archaeological Museum and the Grand Bazaar are also in this area.

- The Archaeological Museum has a collection of antiquities dating back over 5,000 years and includes the sarcophagus of Alexander the Great.

- The Grand Bazaar comprises 65 streets lined with 4,000 shops arranged according to their products, including precious metals and everyday goods. It's one of the world's largest covered markets.

- The Golden Horn is a flooded river valley and a natural harbour flowing into the Bosphorus. Lovely parks and gardens line its shores.

- Crossing the Galata Bridge is an important part of any visit.

b. Students should use their notes to write a summary of what Passage B says there is to see in Istanbul's Old City and why it is an interesting place for tourists to visit. They must use continuous writing, not note form, and their own words as far as possible. The summary must be 100–150 words long. Award up to 5 marks for style and accuracy (total of 15 marks for question 3).

Total of 50 marks for Questions 1, 2 and 3.

Markscheme for Reading Passages – Extended

Part 1

1. Students must write a report to the committee that organises the school debating group. They must give reasons as to whether or not Dr Zinc should be invited to speak at one of the debates. Answers should be written in an appropriate report style and may use subheadings and bullet points. Ideas must be based on details from the passage. The report must be 250–350 words long. Award up to 15 marks for content and up to 5 marks for style and accuracy (total of 20 marks). Points for inclusion:

For:

- He will make an impact (both in appearance and when talking).
- He has a very strong effect on his audience.
- He will amuse and entertain the audience.
- His rhetorical speech ("Oh terrible, terrible"; "Horrible to relate")
- His love of green fields, animals, happy families
- His warnings are relevant to all of us (good evidence required here).

Against:

- His appearance makes him a poor role model.
- His delivery is monotonous.
- He frightens his audience and causes panic.
- Teenagers might make fun of him (e.g. his movements).
- His warnings are too pessimistic and exaggerated (e.g. an asteroid bearing down).
- Some predictions are very hard to believe (e.g. tornados, half past three).
- He is embarrassing not entertaining.
- He takes "gullible" people in.
- One of his aims is to get people to give money.
- He is not always clear or audible ("mumble something incomprehensible").
- He incites irrational behaviour ("wailed and lifted their hands").

2. **a.** Give most credit for discussions of the idea that Dr Zinc acts in an unnatural, exaggerated manner, that he is ridiculous or peculiar. Some students may realise the writer's intention is to be amusing. Others may suggest madness. Students should write 200–300 words. Award up to 10 marks. Students should examine the effects of some of the following:

- "bizarre" – an impression of abnormality, makes the reader wary of him
- "cadaverous" – the skeletal image is too thin for a normal person
- "gesticulating wildly" – an exaggeration to suggest over-enthusiasm or lack of control
- "in a theatrical manner" – is this a genuine scientist / speaker or an actor?
- "intoning more unreality" – sounds like a bad actor or a priest
- "like a tree in a gale" – exaggeration; branches would be bigger than arms and lashing about could seem frightening but is amusing here
- "melancholy" – is this his real or assumed personality?
- "straggly hair" – stereotype of a nutty professor or mad scientist
- "eccentric fellow" – not to be taken seriously or perhaps an understatement.

b. The audience's behaviour suggests that Dr Zinc has had a powerful effect on them or that they are gullible and believe everything they are told. Their overall behaviour is irrational and the writer appears to be making fun of them. Credit recognition of satire and absurdity. Students should write 200–300 words. Award up to 10 marks. Students should examine the effects of some of the following:

- "deathly pale" – an image to exaggerate their fear
- "clasped their hands" – suggests shock and inability to express thoughts
- "twitched uncontrollably" – "twitched" might be vaguely humorous, as if brain-washed or hypnotised
- "gullible" – gives the impression of rather simple people who cannot think for themselves
- "lean towards him" – a visual imagery suggests hypnotism
- "like pet dogs" – the moaning and sobbing is aural imagery suggesting extreme subordination
- "wailed and lifted their hands" – growing crowd hysteria
- "clasped their cell phones" – a sense of finality as if the phone was their last link with humanity or the last chance for an emergency call.

Part 2

3. a. Students' notes should include ten of the following points. Award up to 15 marks. Points for inclusion:

- Problems can be solved by human ingenuity
- Transport is now relatively cheap
- Cheap and easy to visit relatives in other countries
- Students are given opportunities to see new places
- Experience new cultures
- More students benefit from better education
- Politicians are starting to face their responsibilities
- Beginning to tackle poverty
- Beginning to tackle pollution
- Politicians are addressing the effect of greenhouse gases on the economy
- New cures for cancer and diabetes
- Improved medical science leading to better treatments
- Development of medicines
- Technological inventions
- TV improves understanding of different people and cultures
- Internet is an effective form of rapid communication
- Internet provides ways of obtaining information
- Internet improves and promotes commerce
- International sport is widely available
- Sport enables people to experience and share values (pride and competition)
- People can now attend live concerts or see them on television
- Increasing knowledge and education obliges leaders to move forward not look to the past.

b. Students should use their notes to write a summary of what Passage B says are the positive and encouraging aspects of life in the 21st century. They must use continuous writing, not note form, and their own words as far as possible. The summary must be 200–250 words long. Award up to 5 marks for style and accuracy (total of 20 marks for question 3).

Total of 50 marks for Questions 1, 2 and 3.

Self-assessment

Make notes about Unit 9.

Two texts (poetry, prose or drama) I remember in Unit 9 are:

....

Two new skills I learned are: ....

....

Two things I'm not sure about are: ....

....

I enjoyed doing: ....

I would like to .... *again because*

....

....

Resource 10.1

Reading Passages (Core) (1)

Passage A: A Trading Post in Alaska

It is 1890. Maíre McNair a young woman from Belfast in Northern Ireland has travelled to Alaska in North America to be a school teacher at a trading post. Maíre has grown up hearing stories about Selkie Folk, people who take on the appearance of humans but are really seals and belong to the sea.

A babble of shouts and riotous colour drew her attention from the view above to the shore in front. Unfamiliar words and sounds accosted her ears, as did pungent odours of smoke and fish. Women dressed in bright calico colours, bare feet visible from beneath their skirts, and scarves atop their heads, shuffled small children out of the way in readiness for their landing. Nearby, turbaned men with hair cut rough below their ears began to wade into the water, their dun-coloured trousers rolled to their knees. It wasn't all wild colour and excitement; among these rainbow clothes a few stood out in their darker browns and blacks of merino wool and thick cotton trousers, and the lighter whites and beiges of linen shirts. 5 · 10

Just before the boat could go no further a man from the group moved towards them, parting the fish that thronged the water. He wore none of the bright cottons or dark wools. His chest was bare and he glided through the water with a rhythm so graceful Maíre wondered what the water might conceal beneath his hips. He was truly a creature of the sea with his dark tilted eyes and coal-black hair that hung long and loose about his shoulders, and a body that moved through the current like liquid. 15

He arrived at the boat and reached up for her. Wolf tattoos rippled on the back of his hands as he gestured her to come. Maíre gasped at the sight of such primal markings. The Indian noted her reaction but made no remark, only raised his brow a fraction and gestured once again for her to come.

"Daniel." Mrs Paxson addressed this black-haired man with some surprise. "We don't usually see you at the mission." She nodded to a short wiry man wading through the water in Daniel's wake. "Oh good, George, you're here. You can take me ashore. Daniel is taking Miss McNair, the schoolteacher." 20

… Daniel deposited Maíre on the bank and, without a word, headed to the forest above that quickly swallowed him whole. Where was his home, if not here by the sea? How much claim on him had that forest that absorbed him so completely it was as though he were part of it? What was he, if not of the sea? 25

"Don't just stand there gawking, girl," said Mrs Paxson. "Get yourself up to the trading post and help Mr Paxson unpack the stores. I'll be along in a short while." She turned back to the men surrounding her and continued to issue orders about the cargo.

Suppressing her annoyance Maíre nodded, groped for her skirts and made her way towards the cluster of vertically planked buildings. When she reached the building most likely to be the trading post, she realized she had acquired a group of followers who now crowded behind her. Maíre turned around and smiled feebly at them. Faces, very young and very old, male and female, stared expectantly at her. A young girl dressed in bright red calico pressed forward. 30

"Are you the school teacher?" 35

"Yes, yes." Maíre nodded vigorously. "I am the school teacher." She said it slowly and loudly, hoping they would understand her words. "School teacher," she repeated, pointing to her chest. "Miss McNair."

They all giggled. Had she said something wrong? Just as she desperately searched their faces for a clue to the misunderstanding, a door opened behind her.

"I thought I heard voices," said Mr Paxson. He stepped down beside Maíre, facing the group. "I see you've found yourself a welcoming committee." He spoke to the group using another language, a language full of air and sea. Their language. 40

From *Selkie Dreams*, by Kristin Gleeson (2012)

Reading Passages (Core) (2)

Passage B: An American in India

American student Brian Gallagher went to India on an exchange programme. Here he writes about his experience and what he found so different from his life in America.

It would be difficult to underestimate the value of spending time in a foreign country, especially a country that is so particularly foreign to one's own – as India is to mine. Typically mundane experiences, such as walking down a nondescript and common street, become the most incredible   5
adventures. Surrounded by novelty, the world is suddenly alive and fascinating. I remember very clearly my first impressions of India, and how enamored I was with everything that I saw around me. Nothing could bore me, because everything was colored with the culture of my surroundings – and what a different color it was! I was mystified by the cryptic languages I saw on billboards and the towers of Hindu temples along the roadsides. I was entirely bemused by the animals in the streets, as well as all   10
the rickshaws and the old British-style taxis that I saw everywhere. I was pleasantly amused by Indian courtesy and impressed by Indian attitudes towards marriage and the family. Everything, everywhere, jumped out at my senses and engaged my mind like it could never have at home.

It was these small and everyday things that made India such a wildly different place. The extraordinary things, of course, were impressive; but they were impressive because they were   15
extraordinary. It was far more remarkable to find the merely common things that seemed extraordinary. Each one revealed either something truly singular about India, or something in my own conception of the world that had been clouded by my relatively sheltered life. And recognizing either one was incredibly mind-opening. It was by getting in touch with these common differences that I was able to understand India, at least in a limited sense. By dealing one-on-one with the students and faculty at   20
Manipal, I gained an insight into Indian character and by speaking with friends about their futures, I learned a little about Indian values and aspirations. These tiny and individual experiences eventually add up to the whole that is Indian culture and while I would never pretend to comprehend that whole in its fullness, I am incredibly grateful to have come to understand a portion of it.

By Brian Gallagher, www.iaeste.org

Resource 10.3

Reading Passages (Core) (3)

Passage A: Escape from Málaga

It is 1936, the beginning of the Spanish Civil War. Elizabeth, Alex and Juan are trying to get from the city of Málaga to Almeria in Southern Spain.

As far as she could see, in both directions, there were people, hundreds of people walking in the same direction: wounded men, women, children, old people, goats, donkeys, even some chickens in a crate. The entire city seemed to be on the move. An immense silence hung over them, broken only by the 5 plaintive cries of the children begging for food and the curses and moans of the elderly, who struggled to keep up. There was no need for them to speak; there was nothing to say. They all knew that they had to walk as fast as they could to avoid the danger. If they dawdled they would die; this was a race for their lives and even the youngest among them seemed to know it. They urged their crying children on and when someone's grandmother gave up and sat by the roadside, too exhausted to continue, they 10 walked on without her. They had to reach Almeria and safety at all costs.

"*Que desbandá*," Juan murmured, visibly moved to see so many homeless people.

Elizabeth wondered how far these people had come; some were wrapped in coats and blankets, others had nothing more than a single garment to wear; some were barefoot, their feet tom and bleeding. One old woman sat by the roadside, weeping, her legs swollen with ulcers, the blood running 15 down into her sandals. There were so many children, dozens and dozens of children, most of them under ten years old. Some were lucky and sat in baskets astride rheumatic-looking donkeys, others rode on their fathers" backs or lay in their mothers" arms, but many more ran behind, their tiny legs trying to keep up with their families, terrified they would get lost, and all of them crying for food.

"Exactly how far is it to Almeria?" asked Elizabeth. 20

"Well it's a hundred miles from Málaga; so we're looking at another three days and three nights, if we can keep up the pace," answered Alex.

Elizabeth groaned; she did not want to tell them, but already she felt unable to walk any further. Her feet were sore and she was frightened to remove her shoes in case she could not put them on again; her back hurt and she was still desperately hungry. 25

"Keep an eye out for a lorry. Maybe we'll be lucky and be able to get a lift," Juan said, but with little conviction.

The fishing village of Torre del Mar lay before them, in the estuary of the river Vélez. The mountains had receded inland, bare granite outlines on the horizon, leaving at their feet a wide flat valley, a fertile plain of orange trees and avocados. She saw a moving column of black shapes was snaking its way 30 along the valley floor, a second stream of refugees arriving to join the exodus.

"Look at all those people; where are they coming from?" she asked.

"I don't know," Juan answered. "From the *pueblos*, I suppose."

He stopped a woman who was pushing an old pram, laden with bedding. Her face was the colour of a walnut and just as wrinkled; her eyes peered out at him, suspiciously, from beneath a wide straw hat. 35

"*Señora*, where are all these people coming from?" he asked.

She stared at him, amazed at his ignorance.

"They're running away from the soldiers, of course" she said.

"The *fascistas* have taken Zafarraya and broken through the pass; they'll be in Vélez any day."

Then, not waiting for him to reply, called her children to her and hurried on her way, disappearing 40 quickly into the crowd.

"So Málaga will soon be surrounded," he said.

"What's this?" Alex asked.

A huge cloud of white dust was being thrown from the dirt road by a convoy of lorries that was heading towards them. The drivers drove fast, honking their horns continuously with the expectation that everyone would jump aside in deference. They cut a swathe through the exhausted pilgrims, who 45 stumbled and fell to avoid being mown down. As the first lorry reached them Alex and Juan leapt to one side, pulling Elizabeth with them.

From *Between the Sierra and the Sea*, by Joan Fallon (2011)

Resource 10.4

Reading Passages (Core) (4)

Passage B: Escape to Gibraltar

It is 1936, the beginning of the Spanish Civil War. Hubert Caetano lives with his parents in La Linea, a town on the coast across the narrow isthmus from Gibraltar in southern Spain. Hubert's father is a worker's union representative in the hospital where he works.

At dawn there was a violent banging on the door and when my mother tentatively opened it, it was torn aside by rough soldiers who burst into their bedroom and unceremoniously dragged my father   5
out with them, hitting him as they went and calling him a Red traitor. […] We were unable to find out what was happening to him, not even where he was being kept. There was chaos everywhere. Then, two days later, just as suddenly as he had been taken, he was back. Bald, battered and bruised from many beatings. […]

As the days went by the situation became more dangerous, but what finally convinced my father   10
that we should try to leave was the presence of the dreaded Moorish troops. Now though, it was impossible to get across the isthmus into Gibraltar, the obvious place to flee to. Desperately he searched for ways to get us all away from the anarchy in the country, but to no avail, no one wanted to risk the wrath of the merciless Nationalist soldiers and their followers by helping suspects to escape. He had practically given up hope when, very late one night, there was a knock on our door. We froze, but it was   15
only a frightened old fisherman who had spent a long time critically ill at the hospital and was grateful for my father's care of him. He just came in to say that the following night he would leave his oars inside his boat on the beach and was quickly gone.

And so it was that on that moonless night we carefully made our way on to the beach. Down by the fence we could just make out the lights of Nationalist soldiers patrolling the frontier. With difficulty we   20
managed to launch the boat that had fortunately been left near the waters edge and, as noiselessly as possible, rowed out into the darkness. It was just a short distance really though our great fear made it seem an interminable journey. Even in the darkness we could make out the imposing north face of the Rock rising vertically into the black sky. What a welcome sound that muffled crunch was as the boat's keel dug into the soft beach sand.   25

From *Gibraltar: Rock of Ages*, by Hubert Caetano (2003)

Reading Passages (Extended) (1)

Passage A: A Street March

It is 1936. Bill Maguire, a British journalist is in London to report on a fascist demonstration.

On the left, towards Tower Bridge, Bill could make out the darker, more orderly mass of the fascist troops, and hear the thud of a band in the middle distance. The stretch of road separating the two factions was no more than a quarter of a mile long, but was occupied by a veritable army of police over 6,000 overall had been drafted into the area for the day – both on foot and on horseback. It was raining   5 slightly and a faint, acrid smell rose from the damp rubber capes of the men and the steaming coats of the horses. The officers on foot carried batons at the ready. All the men wore that look of phlegmatic preparedness that Bill had seen on the faces of police everywhere.

The anti-fascist crowd seemed to be increasing both in size and confidence by the minute, the narrow line of police delegated to hold them back bulged and leaned dangerously, strained to near   10 breaking point by the explosive pressure of so many angry bodies. Bill turned right, his intention first to speak to the police, and then get into the crowd behind the cordon for the point of view of the protesters. A few intrepid commercial vehicles – baker's and newsagent's delivery vans, and a horse-drawn milk float – had entered Royal Mint Street from the north side, and belligerent drivers, determined not to be cowed by the situation, bellowed abuse at the police and both political factions.   15 Blaring horns, revving engines and the panicky whinnying of horses combined with the mounting clamour on both sides to create a deafening din.

Suddenly, a boy darted from the crowd in Cable Street, ducking beneath the linked arms of the police, and hurled something into the middle of the road. The firecracker skittered and fizzled for about thirty yards before exploding in a series of sharp reports and a plume of sulphurous yellow smoke. The   20 reports, so like gunfire, galvanized the police. The boy was overwhelmed in a moment, the firecracker kicked aside, but not before the horse pulling the milk float had shied violently, its hooves clattering and skidding on the wet road. The float lurched, and a crate tipped off the far side, sending shards of glass, borne on a widening river of milk, flowing across the road towards the gutter. Unsettled, one of the police horses reared and then side-stepped rapidly, mounting the pavement opposite Bill, its head, wild-   25 eyed, snapping up and down, its massive hindquarters bunched beneath it.

Bill flattened himself against the wall of the warehouse, but still it kept coming until its enormous flank buffeted him, winding him, and the flailing boot of its rider grazed his cheek as he fell. As the officer regained proper control, his shout of apology caused the horse to kick out one last time with its hind leg, as if in retaliation, catching Bill a painful blow on the point of the elbow. For a moment he   30 was nauseous with pain, and sat slumped against the wall with his head bent forward. He was shocked, the sense of freedom and exhilaration that had been his only a minute ago had been completely knocked out of him, along with his breath. To his right, opposite the warehouse doorway, there was no kerb, and a river of milk, now grey with dirt, washed around him.

He began to struggle up, his head still swimming. Hands grabbed his arms and hauled him, a voice   35 shouted in his ear: "Not a good place to be, sir, if I may say so, why don't you cut along home?"

There were policemen on either side of him, anxious to remove him as soon as possible. Bill ran his hands through his hair and felt in his breast pocket for his press card.

"Thanks. Sorry I'm in your way. I'm press." The big sergeant gave his card a cursory and disparaging glance.   40

"We've got our work cut out here, sir."

He moved off towards Cable Street, but as he did so the crowd suddenly and violently broke through the police cordon, with an effect like a dam bursting. The street was filled with a torrent of yelling men, some brandishing their placards like spears, others clutching an assortment of missiles ranging from stones to tin cans and coins. Oblivious once more to everything but the excitement, Bill   45 turned and keeping level with them ran back the fifty yards or so to the top of Thomas More Street.

From *A Flower That's Free*, by Sarah Harrison (1984)

Reading Passages (Extended) (2)

Passage B: Crowd Behaviour during the French Revolution, 1789

This is an examination of how people in the street behaved during the French Revolution.

[...] A man looks down the street to see what is occurring. He sees an army of women marching through the streets, followed closely behind by an equally large legion of their men folk. [...] He hears thunderous shouts. These voices ring in his ears. They sound like a unison chant from a demonic horde. Not a vocalized unison, but more of a unison of purpose, of emotion. His desire to escape has   5
been to no avail. Just as he feels he has made it to freedom, he hears a familiar voice among the crowd. It cries out, "Long live the Third Estate". The voice he recognizes as his own. It has found a feverish pitch, matching the crowd's, and chants the slogans that are being strewn all around. Softly at first, but with each repetition it grows louder and more animalistic in demonstration. Feverishly he roars, "Death to the *calottins*" [a type of clergy]). Falling into line with the others who are flooding the streets,   10
he is carried away by the crowd. Carried to a destination he does not know, he finds himself where he desires to be. Years of frustration and hatred toward a government in which he has no voice finally find an outlet. He marches to depose a dictator and establish a life of liberty.

This is the scene that many people think of when asked about the French Revolution. This subject brings to mind pictures of men standing near the guillotine holding aloft a freshly severed head. This   15
period is probably one of the bloodiest periods in the history of France. Is this, however, all there is to it? Is the French Revolution nothing more than a horde of blood-thirsty savages running around looking to kill someone? For many the answer would be yes. This, however, is not the case. The French Revolution has another side, an often unexplored side. This is the side of the Revolution that brings a level of humanity to the chaos. It shows that the people were not originally out for blood. The crowds   20
that formed in Paris at this time were merely trying to survive. During the period of 1787–1789, the crowd formed of necessity, not of savagery. They formed, as did any other pre-industrial crowd, in order to combat the rising food prices. Their wages had been stagnant for years, but the price of bread had taken a dramatic upsurge. In an attempt to survive, the peoples of Paris took on the role of the crowd.   25

Indeed the grain shortage became so bad in 1789 that Mayor Bailly recorded in his journal,

The nearer 14 July came, the greater became the shortage of food. The crowd, besieging every baker's shop, received a parsimonious distribution of bread, always with warnings about possible shortages the next day. Fears were redoubled by the complaints of people who had spent the whole day waiting at the baker's door without receiving anything.   30

There was frequent bloodshed; food was snatched from the hand as people came to blows; workshops were deserted; workmen and craftsmen wasted their time in quarreling, in trying to get hold of even small amounts of food and, by losing working time in queuing, found themselves unable to pay the next day's supply.

The bread, moreover, seized with such effort, was far from being of good quality: it was generally   35
blackish, earthy and sour. Swallowing it scratched the throat, and digesting it caused stomach pains.

He also revealed that [...] while the bread the peasants could obtain was mouldy and rotten, the king and his ministers were fed with fresh bread of the finest quality. All of this worked together to fuel the anger of the crowd.

From *The Heart of the Crowd: A Study of the Motives of the Peasant Class in the French Revolution,*
by Nathan Kinser (1999)

Resource 10.7

Reading Passages (Extended) (3)

Passage A: Travelling in the Desert

In this passage a British journalist describes a visit to the Libyan desert in North Africa.

The plateau, the high dunes, the dry wadi beds and the verdant oases of the South Western desert are
a veritable open air museum. The "Fezzan" is littered with millions of pre-historic spear heads; arrow
heads; crushing and cutting tools; shards of pottery; and even the eggshells of ostriches from pre-
history. On my very first day, lunching in the shade of an acacia tree, I picked up a Stone Age cutting   5
tool that was literally lying at my feet.

Twelve thousand years of civilization can be charted through the engravings and delicate rock
paintings demonstrating the slow march of climate change - the shift from hunting to pastoral pursuits;
tribal differences; mysterious religious ceremonies; the introduction of the horse; and finally, as the
desert encroached, the camel.   10

The talented artists who engraved their observations in the rocky cliffs above the winding river beds
had a purity of line of which Picasso would have been envious. I saw the gentle movements of giraffes,
the lumbering bulk of rhino, the last moments of a dying elephant and the lassooing of a group of
ostriches.

As we wandered the desert we saw a camel giving birth; we ambled through wadis accompanied by   15
chirping mulla mulla birds; we came across cracked, salt lakes where strange, bulbous trees live and
die; snowy white patches of gypsum; swathes of green plants with pale purple flowers, (a consequence
of only three days rain two months before); we raced in 4x4's our Tuareg drivers vying with each other
to get there first (wherever "there" was) and we leapt over impossible, impassable dunes whipped into
geometric knife-edges by the ever-present desert wind; and unforgettably lazed beside the great blue-   20
green slashes of still water, fringed with succulent date palms and stands of pampas grass that comprise
the beautiful oases where turtle doves flutter through the air, tiny pink shrimps swirl in the water and,
on one occasion, a solitary white camel was tethered on the shady bank.

White camels are highly prized and our driver told me that his family had won races across the
Arab world with his fifteen-strong herd. When I explained that England has no desert, he exclaimed   25
sadly "then there is no yellow". The Tuareg are not of Libya, Algeria, Niger, or Mali, they are the people
of the Sahara. Proud, honest and exceedingly generous, they are a joy to be around. They acted as our
drivers, guides and cooks, regaling us with traditional songs, dispensing chilled water from goat skin
bags, and on one occasion picking herbs from a desert bush to alleviate constipation! Every day after
lunch they brewed Tuareg champagne - strong green tea boiled over a driftwood fire, poured from   30
a height to make cappuccino-like foam, then reheated and poured into small glasses with plenty of
sugar. They seemed to genuinely enjoy showing us their territory. But they have had to adapt, choose a
nationality, settle in villages and learn Arabic, French, Italian and English.

The Tuareg were a thorn in the side of ancient Rome, plundering the trade routes from Africa to
the port of Leptis Magna (one hour east of Tripoli). Eventually the Romans were forced to make peace.   35
To safeguard the vital shipments of ivory, slaves, and the thirty-five thousand wild animals that were
sent to Rome for gladiatorial displays graphically shown in Ridley Scott" s box office smash Gladiator.
The decadent Emperor Commodus made Leptis Magna rich and one of its citizens, Septimus Severius,
became Emperor of Rome. The remains of the city, with its theatre, temples, courts of justice, market,
saunas, latrines, hunting baths, and lighthouse were intact before the war.   40

The historical monuments, the pre-historic rock paintings, and the camaraderie of the fiercely
loyal, intelligent and resourceful Tuareg people combined to make this my most highly prized journey
throughout the world. Not to mention the romance of the desert.

By Angela Clarence, *The Observer* (21 May 2000)

Reading Passages (Extended) (4)

Passage B: Travelling in the Desert in the 15th Century

This is a passage from a novel set during the 15th century. Nicholas, a Flemish merchant, and his friend Umar from Timbuktu are part of a camel caravan transporting goods from Timbuktu to the North African coast across the Sahara Desert, via the oasis settlement of Arawan.

There are few wells in the Sahara, and the journey between them depends on navigations as exact and as strict as that employed by a captain at sea, venturing out of sight of his port, and into waters unknown. In   5 time of clear skies, the Sahara caravan makes its way as the birds do, and the captains: by the sun and the stars, and by whatever landmarks the sand may have left. But the winds blow, and dunes shift, and the marks left by one caravan are obliterated before the next comes. And so men will wander, and perish.

The guide Umar had chosen for Nicholas was a Mesufa Tuareg, and blind. For two days, walking or riding, he turned the white jelly of his sightless eyes to the light and the wind, and opened his palpitating   10 black nostrils to the report of the dead, scentless sand, which was neither scentless nor dead, but by some finesse of aroma proclaimed its composition and place. At each mile's end, he filled his hands with the stuff and, rubbing, passed it through his brown fingers. Then he smiled, and said, "Arawan".

"Umar," Nicholas said. "I hope you know what you're doing."

To begin with, they spoke very little. With the rest, they walked through the first night and part of   15 the day, halting rarely. Sleep was brief, and taken by day. During the worst of the heat, they lay with the camels under the white, shimmering sky, and ate, and rested.

Their drovers made tents of their mantles, but Umar's hands erected the light, makeshift awning that sheltered Nicholas and himself, and arranged the cloths, coated by Zuhra with mercuric paste, which they wore against the sting and bite of the pests of the desert. Then, mounting while the sun still glared   20 upon them, they rode until dark, each man his own tent, alone under his own cone of shelter. The chanting, the chatter stopped then, and even the goats became silent.

The nights were marginally cooler. Then the riders revived, and dismounted, and unlashed the bullock-skins of warm water, and drank, and filled the leather bags at their sides. And the camels had their one meal of the day, from the fodder they carried themselves.   25

The company was congenial enough, and consisted of men and women and children, for there were families going to Arawan. As the heat became less, they grew lively. Every hour, the ropes on the loads needed adjusting: a camel would kick and bite and, roaring, disrupt the procession; the goats would stray; a dispute would break out over some trifle. At such times, the caravan carried its own clamour with it, like a long, narrow household perpetually singing, arguing, quarrelling, cackling. They hardly   30 stopped for food, except during the enforced sleep through the heat, but passed between them gourds of maize and sour milk or rough bread. The fresh food had spoiled by the second day.

On the second day, the blind man came to them both and said, […] Many horsemen have passed this way to Arawan recently. Not today. Perhaps three days ago."

Nicholas said, "Someone told you?" The pale, shining sands were everywhere pristine.   35

"My nose," said the man. "The manure has been covered while fresh. It is unusual."

"It's Akil," said Umar, when they were alone. […]

Nicholas said, "Would Akil's men dare to attack us?" […]

"We could avoid Arawan," Urnar said. […] "Two or three hundred camels are rather few against troops of armed Berbers."   40

"Six would move quickly," [...]

"Until the nomads observe them," said Umar. "And it means only six camels to carry food, fodder and water, our belongings and us, if we tire. It leaves no margin for sandstorms or straying or accidents. And lastly, if we don't get to the water at Arawan, there are exactly two hundred miles between the first well after that and the next one."

45

From *Scales of Gold*, by Dorothy Dunnett (1991)

Directed Writing and Composition (Core and Extended) (1)

Not Alone Tours advertisement

You want to see the highlights of America's Grand Canyon – the ancient capitals of Europe – the cities and culture of North Africa – the Great Wall of China ...

You want to travel and experience real adventure!

But you know setting off on a journey of discovery all by yourself, or even with a friend, can be complicated, and sometimes even dangerous.   5

Not Alone Tours is the answer.

With **Not Alone Tours** you can see the sights and enjoy a real holiday without nasty surprises on the way. Visit towns you've only ever heard about and stay in safe, comfortable hotels. Get to know a region properly with experienced, English-speaking local guides. Let **Not Alone Tours** take care of your accommodation and transport, and relax. Our friendly and experienced Tour Managers take care of   10 the details of your trip, as well as being a mine of information on the history and culture of the places you visit.

Join like-minded singles for a safe, totally enjoyable touring holiday with Not Alone Tours.

Resource 10.10

Directed Writing and Composition (Core and Extended) (2)

Not Alone Tours online brochure

Taking your first vacation on your own is a big step. But remember, with **Not Alone Tours you're not alone!** This is why we're the number one choice for singles holidays.

Not Alone Tours guarantees you years of experience and expertise in tours for single travellers.

Accommodation

On our tours, the price you see is based on a single room. You'll never have to share. You'll also have   5
the time, but be careful to use your own words to read or relax as you choose, if you want to be by
yourself for a while.

Tour leaders

Your holiday will be arranged and led by one of our friendly, professional tour leaders. He/she will tell
you everything you want to know about your destination, culture and currency. Our tour guides are   10
fluent in the local language.

Destinations

We offer famous, interesting and secret destinations in more than 20 countries around the world.
Whether you want an exciting coach tour through the Rockies, an informative tour of Edinburgh, a
hike along the Great Wall of China, we've got something for you.   15

In good company

You won't be the only one feeling nervous and excited! Before your trip, you can use the **Not Alone
Tours** website to network with fellow travellers and ask for advice from people who've already made
your trip. After your trip, you can keep in touch with new friends and share your photos, memories and
useful tips.   20

At the airport

Airports are stressful places. But we make sure you're met by your tour leader, who will help you check
in and answer any last minute questions.

Emergency 24-hour service

It's unlikely you'll have problems while you are away, but if you do, help is one phone call away – an   25
emergency phone line 24-7. You can be sure we won't let you down.

Call us on 011 99 7301110 or email us: info@notalonetours.com

    173

Directed Writing and Composition (Core and Extended) (3)

The Island News

Opportunity or Disaster?

Tiny Tanuca to have huge new hotel resort and golf course

Prior to actual purchase, Compton Hotel Resorts have submitted a planning proposal to Tanuca Council for a new luxury holiday resort complex on Tanuca Island. Compton's newest and, they say, largest resort is to be built among the hills of the idyllic little island of Tanuca, overlooking Tabeira Cove with its crystal clear waters and multi-coloured fish. The London-based Compton group has also announced   5 that a large area of natural, undeveloped land will be transformed into a golf course on the north side of the island. This, they tell me, will require extensive landscaping as hills will have to be "smoothed down" and natural sand dunes on the coast converted into "sand-bunkers".

Building plans

The proposed Tanacu Island Hotel Resort will be accessible by a new ferry service from the mainland.   10 The 300-bed luxury hotel resort will include bungalows for employees brought in from the mainland; the golf course will have a time-share apartment complex. There are also plans to construct a "floating lounge restaurant" in beautiful Tabeira Cove.

Conference facilities for business people in the hotel itself consist of over 3,000 square metres of function space spread over three floors to host meetings and private functions such as weddings. The   15 health spa and gym will have seven treatment rooms, an outdoor Olympic-size swimming pool and three outdoor tennis courts.

Employment and infrastructure

The current owner of the land, Maria Gracia Lanetti, says she has been assured that all buildings will be integrated into the environment. She is delighted that the Hotel Resort will offer employment   20 opportunities for the local community and people from the mainland. At present there are no plans to build a school or medical facilities on Tanuca, but Compton does not rule out the need for these in the future.

Tanuca's inhabitants

Tanuca, a hitherto tranquil and unspoilt island, is home to just 400 inhabitants. Its idyllic natural beauty   25 is the last safe haven for wildlife and birds in the Mediterranean. But Tanuca is all set to be transformed into a vacation paradise for the wealthy. Ecologists, conservationists and animal lovers are concerned that the native birds and mammals, which include the very rare Spindling Warbler and the minute Tanuca Shrew, will be disrupted, if not destroyed. Natural habitats will be razed for the resort complex. Watering the golf course alone means re-routing the only two streams on the island, where there is very   30 little annual rainfall.

Fishing and the sea

Fishermen say the constant movement of ferries and boats travelling to and from Tabeira Cove will ruin the fishing; they fear the waters will be permanently polluted. The local seal and sea lion populations, which use north coast of Tanacu for their breeding grounds, are already in decline from oil spills and   35 mercury poisoning; this will end their stay on Tanuca forever.

We at *The Island News* say there has already been far too much development on the other islands around Tanuca. It's time the government stepped in to prevent foreign companies such as Compton destroying our islands. Tanuca Island Council needs to consider how so-called progress and employment opportunities might lead to the end of our natural Island life.   40

By Alexis Bruni on Tanuca Island, 27 September 2012

Resource 11.1a

A short history of English

1. Word invaders

Modern English is used in different forms for many purposes across the world. It is the language of shipping and aviation; it is used for diplomacy, technology and commerce. Most people associate the English language with Great Britain, but English has not always been the language of the British Isles.

The original inhabitants were tribes that spoke versions of what we now call Gaelic and Welsh. They lived alongside the Romans when Britain was occupied from 55 AD until early in the 5th century.

In 449 AD, the British Isles were invaded by warlike Germanic peoples: the Angles, Saxons and Jutes. These Anglo-Saxons gradually pushed the native Celts and Britons to the less fertile western and northern regions of the islands, keeping the fertile areas of southern England and the Midlands for themselves.

From 750 AD until well into the 11th century, people from what is now modern Scandinavia colonised the north-east of Britain and regularly made attacks on the richer coastal regions of the south. They were known as the Vikings.

In 1066, the Normans (descended from other Vikings who had settled in Normandy in northern France) invaded England. The Normans brought a form of French that was influenced by Latin.

As a result of these invasions, many dialects and entirely different languages were being spoken in the British Isles in the Middle Ages. Gradually, as people moved around the local dialects and languages intermingled to form the language we know as Old English.

English today still reflects its different roots, words are pronounced differently around the country and certain words are used in very specific ways. We speak and write Standard English in some circumstances and colloquial English in others. For example, at school you use at least two styles of English: the way you chat to your friends will be quite different to how you write school essays.

Some words are used in one context and different words, often with the same meaning, are used in other contexts. For example, after the Norman invasion, lords and ladies in manor houses and palaces spoke a form of Norman French, while peasants and townsfolk continued to use a mixture of old Celtic, Norse and Anglo-Saxon. Milord and lady in the manor ate mutton and beef, but mutton and beef were called sheep and cows in the fields. Similarly, professional men and women involved in the law, science and medicine today use far more Latin words than people working in shops or factories, and French is still used to make things seem more elegant or better quality. What is the difference, for example, between *cuisine* and *kitchen*, *cook* and *chef*? The word *fashion* comes from Middle English *facioun*, but is fashion the same as *haute couture*?

1. Complete the table below, using the words in the box. Use a dictionary to help you.
   Hint: the words make pairs.

~~smell~~	~~ask~~	~~odour~~	job	exterminate	enunciate	consecrated	forebear
folk	holy	speak	kill	ancestor	profession	kingly	teacher
regal	extend	professor	spread	interrogate			

Old Norse or Old English	Norman French or Latin
smell	*odour*
ask	

2. Choose two different words for the same thing and write a sentence to explain how and why we use them differently.

....

....

....

....

Resource 11.1b

A short history of English

2. Shakespeare's English

Shakespeare wrote from about 1584 to 1613, during the reigns of Elizabeth I and James I. Reading his English aloud can be challenging because the spelling and pronunciation are often different to modern English. Some of his words and expressions have also gone out of use or changed their meaning. For example, *ambition* is seen as a positive thing now, but for the Elizabethans it meant the unscrupulous pursuit of power and had very negative connotations. Think about what happens to Macbeth and Julius Caesar!

1. Match the following words and expressions from Shakespeare's plays to their original meaning.

Shakespeare's English	Original meaning
Anon, anon!	At once
Betimes	Cheat
To cozen	Grey
Grizzled	In a minute! / Just a minute!

2. Suggest meanings for the following words and expressions in Shakespeare's plays.

a. brainsickly ....

b. husbandry (2 meanings) ....

c. hence ....

d. hurly-burly ....

e. marry! ....

f. mountebank ....

g. prithee ....

h. star-crossed lovers ....

i. tetchy ....

j. varlet ....

A short history of English

3. New words and new worlds

With the discovery of new shipping routes in the early 16th century, Britons travelled around the globe. Some settled in distant countries where they continued to use their mother tongue, but adopted and adapted local words for food or goods that had no equivalent in English. As merchants trading in Asia and the New World returned to Britain with tea, tomatoes, potatoes, coffee and chocolate, the original words for these new products were incorporated into English. In fact, tea and potatoes are now so English it's hard to remember that they are foreign imports.

English today is, therefore, the result of a two-way process: words have come into English from places such as Norway, France and China, but have also Britons taken English to distant places such as Australia, India, Jamaica and Ghana, where it has been adapted. Business people have used English as a *lingua franca* (common tongue) for centuries and now the Internet takes English into homes all over the world. In this way English continues to travel, adopting new vocabulary from other countries and infiltrating other languages.

Here are some surprising words that came into common English usage before the 20th century: *bungalow* from India, *sofa* from Arabia, *ketchup* from China.

1. Find out where the words below may have come from. Use a dictionary to help you.

    a. shampoo ....

    b. cotton ....

    c. freckles ....

    d. yacht ....

2. Write down five more words used in English that come from places outside Britain.

....

....

....

....

....

Resource 11.1d

A short history of English

4. New words for the New World

After 1620, many more people from Europe began crossing the Atlantic to North America in search of land and religious freedom. In the new territories, British immigrants came into contact with many different languages, including those of the American Indian tribes, although surprisingly few new words or phrases entered the English language at that time. British settlers kept to themselves and kept their old language intact. Nevertheless, words from the native tribes were needed to name the food, birds and animals settlers had never previously encountered. They adopted and anglicised words such as *asquutasquash*, which became *squash*, as a kind of pumpkin.

Life in the New World resulted in new experiences and inventions. For example, when settlers chopped down trees to build their homes, they put up log cabins using lumber – a word used to describe rubbish in London now referred to the wood of felled trees. The word *settlement* was employed to describe a newly colonised area; a *settler* was a person who lived there. Some previously unknown animals and birds were named after familiar creatures at home: an American hare was called a rabbit and a bird with a red breast was called a robin. Things that had no equivalent were given descriptive names, such as *rattlesnake*. British immigrants also gradually adopted words from other immigrant languages, such as cookies from the Dutch koekje and bayou from French. Some of the vocabulary used by those early immigrants, words that have fallen out of use in Britain, such as *quit*, *gotten*, *fall* (autumn), *sick* (ill), *mad* (angry), *yourn* (yours) and *sassy* (from saucy, which originally meant provocative) are still used in the USA today.

Over the last century, American and British English has merged more closely. Now we all use a mixture of words – but which do you use more?

Here is a selection of words to name the same thing on opposite sides of the Atlantic. Circle the words that you are more familiar with.

British English	American English	British English	American English
biscuit	cookie	maths	math
block of flats	apartment building	motorbike	motorcycle
chemist's shop	drugstore, pharmacy	naughts and crosses	tic-tack-toe
chips	fries, French fries	pavement	sidewalk
drawing-pin	thumbtack	pet hate	pet peeve
crisps	potato chips	pocket money	allowance
dustbin	garbage can, trash can	post	mail
handbag	purse, shoulder bag	postcode	zip code
holiday	vacation	sweets	candy
lift	elevator	tin	can

Spelling irregular plurals

The irregular history of the English language explains why there are so many irregular plurals. For example: *boy* and *boys*, but *man* and *men*.

1. From memory, write the plurals for the following nouns.

   a. wife ....

   b. lady ....

   c. echo ....

   d. piano ....

   e. brother-in-law ....

   f. child ....

   g. cloth ....

   h. leaf ....

2. From memory, write the singular form of the following plural nouns.

   a. fish ....

   b. foxes ....

   c. sheep ....

   d. geese ....

3. Compound nouns change in different ways to become plural. For example: *step-brother* becomes *step-brothers*, but *passer-by* becomes *passers-by*. Change all the singular compound nouns to plural in these sentences. (You will also need to change the verbs in each sentence so they make sense.) The first one has been done for you.

   a. In the olden days, a royal man-at-arms wore a coat-of-mail.

   In the olden days, the royal men-at-arms wore coats-of-mail.

   b. The prisoner was given a pack of cards and a chess set.

   ....

   c. At an English church wedding a bride is followed up the aisle by her bridesmaid.

   ....

   d. The field mouse was caught in a mousetrap.

   ....

   e. The sheep farmer left his farm to his son-in-law.

   ....

   f. An onlooker watched as a policeman arrested a car thief.

   ....

Resource 11.3

Using idioms

An idiom is a phrase that means something different from the meaning of the actual words. For example, the expression "still waters run deep" is a metaphor for someone who says little but thinks a lot.

1. Write the meanings of the following expressions. The first one is done for you.

   a. To be in hot water *to be in trouble*

   b. In deep water ....

   c. To wash your hands of something ....

   d. A wash out ....

   e. Mouth-watering ....

   f. It'll all come out in the wash ....

2. We have used the word *green* in many different ways over the centuries. For example, *Greens* can mean a political organisation dedicated to improving environmental awareness and sustainable development, as well as the green vegetables that are good for you.

   Write the meanings of each of the phrases below. The first one has been done for you.

   a. To go green *to feel sick or to go green with envy*

   b. greenstick fracture ....

   c. greenhouse gases ....

   d. the greenhouse effect ....

   e. green belt ....

   f. village green ....

   g. to get the green light ....

   h. green fingers ....

   i. green-eyed monster ....

   j. greenery ....

3. How many other expressions do you know using colours? Write them down and explain what they mean. For example:

   To see the world through rose-tinted glasses means to have a positive or optimistic outlook on the world and see everything as "rosy".

   ....

   ....

   ....

Spelling words that end with *ence/ance* and *ent/ant*

Many verbs form nouns that end in *ence* or *ance*. For example the verb to *differ* becomes the noun *difference* and *to resist* becomes *resistance*.

Similarly, some verbs form nouns for people that end in *ent* or *ant*. For example to *assist* becomes an *assistant*.

Some adjectives also end in *ent* or *ant*. For example: *convenient* or *distant*.

Complete the sentences below using an appropriate noun or adjective derived from the words in brackets. The first one has been done for you.

1. Despite his *appearance,* he lacks self-*confidence.* (to appear / confident)

2. The first . . . . of the play was not a success, largely because of the un . . . . scenes of violence in the first Act. (to perform / to please)

3. The oldest . . . . of the village has all the power in this society; there is no form of democratic . . . .(to inhabit / to govern)

4. . . . . crime in this country is blamed on easy access to guns: too many . . . . people are killed or injured each year in shooting . . . . (violence/innocence/incidence)

5. Joan was an . . . . pupil, but her frequent . . . . from school meant she did not perform well in exams. (intelligence/absent)

6. Her elderly grandfather is . . . . on the small income he obtains from selling garden produce because he refuses any form of government . . . .(to depend/to assist)

7. They are going to an international . . . . on the environment. Many schools will be in . . . . and many national radio . . . . will be covering the event. (to confer / to attend / to correspond)

8. Milo walks a long . . . . to school every day; bad weather has no . . . . effect on how long it takes him to arrive. (distant / to signify)

9. After examining the two skeletons, it was decided they were probably . . . . of a warlike clan whose . . . . in the area dated back to the 3rd century. (to descend / to exist)

Notes

Notes